The Sleeping Giant Has Awoken

The Sleeping Giant Has Awoken

The New Politics of Religion in the United States

Edited by
Jeffrey W. Robbins and Neal Magee

Introduction by
John D. Caputo

Postface by
Slavoj Žižek

continuum

NEW YORK • LONDON

2008

The Continuum International Publishing Group Inc
80 Maiden Lane, New York, NY 10038

The Continuum International Publishing Group Ltd
The Tower Building, 11 York Road, London SE1 7NX

www.continuumbooks.com

Copyright © 2008 by Neal Magee and Jeffrey W. Robbins
Introduction copyright © 2008 by John D. Caputo
Afterword copyright © 2008 by Slavoj Žižek

Unless otherwise identified, Scripture is from the *New Revised Standard Version Bible,* copyright 1989, by the Division of Christian Education of the National Council of the Churches of Christ in the USA, and is used by permission.

Printed in the United States of America

Library of Congress Cataloging-in-Publication Data

The sleeping giant has awoken : the new politics of religion in the United States / edited by Jeffrey W. Robbins and Neal Magee ; introduction by John D. Caputo ; afterword by Slavoj Žižek.
    p. cm.
  Includes bibliographical references and index.
  ISBN-13: 978-0-8264-2968-1 (hardcover : alk. paper)
  ISBN-10: 0-8264-2968-8 (hardcover : alk. paper)
  ISBN-13: 978-0-8264-2969-8 (pbk. : alk. paper)
  ISBN-10: 0-8264-2969-6 (pbk. : alk. paper) 1. Evangelicalism—United States. 2. Conservatism—United States. 3. Christianity and politics—United States. I. Robbins, Jeffrey W., 1972- II. Magee, Neal. III. Title.

BR1644.5.U6S54 2008
322'.10973—dc22

2007046980

Contents

Preface

This book grew out of a series of conversations between the authors immediately following the 2004 presidential election. Even before gathering in person a few weeks later for the annual meeting of the American Academy of Religion, we had been discussing the twists and turns of the particularly bitter run-up to Election Day and how to parse that day's turnout. As scholars of religion, we could not help but recognize the place religion now held in the political campaigns: in the evangelical Right's mobilization against gay marriage in several states; in Cardinal Joseph Ratzinger's order that open supporters of abortion (even mentioning John Kerry by name) be denied the Eucharist; in George W. Bush and his strategist Karl Rove's moves to garner conservative Christian votes even more effectively than in 2000; in the Democratic candidate's inability to connect with religious voters or even comfortably speak their language even though he was a lifelong Christian. We realized that the terrain had somehow changed, but that understanding it required moving beyond bald charges that evangelicals were power-grabbers, that Bush and Rove played heavily on fear, or that Democrats were utterly disconnected from religion.

This time around, with less than a year before the 2008 presidential elections, evangelical Christians have so far been unable (or unwilling) to rally behind one candidate. Their commitment to the Republican party is for the most part not in question, but the division occurs between whether to support the more "principled" or the more "electable" candidate. We also now see the emergence of "Green" evangelical voters, as well as those put off by unmet promises, strident Christian leaders who threaten moving to a third party, and other Christians who feel that their own leadership is now overly political. Perhaps 2008 will never have a chance to be what 2000 and 2004 were, with near-perfect storms of widespread disgust with presidential behavior, a strengthened Republican party that took the time to think through a comprehensive and disciplined strategy, and an exceptionally well-organized Christian grassroots campaign in most states, all underwritten by a very real fear of terrorism. And perhaps 2008 will be missing a figure like Rove, who could see and realize the political possibilities like few before him for recognizing an untapped electoral demographic. As far as we can tell, the "sleeping giant" about which this book was written is best seen in those earlier elections, and it was awoken with a clarion call by Rove, George W. Bush, and others. Elections next year and beyond will deal less with waking up the giant than with what it does now that it is awake.

However, we recognize that this sort of convergence is not new. In the 1960s another political-religious alliance was formed, that time on the other end of the spectrum, in the form of civil rights and a revitalized call for equality in the United States. The Rev. Dr. Martin Luther King Jr. and many of his contemporaries articulated a far more liberal vision of America, which was also based on plainly Christian, biblical values. And they had no qualms with going into churches to stir up people's passions enough to go out and vote. Therefore, this book hopefully begins to answer one of the underlying questions: How is this new alliance different? Certainly this union follows up on the first, as a corrective to the cultural throes of the 1960s and the Vietnam War. But in another way, the slumber of our particular giant can be found in a long history where evangelicals existed on the margins of American politics and could find no way in. And how they found their way in sets their way apart from that earlier movement.

Much has been said, rightly so, of the commingling of religion and politics in the person and presidency of George W. Bush. Each chapter of the book that follows is in part a contribution to that discussion: a series of attempts to understand the nexus between the political and religious Right. However, the authors also have taken such reflection as an opportunity to see the awakening of the sleeping giant as somehow symptomatic of our culture at large. Perhaps the best way to understand the correlation between or codependence of religion and politics in the United States is not simply to focus on Bush, or evangelicals, or the Republican party. Given the current milieu, those are fine places to begin, but the analysis must go further. To do so would be a mistaken attempt to remove ourselves from the formula and pretend that religion is not already somehow interwoven with the American political scene. It would be to misrecognize the greater relationship between politics and religion today. For instance, we might want to understand the ways our nation is shot through with various forms of "faith": in politics, ideology, religion, but also in the market, in transcendental beauty, in the fundamental goodness of humans, and so on. What remains of a Left in this country does not cling tightly to the term "faith," figuring it to be something that progressive Americans rid themselves of decades ago, leaving it to those deluded religious types. And yet they walk with reverence in museums and galleries in awe of a mysterious thing they call "Beauty," call for universal human rights in the name of "dignity," and celebrate a political theory known as "democracy."

The classical formulation by Marx is that if people only understood what they were doing and what they were a part of, they would throw it off and demand otherwise. However, what George Bush has given us—despite running the most secretive administration in the history of the United States—is a much-clearer window onto the political realm: We see Bush's unwavering loyalty to cronies he has appointed at every level. We see the incredible disconnect between someone who can raise hundreds of millions of dollars and someone who understands how to govern effectively. We hear his claims never to govern by polling and yet know that he tests phrases with focus groups. We see a man who undoubtedly has a faith but who harnesses his Christian self-identification with an eye toward elections.

Bush is certainly not the first on any of these counts. But in the presidency of George Bush, we can now see that Marx's formulation has to be shifted: people know very well what they are doing, and still they are doing it. This recognition comes to us by Slavoj Žižek, who kindly contributed a postface to this book. These disconnects that we experience are in many ways muted by this attitude, but they are also endemic to democratic politics in the twenty-first century. We know very well that sound bites do harm to political discourse and yet we love them. We also well know that Presidents (among others) constantly manipulate their images and messages, and yet we enjoy and accept them as authentic. What this indicates is that a sophisticated electorate must absorb a host of gaps and contradictions because *that is what is required to participate* in what is currently called "democracy." It is this need, or impulse, that is for us profoundly religious. Religion is usually quite at home with gaps and contradictions. Certainly the rarified religious language called "theology" has grappled with them for millennia in various forms: God in three persons; immanence and transcendence; a God that takes human form and is somehow executed; in surrender comes freedom. And so the authors all agree that the awakening of the sleeping giant, besides an expression of the expediency of a mutually beneficial coalition, is a wonderful moment for religious reflection. Our hope is that this book will somehow offer readers a different set of lenses by which to assist that reflection. We also hope that somehow a book that takes on the twin poles of politics and religion might also inform both subjects on their own.

The editors want to thank all of the authors for their creativity, patience, and willingness to spontaneously write a book on this subject. Special thanks are reserved for Professors Žižek and Caputo, whose contributions serve as the bookends between which a younger generation of scholars working at the critical nexus of religion, politics, and culture are invited to reflect upon and in some cases even chart a new course in the study of the politics of religion in the United States. We also want to thank Burke Gerstenschlager of Continuum for his enthusiasm for this project from the beginning and his support and professionalism throughout. Finally, we are both deeply grateful to our wives and children. They know all too well the times when writing and the time to write did not come easily.

N. E. M. & J. W. R.
November 2007

Introduction

A Taste for Theory

John D. Caputo

Releasing the Event

One way to think about critical theory is that it proceeds on the premise that our beliefs and practices, our institutions and structures, contain something that they cannot contain, that they are possessed of something, let us say something that stirs within them, something nascent, restless, and disruptive, which at the same is trapped, repressed, or bottled up by these institutions. We might even say that our institutions bear something within themselves that they cannot bear! Let us call this uncontainable something or other the "event," to choose a word that has a rich history in continental European philosophy from Heidegger (*Ereignis*) through Deleuze and Derrida, up to our own day in Badiou. On this accounting, the role of critical theory is to release the event, to liberate it from all the forces that would prevent the event. This means that critical theory, however critical, is fundamentally an affirmative operation, an affirmation of the event. For those of us who are interested in bringing the resources of theory to bear upon the analysis of religion, this implies that theory is an exploration of the event that stirs and simmers within religious beliefs and practices even as that event is bottled up by religion. Religion, like everything else, works against itself even as it tries to work something out. Theory feels about for the event the way we might feel the pockets of a jacket for a lost key or coin.

On my own accounting, which I draw from Derrida, the event that stirs within religion—within everything, in way or another, but within religion in a particularly palpable way—goes under the name of *the impossible*. By *the* impossible we do not mean a simple contradiction in terms, like (p & ~p), but something that shatters our horizon of expectation, something surprising, overtaking, that comes over us, landing like a blow, a certain salutary trauma, or a not so salutary one, since nothing guarantees that the event will not be one of unimaginable evil. The democracy to come, which we affirm, is haunted by the specter of a national socialism to come. Religion, or religious experience, is a paradigmatic form of human experience, one very close to the human heart, so that without it we would not be simply missing one more experience, but experience itself. Experience is what it is only when it runs into the impossible; otherwise we are just running on automatic pilot. Hence, one of the main things we in the West mean when we speak of religion, which is a Western word, is a kind of pact with *the* impossible, let us say even a covenant, but not so much in the sense of a deal or a contract we have cut with it, which would be a matter of economic exchange, but an allegiance, a vow of fidelity to the impossible, an affirmation of the impossible. Human experience generally, but religion in particular, is an affirmation of the impossible, of the possibility of the impossible.

That is one reason religion and politics so easily bleed into each other. When Robert Kennedy said, "There are those that look at things the way they are, and ask, Why? I dream of things that never were, and ask, Why not?" he was speaking about politics, but he spoke with a religious passion, a prophetic passion about the political future, and his speech was palpable with the event. The event is not something that is, but something going on within what is, making what is restless with the future, making being itself restless with the good, making things restless, for better or for worse. What exists at present, now that it is actual, was all along possible. But the event, as what disturbs what exists, is never present, is always stirring, as *the* impossible, the promise of something impossible. That unsettles things—aesthetically, cognitively, ethically, politically, religiously.

Still, however futural, however much it solicits and draws us beyond itself and toward what is coming, however much it belongs to an absolute and unforeseeable future—the event also belongs to an immemorial past, to an ancient memory, which as Walter Benjamin pointed out, constitutes a *dangerous* memory. On Benjamin's account, the event has a peculiar messianic status: for we today are in the messianic age; we are the ones for whom the dead were waiting, and it is our responsibility to see to it that the injustice of their death is redressed, that their death, as Abraham Lincoln proclaimed, "will not have been in vain," this "will not have been," this "future anterior," cutting to the very essence of messianic temporality for Benjamin. So the event that calls us forward to a messianic future, to the children, is no less the event that calls us back, awakening our messianic memory of the dead.

The moment of the event is the distance between this immemorial past and the unforeseeable future, which solicits the response, the responsibility we experience under the impetus of the event, the need to make ourselves worthy of the events that happen to us, as Deleuze put it so felicitously.

Releasing the Christ Event

I say all this as a way of framing the essays that follow, which I see as proceeding from the premise that Christianity contains something it cannot contain, which forms the framework for a critical consideration of Christianity and its relation to the idea of a radical democracy. Like any work of theory worthy of the name, this critique would not simply be a negation but an affirmation of the event that transpires in Christianity as opposed to the current or at least the dominant and deeply reactionary form in which we find Christianity today, which is what we nowadays call the Christian Right. The capacity of religion to work against itself, to prevent the event by which it is shaken, to discharge its passion resentfully, is here diagnosed and charted. But what event? In the case of Christianity, the event is nothing other than the memory of Jesus, or the promise of Jesus, an event that calls from the immemorial memory of Christian and prophetic religion, which also calls us forward, soliciting us to make that memory come true. The event is the kingdom—"commonwealth" might be a better word today—that Jesus announced, the rule not of the "world" and its powers, but of God:

> Blessed are you who are poor, for yours is the kingdom of God. (Luke 6:20)
>
> Woe to you who are rich, for you have received your consolation. (6:24) The Spirit of the Lord is upon me, because he has announced me to bring good news to the poor. He has sent me to

proclaim release to the captives and recovery of sight to the blind,
to let the oppressed go free, to proclaim the year of the Lord's favor.
(4:18–19)

In his teaching, Jesus advised a life of uncompromising simplicity and
nonacquisitiveness, like the birds of the air and lilies of the field, which
is not bent on providing for oneself and building up a stock against the
future, which trusts God to provide. He said enough disturbing things
about the coming of this kingdom, the rule of mercy, forgiveness, and
nonviolence, to make the powers that be uneasy. Saying things like that
in an occupied country brought him to an early grave and a cruel if not
uncommon execution at the hands of an imperial power. But in death,
he was no less forgiving and nonviolent. His earliest followers led lives of
exemplary commonality, sharing all things in common, distributing to
each what they needed. The first debate that broke out in what we today
call Christianity was whether this complete commonality was being
observed perfectly.

But the dominant form of American Christianity today, the Christian
Right, has sat down to table with virtually every power and domination
that Jesus contested in his own lifetime, with the very powers of imperial
rule, the rule of the world, which took his life. It stands for authoritarianism, nationalism, and militarism that contradict the letter and the
spirit of Jesus' words, who said to love one's enemies, and if one is struck
on the cheek, to turn the other cheek. It enthusiastically supports a war
that cynically flaunts the classical conditions of just-war theory, "just war"
itself being a strange turn of phrase to be found on the lips of a follower
of the author of the Sermon on the Mount. It marches arm in arm with
an unbridled capitalist greed that has recklessly permitted the rich to
grow ever richer while grinding up the poor—flaunting the very ministry
Jesus announced for himself. By lending its shoulder to laissez-faire capitalism, the Right undermines everything it might have been believed to
stand for. Unchecked capitalism wrecks family values by impoverishing
families and leaving children homeless and parentless. As Lou Dobbs—
not exactly a member of the Left—has documented, the economics pursued by the Right constitutes an all-out attack upon the middle class,
where family life is the mainstay. Unchecked capitalism turns sexuality
into commodity; it seeds the fields of abortion, prostitution, drugs, and
crime by holding its heel to the neck of the poorest and most defenseless
people in society. Where Jesus found strength in the weakness of God, in

forgiveness and nonviolence, the Christian Right openly lusts for a Christian Empire, even as it was an earlier Empire that took the life of Jesus.

The cruelest and most bitter irony is that the Christian Right does all this in the very name of Jesus, asking us, "What would Jesus do?"—as if Jesus were a capitalist out to make millions and a militarist with aspirations for imperial power, in search of a kingdom very decidedly of this world. What is this if not the will of humans in love with bare-knuckled power, with themselves and their own will, cloaking themselves in the name of the weakness of God and the nonviolence of Jesus? It is an ancient ruse but one that invites its own undoing if, as we maintain, religious structures contain something that they cannot contain. To ask, "What would Jesus do?" is to ask a dangerous question, to call upon a dangerous memory, to call for a future that endangers the present; it is a question with the power to turn itself on those who hold the question on their leash as a way to intimidate their enemies. The question belongs to a recurring scenario of the Christian imagination. What would Jesus make of us all if he were to return and see what is going on in his name? Dostoyevsky famously staged such a scene in fifteenth-century Seville. His Eminence, the Lord Cardinal Grand Inquisitor, recognized Jesus in a crowd outside the cathedral, teaching and healing, and had him arrested and condemned to death as a heretic, that is, as someone who had come to interfere with the work of the church.

But there is another example of this scene, one much closer to home. The question comes from a book written by Charles Sheldon in 1896 titled *In His Steps*, which bore the subtitle *What Would Jesus Do?* The book was simultaneously published in serial form in a religious weekly entitled the *Chicago Advance*. Sheldon was a pastor in Topeka, Kansas, and the book is a compilation of a series of Sunday sermons he had given, which became immensely popular in their day. Largely forgotten today, it was one of the best-selling books of Christian spirituality of all time. There are estimates that it sold some thirty million copies, but no one knows, because Sheldon took no pains to file a proper and secure copyright, which actually allowed the text to be widely reproduced. The book opens with a man dressed in rags seeking food and shelter from the good people of Raymond, Kansas. He knocks on the door of the pastor, the Reverend Maxwell, who cannot be interrupted from the preparation of his sermon on 1 Peter 2:21: "For to this you have been called, because Christ also suffered for you, leaving you an example, so that you should follow his steps." The vagabond next shows up at the Rev. Maxwell's

Sunday morning services, breaking in upon the decorum of the well-heeled congregation. He tells the good people a story of misfortune, a lost job, a family broken up by poverty, the futility of his efforts to find relief among the congregation, who just might then have been reminded of Matthew 25:35–40: "Lord, when was it that we saw you hungry and gave you food?"(25:37). Then he adds:

> It seems to me there's an awful lot of trouble in the world that somehow wouldn't exist if all the people who sing such songs went and lived them out. I suppose I don't understand. But what would Jesus do? (16)

The novel goes to chronicle the transformation of the lives of Rev. Maxwell and his congregation in response to the appearance of this Christlike figure in their midst. They abandon careers, give up lives of comfort, sell what they have, and give themselves to serving the poor, passing their time in the most dangerous neighborhood in their city. Sheldon's book touched the hearts of millions of people. He was an important formative force in the Social Gospel movement, and he invested a considerable effort in "Tennesseetown," Topeka's worst ghetto, one of the more-important points of the aspiration for a radical democracy converging with the prophetic heart in the history of American Christianity. He was an outspoken critic of ecclesiastical racism and of the Klu Klux Klan and an outspoken advocate for women's rights, in the church and in secular society at large.

So that famous question with which the Christian Right has tried to beat us half to death arises from a writer whose answer was clear: spend everything you have on the least among us, make your ministry in the most dangerous neighborhoods in the worst cities in the country, see the face of Jesus on everyone whom the wheels of capitalism have ground into the dirt. The more recent editions of *In His Steps* come with pictures on the cover of a very smarmy looking Jesus, with his eyes cast heavenward. They should have a picture of Tennessee town, or better still, perhaps a scene from *The Wire*, the brilliant HBO series that depicts one of capitalism's most obscene effects, the desperation of the inner-city drug scene: "the street." *The Wire* portrays the attempts of people to work out a life where it is impossible to live, and also the work of *the* impossible, the people trying to address the violence. That work, Sheldon maintains, is the ministry of Jesus, what Jesus would do. So the question that has become a bumper sticker for the Christian Right contains a surprise for those who would use Jesus as a club with which to abuse their enemies. The question is a good one (although it harbors a host of hermeneutical problems!) and this because it contains something it cannot contain. I do not think the Christian Right really wants to know the answer!

How have we come to the present turn? How has this question come to have exactly the opposite effect than the one Sheldon intended? How is it put to work by Christians to serve the interests of oppressing the poor, promoting the proliferation of guns, and waging a "preventive war" under the cover of the name of Jesus? The fate of this question is a symptom of the religious and cultural tendency analyzed in this volume.

Releasing the Book Event

The essays that follow variously chart the migrations and mutations, contortions and distortions, that have led us to this point. It begins with an examination of the historical contribution made by both radical religion and the radical critique of religion to American-styled democracy. Though a familiar story, with the recent ascendancy of the religious Right, it increasingly occupies a minor position in the narrative of America's founding vision. Thus, in the place of the oft-repeated claim that the United States is a Christian nation, the authors here offer up an important reminder that the story is not so simple and clear-cut, and that the religious influence in our ongoing political experiment cuts both ways as both the religious visionaries and skeptics have sought to find a home. From this first chapter, the volume then proceeds to a sustained and multifaceted look at conservative religious thinking over the last several years, offering a contrast between the conservative evangelical vision and what Peter Heltzel terms "prophetic evangelicalism," demonstrating the troubling and largely unexamined pact between religion and consumerism, together with what some consider to be the fascist and theocratic trends within the new politics of religion. Moreover, these chapters discuss the effects of the growing alliance between conservative politics and evangelical Christianity that blossomed most powerfully/effectively in the run-up to the 2000 presidential election with a candidate named George W. Bush. Some of these chapters are written by scholars within the Christian tradition who have much to say about how the church has undermined itself by participating in such bald partisanship, and thus losing its prophetic voice and critical distance. Others in this first half draw upon theory to address the possibilities if this alliance were to unfold even further, its origins and logical consequences, and the unsustainable contradictions necessary to support it.

The second half of the book takes a different vantage point, generally starting with examinations of the political and the ways this injection of the religious disrupts, confuses, and leads or misleads it. Here theory continues to bring other lines of thinking to bear upon this nexus of Christianity and the political by offering a critical analysis of key terms for understanding contemporary politics, culture, and religion: capitalism, immanence, sovereignty, history, shopping, media, symbols, and power. In these latter chapters, the motivating question for the authors is a question regarding the viability of our current discourse, a question about whether the language we use and the images that circulate have any meaning beyond the most perverse and cynical. The authors strive for a critical examination of this particular political moment, but also for a vocabulary and approach to understand other possible formulations of politics and religion in the American context.

The authors are historically erudite, but they have a taste for theory, which animates their erudition. The authors are not interested in reducing religion to rubble but in feeling about for the radical and prophetic event that is stirring there amid everything that prevents that event. As a result, the volume reads as both an exposé and a call for response and reclamation. What is more, it should be read as a critical intervention— an intervention into the sleeping giant that has awoken by the ascendancy and consolidation of the powerful nexus between political conservatism, evangelical Christianity, and American consumerist culture, and an awakening of its own by a new generation of scholars committed to both the emancipatory promise of religion and the future of democracy.

Martin Luther King Day,
January 15, 2007

John D. Caputo
Thomas J. Watson Professor of Religion and Humanities
Syracuse University

1

Radical Religion and American Democracy

Jeffrey W. Robbins

I do not want to be numbered among those who sold their souls for a mess of pottage—who surrendered their democratic Christian identity for a comfortable place at the table of the American empire while, like Lazarus, the least of these cried out and I was too intoxicated with worldly power and might to hear, beckon, and heed their cries.

Cornel West, *Democracy Matters*

We have it in our power to begin the world over again.

Thomas Paine, *Common Sense*

The story of the emerging democracy during the American Revolutionary period is incomplete without telling the contribution made by both radical religion and the radical critique of religion. Though most Americans are familiar with the Pilgrim past of America's founding, we have forgotten the equally formative role played by the religious outsiders, whether they be on the side of religious change and reform or the dissidents and skeptics. While we have enshrined our Pilgrim forebears in the sacred story of our mythic origins, we have relegated the rest to the back pages of our historical memory.

The story we know is that early settlers of the American colonies embarked on the risk of the arduous journey across the Atlantic in order to escape religious persecution and to practice their own religion freely. Among these settlers were those such as John Winthrop, the first governor of the Massachusetts Bay Colony. Winthrop not only led one of the largest groups of Pilgrims over to the so-called New World, but even more significantly, infused this pilgrimage with a profound sense of religious importance. As he famously wrote aboard the ship the *Arrabella* en route to the Massachusetts Bay, America must be considered as a "city on a hill," with the eyes of the entire world upon its people. According to Winthrop's vision, the Pilgrims' journey was divinely appointed; their work was God's work. And if they should fail, the promised land of bounty that was their own to claim would turn into a curse.

This religious motivation for the original journey to America, along with the religious sanction for the Pilgrims' claim on the land, would eventually be coupled with other equally important elements to make up the mythic story of our national origins. Remaining within the colonial period, there is the story of those such as the Quaker William Penn, who provides an interesting counterexample to that of Winthrop. In his evangelical fervor, Penn was every bit the equal to Winthrop. For instance, like Winthrop's vision of the "city on a hill," Penn established Pennsylvania as a "community of brotherly love," with the intention that it be "an example and standard . . . set up to the nations." [1] But whereas Winthrop helped to establish the Massachusetts Bay colony as a specifically religious commonwealth based on church order and spiritual discipline, Penn laid out a strikingly different foundation for Pennsylvania. Most notably, while Massachusetts came to be known by its uniformity and its strongly authoritarian religious overtones, Pennsylvania would be distinguished by rejecting a religious establishment and allowing religious freedom; perhaps not surprisingly, it would eventually become the site of the most egalitarian state constitution of the Revolutionary period.

The final piece to this most familiar American story comes from the period immediately following the Revolutionary War, when a new federal constitution was being drafted and questions over the proposed Bill of Rights were being fervently debated. It is common for us to look at this period and celebrate the heroic efforts by those such as James Madison and Thomas Jefferson to provide the legal framework for the disestablishment of religion, or what would eventually come to be known as the separation of church and state. These three pieces then—(1) the religious founding of America as a safe haven for the persecuted, (2) the opportunity in America for religious freedom, and (3) the disestablishment of state-sponsored religion in America—are integral to our enduring conviction that American-styled democracy still holds out the great promise for the spiritual rejuvenation and political stability of the world.

While I do not mean to question the veracity of this story, I do question its completeness. And if the story is incomplete and overly selective, then we must also question how effectively it conveys the truth of the actual forces, institutions, and ideologies that shaped the emerging democracy in the United States. In other words, this might be a case, like many other mythic stories, that is a truth also hiding certain truths. In this case, at least one of the hidden truths would be the essential role played by the religious radicals, dissidents, and skeptics, the history that has not been purveyed and sanctioned in our textbooks, the messier (which is not to say revisionist) account that helps to correct and complete the historical record. In the words of Edwin Scott Gaustad, who draws upon Reinhold Niebuhr in his classic study *Dissent in American Religion*, although "consent makes democracy possible, dissent makes democracy meaningful."[2]

For instance, the story we must remember is that even as the Pilgrims escaped religious persecution in Europe, they would become the persecutors on the new soil in America. This transition from being the persecuted to becoming the persecutors can be seen whether in the form of a puritanical moral regime as dramatized by Nathaniel Hawthorne's *The Scarlet Letter* or Arthur Miller's *The Crucible*, a theocratic hierarchy leading to the exile of religious visionaries and dissidents such as Roger Williams and Anne Hutchinson, or the xenophobic relations with the Native American population that provided the ideological justification for the violent takeover of the land and displacement, if not annihilation, of a people.

The story that we must remember also includes how William Penn's Quakers were so often portrayed as irresponsible fringe elements by many of their contemporaries. For one, they were thought to endow too much power in the hands of the people. For every one of those who were pushing for more universal suffrage, there were others who feared the "madness of the multitude." For those who believed that the Protestant ideal of the priesthood of every believer translated into a truly democratic polity, there were still others who valued the established churches for their role in promoting social stability. Not only was the Quaker community feared for actually being *too democratic*, but also because of their commitment to pacifism, once the war for independence broke out, their loyalty and patriotism were also questioned.

And finally, we must remember that before the Bill of Rights was ratified, which in the first amendment guaranteed religious liberty and prevented the establishment of religion, Madison and Jefferson forged an unlikely political alliance with the evangelical community in the state of Virginia in order to pass the nation's first law that completely separated the civil from the religious authority. This law was enacted in the 1786 Act for Establishing Religious Freedom. As chronicled by Susan Jacoby in her book *Freethinkers,* its passage provides the perfect case in point for how politics and religion make for strange bedfellows. In this particular case, Madison and Jefferson, as representatives of the Enlightenment rationalist tradition, were motivated primarily out of a principled interest in religious liberty and out of an awareness of the damage done by state-sanctioned religion in the past. Meanwhile, the evangelicals were keenly aware that they represented a minority religious population and thus stood to lose if any single religious institution was to be given any state support. For this brief moment in time, as Jacoby writes, "the interests of the evangelicals and the Enlightenment rationalists coincided and coalesced in a common support for separation of church and state." Jacoby continues:

> Although evangelicals did not share Madison's and Jefferson's suspicions of religious influence on civil government—indeed, they wished to expand the scope of their own influence—they eventually became convinced that dissenting denominations could best flourish under a government that explicitly prohibited state interference with church affairs. And they were willing to renounce government money to ensure government noninterference.[3]

Thus, while there is a great truth and a proud legacy contained within the mythic story of our national origins, as a sacralization or mythologization of an unruly and contested history, it is precisely that: a truth and a legacy *contained* and thus carefully controlled as it becomes the tool in the ideology of American exceptionalism.

Awakening a Revolutionary Democracy

While for some, this historical amnesia might be merely academic, for others it is a matter of urgent concern if we desire to better understand and redirect the new politics of religion in the United States. The urgency of this endeavor is perhaps best expressed by the American historian Gary Nash, who chronicles what he calls "the unknown American Revolution." As Nash writes, "The American Revolution was not only a war of independence but [also] a many-sided struggle to reinvent America. It was a civil war at home as well as a military struggle for national liberation."[4] By chronicling this "revolution within the revolution," or the struggle for democracy that took place simultaneous with and in some cases even laid the groundwork for the war for independence, Nash reminds us how during the early days of the American republic, just as now, there was a battle between those who placed a premium on freedom, security, and order—versus those driven by concerns for equality and equity. Further, just as independence does not necessarily constitute democracy, democratic action does not necessarily require independence as its prerequisite. Therefore, though the war for independence was eventually won, the democratic revolution for a free, just, and equal society is never complete. In Nash's words:

> To think of the American Revolution as incomplete is very different from arguing that it was a failure, even for those with the most expansive ideas about a truly free, just, and equal society. Revolutions are always incomplete. Almost every social and political convulsion that has gone beyond first disruptions of the *ancient régime* depended on mass involvement; and that in itself, in every recorded case of revolutionary insurgency, raised expectations that could not be completely satisfied. In this sense, there has never been such a thing as a completed revolution.[5]

As for the mass involvement and the raising of expectations that Nash has in mind, integral to this story is the role played by the radical religious visionaries, itinerant preachers, and newly emboldened communities astir with the religious passion coming with the belief that they were direct agents of God. The religious effect on the emerging American democracy can first be seen in what is commonly referred to as the First Great Awakening, a series of religious revivals that swept through the colonies during the middle of the eighteenth century, at least a full generation before the actual war for independence was fought. This outburst of religious enthusiasm has been called "the most powerful—and diffuse—religious movement since the [Protestant] Reformation itself."[6] The main catalyst was the English Calvinist George Whitefield, who toured the American colonies as a traveling evangelist. Whitefield was nicknamed "the Grand Itinerant," indicating that though he was ordained as a priest by the Church of England, though he had a formal theological training within the Calvinist tradition and was a friend and contemporary of John Wesley (the founder of the Methodists) during his studies at Oxford, his primary identity and influence was as "a preacher who is not confined to one particular church and pulpit but who proclaims the Word wherever he can find listeners."[7] With the great success of the emotionally stirring sermons by Whitefield, the colonies had perhaps their first united and unifying cultural experience. It was as though everyone had either heard Whitefield for themselves, or knew of someone who had. In this way, the first Great Awakening proved instrumental in the birth of a national consciousness and the making of a political federation. Hence, an examination of the politics of religion during this period shows how *the cultural led the political* as this shared religious experience helped to form a collective identity.

More native to our present concerns, while the Great Awakening is seen by historians as one of the first common and unifying experiences within the American colonies, equally important was its message of social leveling, which was seen by many contemporaries as especially incendiary. As Nash writes, "Whitefield challenged traditional sources of authority, called upon people to become instruments of their own salvation, and implicitly attacked the prevailing upper-class notion that the uneducated masses had no minds of their own."[8] The effect of this message, again in the words of Nash, was the "[relocation of] authority collectively in the mass of common people."[9] Needless to say, one would imagine that there would be many established interests that resented, feared, and resisted this movement. One contemporary, for instance, accused the traveling itinerants such as Whitefield of being "a set of incendiaries, enemies not only of the Established Church, but also common disturbers of the peace."[10] Worried Anglican clergymen in Virginia were able to convince the governor "to restrain 'strolling preachers' who conjured up a world without properly constituted authority."[11]

Though in hindsight this widespread and emotionally potent series of religious revivals might have proved to be enormously effective in creating a common culture and forging the beginnings of a national identity, during that time its leaders were seen by many as irresponsible and unrefined agitators. The notion that they were conjuring up worlds without the legitimate authority to do so leaves the impression that they worked more as sorcerers and magicians than as authentic preachers of the gospel. They offered an unapologetically radical egalitarian interpretation of the gospel. In so doing, they upset the established social order and planted the seeds of democracy within the emerging culture of the American colonies. Nash spells out the radical democratic implications of this movement well:

> The Great Awakening provided a "radical model" for revolutionary activists. . . . The Awakeners created a mass movement; they challenged upper-class assumptions about social order and the deference due to established figures; they seceded from churches they regarded as corrupt and built new, regenerated ones in their place, even without license; they forced religious toleration on those arrayed against it and broke apart attempted unions of church and state; they fractured established churches such as those in Virginian and thereby threatened the existing social order.[12]

In short, neither the revivalist preachers nor the converts they attracted knew their place or observed the proper decorum. The First Great Awakening can and should be seen as a democratic movement not only because it endowed individuals with the gumption, if not the right, to question authority, but also because it left individuals organized and mobilized as collective congregations in its wake. It is not that the emphasis on personal conversion merely undermined the authority of established churches and the existing social order, but rather that a new locus of authority was established—an authority whose legitimacy lied squarely with the people acting as agents of God.

The Revaluation of Revolution

This brief survey of the social effects of the First Great Awakening provides a glimpse into how the radical religious element might and actually did contribute to generating a revolutionary fervor for democracy and independence. But recalling Nash's earlier statements about the revolution within the revolution and how the American Revolution was not only a war for independence but also a struggle to reinvent American society, it should be no surprise that the forces for democracy and independence were not always in line. It is one thing to upend an established social order and even overthrow a political regime, as was accomplished in the American Revolution, but it is something else to establish a democracy in which it is actually the people who rule. This is perhaps best illustrated by contrasting John Adams and Thomas Paine, both in terms of the respective positions they held in society and how they have been remembered in history.

With regard to John Adams, he is one of the most revered figures in U.S. history. He was the first Vice President of the United States and the second President; he was the cousin of the Boston Patriot Samuel Adams and father of John Quincy Adams. He was one of the principal architects of the tradition of American republicanism. Still today numerous biographies and critical studies of Adams's impact on the American political system are being published, to great acclaim and popularity.[13]

Captivating perhaps, and by almost every account, and in spite of his leadership in rallying support for declaring independence from England, he was also deeply conservative, placing great emphasis on social order and decorum. For instance, he once complained to his wife, Abigail, that "our struggle [for independence] has loosened the bands of government everywhere. That children and apprentices were disobedient—that schools and colleges were grown turbulent—that Indians slighted their guardians and Negroes grew insolent to their masters."[14] This aristocratic sensibility was somewhat ironic considering that Adams was one of the few founding fathers who was not independently wealthy.

There is also the famous and illuminating exchange between John and Abigail Adams in which she implored him to "remember the ladies, and be more generous and favourable to them than your ancestors." After all, she argued, the same "passion for liberty" that was deemed noble in the American Revolutionary effort also animated a growing number of women with regard to their own social and political status. Therefore, she warned: "Do not put such unlimited power into the hands of the husbands. Remember, all men would be tyrants if they could. If particular care and attention is not paid to the ladies, we are determined to foment a rebellion, and will not hold ourselves bound by any laws in which we have no voice or representation."[15] For the most part, Adams's response to his wife was one of patient condescension. He indulged her almost like a parent would a child. While he heard her admonition, he never quite saw or understood its legitimacy compared with the great matters of war and state with which he was primarily consumed.

Because Adams's first concern was liberty but not necessarily equality, or order but not necessarily democracy, his struggle in the American Revolutionary effort was deemed complete whenever the English crown conceded independence for the colonies. The end of the war for independence marked a turning point as the business of government took priority over the cause for equality, meaning that we are faced with a certain contradiction not only within Adams's character, but also within the founding of the American republic. As Nash describes this contradiction, "Adams saw the Revolution as a 'people's war,' but he was unwilling to have a people's war produce a people's polity. Adams loved liberty but not equality, and from this position he would not budge through the entire course of the long Revolution."[16]

Turning from Adams to the radical pamphleteer Thomas Paine, we discover an individual who lived a much more turbulent life, seemingly forever displaced. English by birth, he did not arrive in the American colonies until 1774, when his trip was personally arranged by Benjamin Franklin, whom Paine had met in London a few months earlier. His pamphlet *Common Sense*, first published in January 1776, eventually became the best-selling work in eighteenth-century America and is credited with convincing many colonists, including George Washington, to declare independence from England. Paine was an almost rabid advocate for personal liberty and limited government. He also became an outspoken champion for universal suffrage, which Adams roundly dismissed as one of Paine's "absurd democratical notions." Though Adams was forced to admit that "I know not whether any man in the world has had more influence on its inhabitants or affairs for the last thirty years than Tom Paine," he privately confessed his distaste, writing that Paine was "a mongrel between pig and puppy, begotten by a wild boar on a bitch wolf," and that "never before in any age of the world" was such a "poltroon" allowed "to run through such a career of mischief."[17]

Adams's opinion of Paine notwithstanding, Paine's influence and renown extended beyond America since he was also an enthusiastic supporter of the French Revolution. His book *The Rights of Man*, first published in 1791 after Paine had returned to Europe, continued the arguments first developed in *Common Sense*, though now they were applied more universally as a general critique of all monarchies and European aristocratic institutions. As the French Revolution degenerated into the so-called Reign of Terror, Paine's situation grew worse and worse, to the point of his being imprisoned and sentenced to death. While in prison, he completed his scathing attack on revealed religion in a book called *The Age of Reason*.

This work proved once again that Paine was not afraid of controversy, and for our purposes, it demonstrates the connection between democratic ideals and religious dissent. Only here, in contrast to the examples examined previously from the first Great Awakening, Paine's views on religion represent an almost opposite extreme. The only thing that Paine's rationalized deism had in common with the enthusiastic form of piety preached by the likes of Whitefield is that they were both anti-institutional and antiestablishment. But while Whitefield helped to contribute to a widespread cultural movement that gave great momentum to the American Revolutionary cause for independence, Paine's religious writings came only after independence had been won. Therefore, the fact that he stood outside the mainstream as a critical voice of dissent meant that many of those who celebrated the rhetorical force of his polemics in *Common Sense* now distanced themselves from his ideas and even from Paine personally. In short, a new politics of religion had taken root in the post-Revolutionary American society. The result was that after Paine was released from prison and returned to the United States, he spent his remaining years in isolation and despair.

This despair is most clearly expressed in a series of public letters "To the Citizens of the United States" that he wrote in 1802, soon after he had first returned to the United States from Europe. Paine called these letters "sparks from the altar of Seventy-Six." They hearken back not only to the words of *Common Sense*, but also to the vision of the New World as articulated by Winthrop, Penn, and so many others before him: "The independence of America . . . was the opportunity of *beginning the world anew*, as it were; and of bringing forward a *new system* of government in which the rights of *all* men should be preserved that gave *value* to independence."[18] Reflecting on this lament from Paine, Nash writes that clearly "matters had gone amiss [for Paine]. The rights of all men had never been fully acknowledged, and in the years [Paine] had been away, the accomplishments of the radical revolutionists to begin the world anew had been sullied."[19] As Jacoby describes it, "The America [that] Paine found when he returned in 1802 was far less hospitable . . . than the America [that] Paine had left fifteen years earlier."[20]

This is why the story of Paine's last years is especially painful. For instance, at the time of his death in 1809, the notice in the New York newspaper that was reprinted around the country read, "He had lived long, did some good and much harm." Only six individuals came to his funeral, two of whom were freed slaves. It was as though his democratic ideals were useful in throwing off the yoke of British imperial rule and in fanning the flames of Revolution, but once the power had changed hands, he had no place to call his home in the very society he had helped to create. "To this day," Jacoby writes, "the received opinion about Paine . . . is that he was an important revolutionary propagandist but an unimportant thinker."[21] The problem with this, however, as Jacoby points out, is that Paine himself had remained remarkably consistent through the years—the same firebrand, the same enemy of monarchy and organized religion. In Jacoby's words, "Paine the theologian and Paine the politician were not different men—even though many historians, wishing to credit the author of 'Common Sense' but not the author of *The Age of Reason*, have tried to make the case that they were. The antimonarchical and antiecclesiastical Paines were united in the belief that there could be no legitimacy in forms of government or forms of religion that defied reason and nature."[22]

So if not Paine, then what did change? For one, there was the consolidation of power within the U.S. government, most notably in the Alien and Sedition Acts that the Adams administration had passed in 1798. Under the Sedition Act, anyone "opposing or resisting any law of the United States, or any act of the President of the United States" could be imprisoned for up to two years. It was also illegal to "write, print, utter, or publish" anything critical of the President or Congress. The Alien Enemies Act gave the President the authority to apprehend and deport resident aliens if their home countries were at war with the United States. Though partly responsible for Adams's defeat to Thomas Jefferson in the 1800 presidential election and partially repealed in 1801, these acts nevertheless had the effect of stifling all criticism of the government and greatly enhancing the power of the executive branch of government. Indeed, the Alien Enemies Act still remains in effect today and has been crucial in making President Bush's case for the post-9/11 legislation known as the USA Patriot Act as well as the more recent Military Commissions Act, which gives the President the authority to suspend the writ of habeas corpus for those deemed "unlawful enemy combatants" of the state.

Additionally, there was a revaluation of the very idea of revolution itself. After the American Revolution successfully won independence for the United States, two other revolutions followed quickly in its wake, both of which helped give the idea of revolution a bad name for many within American society. The first was the French Revolution, which lasted from 1789 to 1799. The history of the French Revolution is well known. It includes the democratic rallying cry of "Liberty, Equality, Fraternity, or Death," the harsh and abrupt policy of de-Christianization, as well as the "Reign of Terror," a period of brutal repression during which virtually all the hard-won civil liberties were suspended by the ruling political regime. Closer to home was the slave uprising in Haiti (1791–1804) that led to the establishment of Haiti as the hemisphere's first and only free black republic. Although the French Revolution is seen by many as a major turning point in Western civilization, it was the Haitian Revolution that threatened all those in the United States still reliant on a slave-based, plantation economy.

The result of this widespread distancing from, if not disavowal of, revolution, at least in the minds of those such as Paine, was that democracy was sacrificed at the altar of independence. For instance, it would be over half a century before slavery was outlawed, and only after a brutal civil war. In spite of Abigail Adams's pleadings, it would be over a century before women were given the right to vote. Native Americans were stripped of their land, their dignity, their autonomy, and for all too many, even their lives. Recalling Nash again, the democratic revolution within the Revolution was not only incomplete, but in many ways also utterly abandoned as the nation grew from its Revolutionary beginnings to its current status as the world's great power.

In the meantime, the politics of religion in the United States has also undergone a dramatic transformation. As the sociologist of religion Robert Bellah chronicles, the United States developed its own distinctive civil religion, one that blurs the boundary between church and state; especially in times of national crisis, it easily becomes a tool of the ruling interests, no matter whether their policies and aims are consistent with the civil religion's transcendent principles or not.[23] With this civil religion, both the radical religious element and the voice of religious dissent are tempered by the prevailing national wisdom of diligence, moderation, and individualism, all of which are essential ingredients in the so-called Protestant work ethic that fits hand in glove with the spirit of capitalism.[24] This new politics of religion is a de facto form of religious establishment that gives sanction to the individual and national pursuit of profit above all else. Within this milieu, it becomes increasingly difficult to distinguish between democratic freedoms and the freedom of the open market as our American-styled democracy has been conflated with a particular economic system and ideology. We have fought and died in the name of democracy while the truly revolutionary aspects of democracy in the fight for greater equality, justice, and franchise have been subordinated to our commercial interests.

A Battle for the Soul of America

It is precisely with these concerns in mind that the well-known neopragmatic African-American philosopher Cornel West has recently written a book titled *Democracy Matters*, which forcefully challenges the antidemocratic dogmas that plague contemporary American society and politics. These antidemocratic dogmas include what he calls "a callous free-market fundamentalism, an aggressive militarism, and an insidious authoritarianism." These dogmas blind Americans to their history, deluding us of our racist and imperialistic past, and simultaneously simplifying the great complexity of the hard choices we face now and for the future. Key to the potency of these antidemocratic dogmas is the role played by religion. As West describes it, the contemporary influence of religion in American politics and society represents a "battle for the soul of American democracy," and this battle is "in large part, a battle for the soul of American Christianity."[25]

As someone who still believes in the promise of American democracy, West drinks from the traditional wells of both radical religion and religious dissent, the evangelical waters of the First Great Awakening and the voice of skepticism and nonconformity from Paine's *Common Sense*. Regarding the first, West distinguishes between "Constantinian Christianity" and "prophetic Christianity." "Constantinian Christianity" represents the merger of church and state, whether in the soft cultural form of civil religion or in the theocratic ambitions of an imperial authoritarianism. As West rightly points out, this Constantinian temptation has always plagued Christianity throughout its history, leading to a certain "insidious schizophrenia" in which, according to the logic of the Christian faith, one's loyalty ultimately belongs to God, while at the same time the religion is used as a political tool for unification and conformity. As West writes, "The American democratic experiment would have been inconceivable without the fervor of Christians, yet strains of Constantianism were woven into the fabric of America's Christian identity from the start. Constantinian strains of American Christianity have been on the wrong side of so many of our social troubles, such as the dogmatic justification of slavery and the parochial defense of women's inequality."[26]

On the other hand, prophetic Christianity is more consistent, though its demands are more radical. In the New Testament, it is expressed in Jesus' concern for the poor and the outcasts, and in his primary interest in the kingdom of God as a radically egalitarian and nonhierarchical society. It is also seen in the early church's communal sharing of its wealth and resources as described in the Acts of the Apostles. It places a priority on the message of social justice as opposed to the exclusive emphasis on personal salvation; theologically speaking, it is more eschatological than soteriological. In the United States, this prophetic Christianity led the fight for the abolition of slavery, was the pioneering voice for women's suffrage, was integral to the trade-union movements, and was the impetus and foundation for so much in the civil rights movement. In West's mind, "This prophetic Christianity adds a moral fervor to our democracy that is a very good thing. It also holds that we must embrace those outside of the Christian faith and act with empathy towards them. This prophetic Christianity is an ecumenical force for good."[27]

It is also inevitably a voice from the margins. It should be no surprise that within a short span of time, both John the Baptist and Jesus were executed by the Roman Empire, being branded as subversive figures and enemies of the state. Likewise within the history of the United States, many of the leaders of prophetic Christianity have been branded as radicals, have faced criminal prosecution, and in some cases have even been martyred. The message is challenging since it exposes the fissures that exist not only within our deeply divided society but also within the meaning and interpretation of religion itself. Constantinian Christianity is a permanent temptation because it lures people with "the rewards and respectability of the American empire." It is precisely because of its seductive power, precisely because so many of us have bought into the "idol of money and the fetish of wealth," that the restoration of a radical prophetic voice is so central to the future of our democracy.[28]

But in the tradition of Paine, West also hearkens back to that other nonconformist tradition of religious critique and dissent, especially Ralph Waldo Emerson, who wrote in his famous essay "Self-Reliance" that "whoso would be a man must be a nonconformist." And further, "Nothing is at last sacred but the integrity of your own mind."[29] This voice of critique and dissent applies not only to religion, but more fundamentally, also to the American dream of prosperity that subordinates all other values to its pursuit. This concern with consumerism was such a great and urgent matter for Emerson that he expressed in a number of different ways:

> Trade is the lord of the world nowadays—and government only a parachute to this balloon.
> There is nothing more important in the culture of man than to resist the dangers of commerce.
> Out of doors, all seems a market.[30]

In a story reminiscent to that of Paine, we have in Emerson someone who has observed what the United States has become and, at least to a certain degree, recoiled. On the one hand, the United States is a society that prides itself on equal opportunity and individual merit (e.g., Horatio Alger's rags-to-riches stories of the self-made man), but on the other there is widespread conformity—a tyranny of the majority only made stronger by the market-driven forces of the voluntary nature of American religion. In such a society as this, where the illusion of choice provides an almost unlimited selection of breakfast cereals but virtually no escape from consumer society, from the commodification of everything even including democracy and religion themselves, where do we turn?

By looking to the past, we can be encouraged to know that this struggle is not new, that whatever we make of the new politics of religion in the United States, there are resources within our own tradition that might inform and inspire. And finally, we might do well to remember that the democratic revolution that was begun is never complete. Just as there is a fight and struggle over the proper interpretation of Christianity today, just as there are those on the margins of our society whom we would do well to hear, so too is there hope and a call to action.

Notes

1 Quoted in Peter Williams, *America's Religions: From Their Origins to the Twenty-First Century* (Urbana: University of Illinois Press, 2002), 130.

2 Edwin Scott Gaustad, *Dissent in American Religion*, rev. ed. (Chicago: University of Chicago Press, 2006), 2.

3 Susan Jacoby, *Freethinkers: A History of American Secularism* (New York: Henry Holt, 2004), 21.

4 Gary Nash, *The Unknown American Revolution: The Unruly Birth of Democracy and the Struggle to Create America* (New York: Penguin Books, 2005), 1.

5 Ibid., 453–54.

6 Williams, *America's Religions*, 140.

7 Ibid., 142.

8 Nash, *Unknown American Revolution*, 9.

9 Ibid., 10.

10 Quoted in Henry Mayer, *A Son of Thunder: Patrick Henry and the American Revolution* (New York: Franklin Watts, 1986), 34.

11 Nash, *Unknown American Revolution*, 10.

12 Ibid., 11.

13 See especially David McCullough, *John Adams* (New York: Simon & Schuster, 2001), a best- selling work that was also the winner of the 2002 Pulitzer Prize. Also Joseph J. Ellis, *Passionate Sage: The Character and Legacy of John Adams* (New York: W. W. Norton, 1993), 230: "Indeed, by the time of the bicentennial of the American Revolution, Adams's reputation within the community of professional historians had recovered the lofty position it had occupied at the time of his death. When Robert Rutland reviewed the several modern editions of the papers of the Founding Fathers, he concluded that there was a fresh scholarly consensus: 'Madison was the great intellectual.... Jefferson the ... unquenchable idealist, and Franklin the most charming and versatile genius, but Adams is the most captivating founding father on most counts.'"

14 John Adams to Abigail Adams, *Adams Family Correspondence*, vol. 1 (New York: Athenaeum, 1965), 381.

15 Abigail Adams to John Adams, in ibid., 369–71.

16 Nash, *Unknown American Revolution*, 279.

17 Quoted in ibid., 425.

18 As quoted in ibid., 423.

19 Ibid.

20 Jacoby, *Freethinkers*, 43.

21 Ibid., 59.

22 Ibid.

23 See Robert Bellah, *The Broken Covenant: American Civil Religion in Time of Trial* (New York: Seabury, 1975).

24 See Max Weber, *The Protestant Ethic and the Spirit of Capitalism* (New York: Routledge, 1992).

25 Cornel West, *Democracy Matters: Winning the Fight against Imperialism* (New York: Penguin, 2004), 146.

26 Ibid., 149.

27 Ibid., 152.

28 Ibid., 158.

29 Quoted in ibid., 69.

30 Quoted in ibid., 72.

2

Prophetic Evangelicals
Toward a Politics of Hope
Peter Goodwin Heltzel

The American political establishment's fascination with evangelicals is entering its fourth decade. It began with Jimmy Carter's 1976 candidacy for the presidency and continued through George W. Bush's 2004 re-election. Indeed, no shortage of tools has been used to examine evangelicals. Sociologists have looked at demographics, and political scientists have analyzed tactics, but they have all neglected one important element. To understand politically active evangelicals in all their diversity—from storefront-church Pentecostals to members of the established African-American churches to white suburbanites who attend megachurches—you have to explore their theologies.

Deep theological conviction is what drives evangelicals to political action. Nineteenth-century evangelical abolitionists fought against slavery, and twentieth-century evangelicals fought for the lives of unborn babies: they were united in their desire to embody Jesus Christ's gospel of love and justice. Though many Americans think of evangelicals as otherworldly militant conservatives, there has been another stream of earthly generous activists deeply engaged in the struggle for justice. This group of justice-seeking evangelicals I describe as "prophetic evangelicals."

In this chapter, I define evangelicalism and introduce prophetic evangelicalism, using "progressive" as a contrast term for understanding some of the basic theological logics of evangelicalism. Focusing on the issue of racial justice, I next describe prophetic evangelicalism's roots in the abolition struggle, in the context of antebellum revivalism, and then describe evangelicals' ambivalent relationship to the civil rights struggle. In the context of this historical background, I argue that prophetic evangelicals currently play a vital role in the emergence of a new moral center developing around issues of racial, economic, and environmental justice. Throughout American history, when white evangelicals have been in solidarity with the African-American freedom struggle, they have most fully embodied prophetic Christianity.

Who Are the Evangelicals?

One cannot turn on the television today or open *The New York Times* without meeting a new evangelical. From T. D. Jakes to President George W. Bush, evangelicals are ubiquitous in contemporary American life. Who are these passionate Protestant Christians, and where did they come from?

Contemporary interest in evangelicals is driven in part by the concrete political power this group of conservative Christians wields. Many see President George W. Bush as a symbol of the new evangelical political establishment. As a self-identified evangelical, Bush and his religiosity have been well received among many evangelicals. Esther Kaplan writes, "Bush's religiosity is so widely embraced on the Christian Right that when Pat Robertson resigned as president of the Christian Coalition at the end of 2001, American Values president Gary Bauer told the *Washington Post*, 'I think Robertson stepped down because the position has already been filled. [Bush] is that leader right now.'"[1]

Evangelicals provided an important swing vote in the 2000 and 2004 presidential elections, the foundation of the Karl Rove strategy. One recent Pew survey showed that 87 percent of "traditionalist" evangelicals (10.7 percent of the adult population) voted for President Bush in the 2004 presidential election.[2] Although many evangelicals voted for President Bush in the past two presidential elections, not all evangelicals have categorically embraced him and his domestic and foreign policies. What is clear is that the lion's share of evangelicals heartily agrees with Bush's "pro-life" stand on the controversial abortion issue, the "pro-life" position being a central plank in the platform of the Republican party since 1980.

Evangelical politics experienced a political rebirth in the 1970s through the abortion issue. *Roe versus Wade* in 1973 received the quick attention of evangelicals, but not until the disclosure that abortions performed per year were over one million did evangelicals become galvanized for political action. Not only did evangelicals throughout the nation protest in front of abortion clinics; they also set up crisis pregnancy centers and developed extensive networks of adoption and support for mothers contemplating abortion. When pro-life evangelicals migrated to the Republican party in droves in 1980, they began to play an important role in the ascendancy of Republican politics that has continued to the present. Largely through the politics of the "traditional family" focused on the abortion issue, we have seen a growing identification between evangelicals and the Republican party, an alliance that evangelical historian Randall Balmer calls "blasphemous."[3]

Though the issue of abortion has been central to the political mobilization of evangelical Christians, American evangelicalism is more complex than contemporary recent historical and political accountings would often like us to think. The U.S. media frequently equate evangelicalism with the religious Right. The Left wing blogosphere and sometimes the mainstream media stereotype evangelicals as zealous Republican evangelists who want to reclaim a Christian America. This caricatured accounting of evangelicalism fails to differentiate the religious Right (e.g., Jerry Falwell, Ralph Reed, Pat Robertson) from more justice-oriented evangelicals (e.g., Tony Campolo, William Dyrness, David Gushee, Richard Mouw, Ron Sider, Glenn Stassen, Jim Wallis). I call the latter group "prophetic evangelicals." A thoughtful analysis of the history of American evangelicalism and its current political manifestation shows that prophetic evangelicals today represent a consistent, albeit sometimes a minority, stream of evangelicalism committed to social justice that dates back to the middle of the nineteenth century. They, too, are evangelicals. How is that possible?

British historian David Bebbington identifies four distinctive features of evangelical faith and practice: (1) a conversion to Jesus Christ, (2) a view in which the Bible is the ultimate religious authority, (3) an activism expressed through evangelism and social witness, and (4) an emphasis on Jesus' death on the cross and bodily resurrection from the dead.[4] Bebbington's definition has become a standard in the field of American religious history and provides the basic theological parameters for understanding transatlantic evangelicalism. Bebbington's definition is satisfactory only in the abstract; it is inadequate to the extent that it ignores the varied historical, cultural, and political contexts within which evangelicalism has flourished. A fuller account of the evangelical movement would take into consideration the different ways that the theological themes Bebbington identifies are deployed to further political ends. To understand prophetic evangelicalism in America, we must consider different pockets of American culture, including their histories.

Many historians argue that in the eighteenth and early nineteenth centuries, all Protestant Christians in America were broadly evangelical.[5] Slavery in the antebellum South became the decisive issue that divided evangelicalism in half. Evangelicals who argued for slavery and those who argued against it both appealed to the same Bible to forge their arguments. For evangelicalism, slavery became a hermeneutical, theological, and ethical dilemma of the greatest proportion. Prophetic evangelicalism has its historic roots in the abolition struggle against slavery. Its ancestors are people like Jonathan Blanchard, the founder of Wheaton College; Charles G. Finney, the father of modern revivalism; Asa Mahan, the first president of Oberlin College; and numerous others—particularly leaders of American Methodism, who are discussed at more length below.

Prophetic Evangelicals

Prophetic evangelicals today continue the nineteenth-century radical religious tradition. True to these roots, they are concerned with a whole ethic of life, one that includes addressing racism, poverty, and militarism, and more adequately meeting our needs in education, health care, AIDS, and the environment, among other issues. In all of their struggles for justice, prophetic evangelicals persistently bear witness to the gospel. They are Bible-believing, Christ-centered ambassadors for justice. For prophetic evangelicals, the call to world evangelism and the call to embody an ethic of global justice go hand in hand. The word of God finds its fulfillment in the concrete work of loving the neighbor. Yet at important junctures in American history, prophetic evangelicals are also honest about past failures to be on the side of justice. As we shall recognize below, the civil rights movement is one moment when many white evangelicals chose to sit on the sidelines. Repenting for these sins of omission, prophetic evangelicals seek now to march ahead, bearing gospel witness at the sites of the most intractable injustice. What distinguishes them from other forms of evangelicalism is their distinct commitment to the struggle for peace and social justice, both in this country and in the world.

The struggle for justice is the one reason why prophetic evangelicalism is, or always seeks to be, prophetic. Hermeneutics is the beginning of evangelical politics. Since evangelicals believe that the Bible is their ultimate authority, evangelical politics will always be biblical politics. But the key to interpreting the biblical text, according to prophetic evangelicals, is the Christian obligation to apply Scripture to all dimensions of our contemporary context, including its political and economic realities. This way of interpreting the sacred past is central to biblical prophecy and the prophetic tradition.

Prophecy is a prominent genre in the biblical literature and a theme that spans the breadth of redemptive history. Prophecy is the very word of God that is shared with God's people through a messenger called a prophet: *nabi* in Hebrew (*nāvî'*). An act of prophecy always begins with God. God is the source, the sustenance, and the future of the prophetic word. The prophet's words are vital because they provide a discursive medium to reconnect people of God with their creator.

Prophecy has always played an important role in the apocalyptic imagination of American evangelicals. Typically, however, the evangelical emphasis on prophecy is connected to Christology. Evangelicals focus their understanding of prophecy around predictions of the coming Messiah, a focus representative of their christocentric hermeneutic habit. When evangelicals interpret the Bible, it is often through the lens of Jesus Christ. While other Christian traditions may use alternate hermeneutical strategies, evangelicals time and time again come back to "the words in red," the words spoken by Jesus Christ. Since Christians understand Jesus Christ to be the Messiah promised by the Hebrew prophets, the prophetic motif fits the biblical and christological parameters of the evangelical imagination.

In summary, prophetic evangelicalism more accurately describes the form that evangelical politics takes since it is fundamentally *biblical politics*. American evangelicals, like the magisterial Reformers, see the Bible as their sole source of faith and practice. They frame their contemporary political action with the background of redemptive history. Jesus Christ's teaching, life, and redemptive death and resurrection become the animating locus of social engagement in the world. Prophetic evangelicals are committed to world evangelization, but they see robust social witness as another vital form of evangelical testimony.

Since I am writing this chapter to illuminate the new politics of religion in the United States, I will take a moment to explain why "prophetic" is a better designation than "progressive" for this band of justice-making evangelicals. It is not simply that evangelicals prefer the term "prophetic" because it is more biblical and more christocentric; it also reflects a different philosophy of history than does the term "progressive." The evangelical's allergic reaction to the term "progressive" is in part due to its etymology—its deployment in Marxist discourse to designate being on the right side of the French Revolution.[6] In this system, any given political agent either flows out of this liberation struggle for *liberté, égalité, fraternité* as a "progressive"; or reacts against it as a conservative, a "reactionary." Adopting a Hegelian notion of human history including an inevitable dynamic toward progress as driving the historic process, many early Marxist historians viewed history as moving in one direction (toward socialism). Given this historic trajectory, political agents and collectives need to fall into line with history's flow toward economic democracy. While the Marxist theoretical background of the term "progressive" does not exhaust the term's multiple sources, it has enough of an effective history to be uninviting to most evangelicals. In the context of Marxist thought in general, there are at least two reasons this is the case: atheism and socialist economics.

Evangelical's initial concern with the term "progressive" is the atheist underpinning of Marx's thought. Much of the evangelical apologetic struggle in the twentieth century was spent in focused defense of biblical theism against its atheist detractors. In Marx's thought, religion is part of the problem with political economy. It is a part of the old regime that needs to be shed like the skin off a snake's back. Scientific and economic facility and skill are critical for humanity to progress, while religion is an "opiate of the people" precisely because it hinders this greater societal progress. Marx would interpret contemporary evangelical religiosity as the last gasp for a religion withering as quickly as a tree in an eternal desert. For evangelicals, on the other hand, the Judeo-Christian heritage provides God's moral law and Jesus' ethical example as the common moral center for ordering society.

Evangelicals' second concern with the term "progressive" is the utopian aspirations of socialist economics. Though the French Revolution was primarily a project in political liberation, Marx applied aspects of the revolutionary project to economic liberation. As this conjunction of politics and economics would develop within Marxist analysis, one was "progressive" if working for economic democracy, but "reactionaries" supported free-market capitalism. Marx saw history as moving toward socialism; evangelicals saw history moving toward the second coming of Jesus Christ. Though an evangelical ethic may include cooperative forms of community, it does not see socialism as a necessary economic system or the end of history. Evangelical concern with socialist economics has to do in part with a robust doctrine of sin that casts suspicion on historic attempts to "hold all things in common" (cf. Acts 2:44; 4:32), thus pushing evangelicals more toward a defense of personal property and the creativity necessary in a free-enterprise culture to fuel economic growth.

Evangelicals' concern with the threat of atheism and the false idealism of socialist economics was exacerbated with the escalation of the Cold War. Atheism and communism often became identified with each other in the evangelical imagination, particularly in the fundamentalist flank. The communist threat abroad and the liberal threat at home put many evangelicals on the defensive, inspiring them to fight more heartily in defending the gospel and the American way of life.

As a result of these problems with labeling evangelicals as progressive, I suggest using prophetic discourse as a framework for developing and proclaiming a Christian alternative to the Christian Right. The language of prophecy is biblical, christocentric, and activist, capturing the spirit of any evangelicals committed to lives of justice-seeking and peace-making. Further, it makes possible all that a "progressive" Christian witness today seeks to claim, without the unfortunate inheritance of Marxist progressivism.

But what is the future of prophetic evangelicalism? What can we learn about its potential power from the successes and failures of evangelicalism's past? In what follows in this essay, I will focus on prophetic evangelicals' engagement of racial justice in the abolition movement, the civil rights movement, and in new coalitions for justice. I am particularly interested in how white evangelicals in the North and South have responded to African Americans at moments of crisis and why. My thesis is that white evangelicals have maintained their prophetic character when they were in solidarity with the freedom struggles of African Americans and lost their prophetic character as they refused to participate in these movements for racial justice. If this thesis is sustained, it may contain lessons not only for evangelicals, and not only for all Christians who seek to provide a prophetic witness today, but also for the broader culture seeking to understand the redemptive and emancipatory political power of religion.

Evangelicals, Revivalism, and Abolition

Evangelicalism of all varieties has roots in the transatlantic revivalism of the eighteenth and nineteenth centuries, specifically in the periods known as the First and Second Great Awakenings. Often referred to as "classical evangelicalism," it emphasizes the conversionist and pietistic strands of American evangelicalism. Though much of colonial America bore a Calvinist and Puritan imprint, the eighteenth and nineteenth centuries' revivalism and radical reform is better characterized as Methodist. Wesleyan doctrines of sanctification were often applied to both personal piety as well as societal transformation. With the free-will orientation of Arminian forms of Methodism and a postmillennial eschatology, nineteenth-century evangelicals were often engaged in ministries of social transformation, including the struggle to abolish slavery, one of the great founts of the prophetic evangelical social ethic.[7]

A significant cross-fertilization occurred between white and black evangelicals in the nineteenth century, both shaped by streams of antebellum revivalism. Revivals created a new religious landscape for whites and African Americans to meet on equal footing. Through the great revival meetings, many individuals, regardless of race and ethnicity, were brought to faith in Jesus Christ. John Wesley and George Whitefield arrived in the South during the late 1730s. Meeting his first black slave on August 1, 1736, John Wesley quickly began to share his faith with African Americans. When George Whitefield came ashore in the Carolinas in 1738, African Americans converted in large numbers. As a result of these conversions, a strong African-American Protestant presence emerged in the lower South and Mid-Atlantic States.

At points, revival meetings functioned as a new space for racial reconciliation. At their best, revivals would often provide positive consequences, including blacks and whites worshipping together, some white slaveholders letting their slaves go, and other white slaveholders beginning to treat their slaves more humanely. Within the revivalist ethos were moments of near equality. Mechal Sobel writes, "Virtually all eighteenth-century Baptist and Methodist churches were mixed churches, in which blacks sometimes preached to whites and in which whites and blacks witnessed together, shouted together, and shared ecstatic experiences at 'dry' and wet christenings, meetings and burials."[8] Revivals provided African Americans with both a message of equality before God and a physical space where they were free to express themselves through singing, shaking, running, dancing, chanting, and shouting.

Revivalism provided a new space outside the rigid hierarchies of the plantation for African Americans to sing and dance and express themselves in the rituals and cultural forms of their African past. It also provided an opportunity for many African-American men to preach. For example, Harry Hosier, nicknamed "Black Harry," preached on the circuit with Francis Asbury, and audiences along the revivalist journeys consistently preferred Hosier's passionate preaching to Asbury's staid sermons.[9] Revivalism thus provided a place where African Americans could bring contemporary expression to their ancient African past as well as be empowered to minister to blacks and whites. Revivals created a space for blacks and whites to express their spirituality in an interracial communion. In the context of these revivals, there was also freedom of emotional expression. As whites and blacks were free to express themselves bodily and emotionally in the context of revival meetings, a process of mutual mimicking emerged that becomes a metaphor for present multicultural hybridity within evangelicalism.

In the context of interracial communion that flowed from American revivalism at its best, a growing group of white and black abolitionists emerged. American abolitionism took great inspiration from the abolition movement in Britain. Beginning with a meeting of twelve abolitionists in London, the antislavery movement in Britain culminated in the British parliament voting for slave emancipation in 1833.[10]

During the period of 1840–60, the "new-measures" revivalism of evangelists like Jacob Knapp, Timothy Weld, and Charles G. Finney often led to radical abolition efforts in the North. Preachers in the Oberlin school of Finney sought a higher life of entire sanctification that also had a strong social dimension. Timothy Weld's passionate preaching was a fascinating synthesis of revivalism and reform: he would use altar calls at the end of services to enlist Christians for the abolition movement.

Phoebe Palmer, a popular woman evangelist who focused on an experience of "perfect" love, joined the Oberlin preachers in promoting a more socially engaged Wesleyanism. Jonathan Blanchard, the first president of Wheaton College—founded in Wheaton, Illinois, in 1860—joined the Wesleyan Abolition struggle from his base in the Chicago metro area. While the evangelical abolition movement had more numeric strength in the North, it also had a faithful but smaller remnant in the South. Any black and white evangelicals who joined the struggle for the abolition of slavery are the freedom-fighting forebears of prophetic evangelicals.

Evangelicals and the Civil Rights Movement

As evangelicals moved into the twentieth century, the broader struggle for social justice often became narrowed to matters of personal morality, like drinking, dancing, smoking, and cursing. This fundamentalist focus on personal morality was exacerbated by other factors that marked early twentieth-century evangelicalism: cultural isolationism, a premillennial dispensational eschatology, and anti-intellectualism. Overcoming this fundamentalist retrenchment was the primary theological task of mid-twentieth-century evangelicals.

In the 1940s a new socially conscious neoevangelicalism emerged from fundamentalism as an ecumenical coalition after World War II.[11] This new movement quickly institutionalized through the formation of the National Association of Evangelicals in 1942, the founding of Fuller Seminary in 1947, and the establishment of *Christianity Today* in 1956. The crusades of Billy Graham, including his New York crusade in 1957, which reached out beyond his fundamentalist base to the New York Council of Churches, were also critical to its formation. Neoevangelicals like Carl F. H. Henry and Harold John Ockenga sought to hold on to the primary theological convictions of the fundamentalists, while enlarging the vision to include cultural engagement, political activism, and social transformation.

In 1947 Carl Henry's *The Uneasy Conscience of Modern Fundamentalism* was a splash of cold water in the faces of evangelicals. Henry's "uneasy conscience" was a loud wake-up call to evangelicals to come out from their cultural isolation and join the struggle for broader social transformation.[12] Henry called evangelicals to confront specific political issues of the day, including "aggressive warfare, racial hatred and intolerance, the liquor traffic, and exploitation of labor and management."[13] In addition to taking up the lead issue of "liquor traffic," which drove the prohibition movement, Henry also challenged evangelicals to work for racial justice, economic justice, and international peace. Rooted in the nineteenth-century abolition struggle, this broader evangelical social ethic represented an important paradigm shift in evangelical social action.

Henry began his editorship of *Christianity Today* with hopes of a courageous evangelical engagement of the great social issue of the day, but he met resistance within evangelicalism. While Henry personally spoke and wrote about the importance of racial justice, *Christianity Today* through the 1960s gave the civil rights movement only limited coverage.[14] For example, as editor of *Christianity Today*, Henry sent his colleague Frank E. Gaebelein to cover the Selma March to Montgomery; however, Henry was not allowed to print the stories. Disagreement over editorial policy, where Henry would represent a more prophetic evangelical position, was one of the reasons why Henry would later be asked to resign as editor of the magazine. The fact that *Christianity Today* avoided significant coverage of the civil rights movement, which its mainline rival *The Christian Century* extensively reported, is an illustration of a continued cultural isolationism of many white evangelicals from the struggle for racial justice. These editorial decisions symbolize the great distance between the experiences of many white evangelicals and those of African Americans throughout the country in the 1960s, a problem that has continued to our current day.

Martin Luther King Jr. was disappointed with the lack of white evangelical participation in the civil rights struggle. In his "Letter from Birmingham City Jail," King wrote:

I must confess that over the last few years I have been gravely disappointed with the white moderate. I have almost reached the regrettable conclusion that the Negro's greatest stumbling block in the stride toward freedom is not the White Citizen's Counciler or the Ku Klux Klanner, but the white moderate who is more devoted to "order" than to justice; who prefers a negative peace which is the absence of tension to a positive peace which is the presence of justice; who constantly says, "I agree with you in the goal you seek, but I can't agree with your methods of direct action"; who paternalistically feels that he can set the timetable for another man's freedom; who lives by the myth of time and who constantly advised the Negro to wait until a more "convenient season." Shallow understanding from people of good will is more frustrating than absolute misunderstanding from people of ill will. Lukewarm acceptance is much more bewildering than outright rejection.[15]

King was "gravely disappointed" that white moderates were not joining the struggle for racial justice. During the 1960s, the great majority of white moderates, regardless of their theological or ecclesial identity, were sitting on the sidelines during the civil rights movement. This silence, legitimated by a theological commitment to "order," ensured a noticeable absence of participation in the national struggle for racial and economic justice. Whether mainline or evangelical, white moderates years later were happy to embrace the positive fruit of the civil rights movement; yet history indicates that only a small group of them actually did or said anything to usher it in.

Prophetic Evangelicals in the Twenty-first Century

The African-American freedom struggle has been difficult for many white evangelicals to understand. They have tried to tone down their white power and privilege, in order to fully enter a sympathetic understanding of people of color. New friendships can translate into common actions to dismantle institutional racism. If there is to be reconciliation between white evangelicals and African-American Protestants, white antiracist moderates—the very ones that King called to from the Birmingham jail—will need to wake up and cross the lines to join those on the margin in the struggle for peace and justice.

Though Martin Luther King Jr. and Carl Henry came from quite different places theologically and in terms of their cultural context, they held much in common. They both drew on rhetorical and political themes in their tradition of Baptist revivalism, to "reform" a deeper cultural and political isolationist tendency within their Baptist traditions. They were both prophetic Baptists who thought that the gospel of Jesus Christ challenges the church to have a radical social witness in society.

King and Henry shared a common revivalist tradition within American religion. Mark Noll points to the continuity between the projects of King and Henry by flagging their prominence as great communicators and the way they both effectively applied a common tradition of revivalist rhetoric and public speaking. Henry's manifestos and editorials and King's sermons and speeches galvanized two important social movements because they communicated in ways that tapped into the deepest roots of American populism and spirituality.[16]

Although King and Henry shared a common revivalist ancestry, that strain took quite different historic expressions during the decade of crisis, the 1960s. William Pannell argues that though the black and white churches share a common evangelical heritage embodied particularly in Baptist and Methodist streams, after the Civil War there was a divorce between these two theological traditions.[17] As Henry tried to heal the divorce between theology and ethics within evangelicalism in the 1940s, he also sought to heal the divorce between white and black evangelicalism that began even much earlier than the 1860s. We see intimations of this in *The Uneasy Conscience of Fundamentalism* (1947); particularly in *A Plea for Evangelical Demonstration* (1971), however, Henry presents glimpses of a more rigorously socially engaged antiracist evangelicalism. The first paragraph of *Plea* is a manifesto for a radical evangelicalism:

> This is a call for authentic evangelical protest. A sensitive Christian conscience must openly confront enduring and intractable social injustices. Biblically-concerned Christians need not forego a moment of open identification with those of other faiths and alien views in protesting what all together recognize to be unjust.[18]

From the lead sentence of the book, we see that Henry is really interested in "protest," not "demonstration" in the sense of an apologetic proof for biblical theism. Henry is concerned about inspiring a new generation of evangelicals to embody God's justice in the world.

It is fascinating that in these two first sentences of the book, Henry reclaims that language of "protest" and "confrontation," the language that he had always reserved for the opponents of his previous writing, particularly the neo-Protestant Social Gospelers. Here he takes that language back for an evangelical ethic. Not only should evangelicals protest; they also should do so with atheists and people of all faiths. This is a reference to the coalition politics of the civil rights movement. Finally, and most important, Henry claims that we need to protest "what all together recognize to be unjust," echoing King's comment in the Birmingham jail that "injustice anywhere is injustice everywhere." The Henry of *Plea* is a Henry on fire for lasting social change as a vital expression of our gospel witness.

In this *Plea*, his call to justice in *Uneasy Conscience* is even more clear and intense:

> The Christian is morally bound to challenge all beliefs and ideologies that trample man's personal dignity as a bearer of the divine

image, all forms of political and economic practice that undercut the worth of human beings, all social structures that discriminate in matters of legal rights. He has every reason to confront political powers with God's revealed will in the interest of justice in human relationships.[19]

He goes on to illustrate this evangelical struggle by embodying a multi-ethnic, multi-socioeconomic reality, pushing beyond its "ghetto-mentality," which produces a homogenous community reduced to a "racial or class or ethnic enclave."[20]

Although at first glance one might think that Carl Henry's evangelical politics is far from Martin Luther King's, closer inspection shows their affinities. Both argued that the church should become involved in politics, and both saw racism as an "intractable injustice" that all people of goodwill should organize to eradicate. Though they shared a common vocational call as public prophets, King and Henry came from different contexts and cultures. King came from a culture of slavery and segregation; Henry came from a culture of cultural isolation and white privilege. King and Henry were both frustrated in the 1960s by much of the evangelical world's inaction on the race question. Henry shared and promoted Billy Graham's vision of world evangelism implemented through a strategy of mass crusades, but he did not see this as at odds with a broader struggle for justice. The National Association of Evangelicals (NAE), which Henry helped to found in 1942, became an important gathering for evangelicals, whether fundamentalist, moderates, or progressives. Together they could work for the unity of the church and together "openly confront enduring and intractable social injustices."

After King was assassinated in Memphis, Tennessee, as he organized sanitation workers for just working conditions, the freedom struggle within the churches would live on in the Southern Christian Leadership Conference (SCLC) and in Operation Breadbasket, which would become the Rainbow/PUSH coalition led by Jesse Louis Jackson Sr. Even white evangelicals like Jim Wallis would find inspiration in Dr. King's life and vision, so much so that Wallis created an inner-city community for justice in Washington, D.C. This Sojourners community has since developed into a thriving expression of prophetic evangelicalism and includes the magazine *Sojourners* and a new ecumenical campaign to end poverty: Call to Renewal.

There are many signs of hope for the emergence of a new theological vision for prophetic evangelicals. The NAE's *For the Health of the Nations* document demonstrates that evangelicals in the tradition of Carl Henry embody a worldview that embraces social justice as well as personal salvation, including their recent prophetic stands on the environment. In addition to justice making in the world, King's vision for racial equality and reconciliation continues to open a new horizon of hope.

Black and white evangelical churches have been segregated for too long. It is time to develop new coalitions of justice that are not limited to traditional racial/ethnic constituencies. However, this collaborative move must also be from the standpoint of strong respect for the particularity of different racial realities. White evangelicals must relate to evangelicals and nonevangelicals of color in ways that acknowledge and respect their differences.

We are beginning to witness some positive signs of white evangelicals thinking in more depth about the problem of race.[21] However, unless white evangelicals join a broader coalition for justice, it is unclear how they can truly and effectively work for racial and economic justice. As we move ahead, it is vital that white and black evangelicals lead together as equal partners, joining together with Hispanic and Asian-American evangelicals in the struggle for reconciliation. If there is a future for democratic politics in America, a multicultural evangelical coalition for justice must play a vital role.

Notes

1 Esther Kaplan, *With God on Their Side: How Christian Fundamentalists Trampled Science, Policy, and Democracy in George W. Bush's White House* (New York: New Press, 2004), 7.

2 Fourth National Survey of Religion and Politics, Post-Election Sample (N = 2730, November–December 2004, University of Akron), as cited by John C. Green, "How the Faithful Voted: Religious Communities and the Presidential Vote in 2004," Pew Forum on Religion and Public Life, University of Akron.

3 Randall Balmer, *Thy Kingdom Come: How the Religious Right Distorts the Faith and Threatens America: An Evangelical's Lament* (New York: Basic Books, 2006).

4 David Bebbington, *Evangelicalism in Modern Britain: A History from the 1730s to the 1980s* (London: Unwin Hyman, 1989), 2–19.

5 Mark Noll, *The Rise of Evangelicalism: The Age of Edwards, Whitefield and the Wesleys* (Downers Grove, IL: InterVarsity Press, 2003).

6 I am indebted to Dale T. Irvin for suggesting the etymology of the term "progressive" in Marxist discourse as a way of exposing reasons for why many evangelicals find the term problematic.

7 Timothy L. Smith, *Revivalism and Social Reform in Mid-Nineteenth-Century America* (New York: Abingdon, 1957); Donald W. Dayton, *Discovering an Evangelical Heritage* (New York: Harper & Row, 1976).

8 Mechal Sobel, *The World They Made Together: Black and White Values in Eighteenth Century Virginia* (Princeton, NJ: Princeton University Press, 1987), 180.

9 Nathan Hatch, *The Democratization of American Christianity* (New Haven: Yale University Press, 1989), 106.

10 See Adam Hochschild, *Bury the Chains: Prophets and Rebels in the Fight to Free an Empire's Slaves* (New York: Houghton Mifflin / Mariner, 2005).

11 See George Marsden, *Fundamentalism and American Culture*, 2nd ed. (Oxford: Oxford University Press, 2006).

12 Carl Henry, *The Uneasy Conscience of Modern Fundamentalism* (Grand Rapids: Eerdmans, 1948).

13 Ibid, 17.

14 On the lack of attention to racial justice in *Christianity Today* during the 1950s and 1960s, see Mark G. Toulouse, "*Christianity Today* and American Public Life: A Case Study," *Journal of Church and State* 35 (Spring 1993): 255–57, 272–74; and Michael O. Emerson and Christian Smith, *Divided by Faith: Evangelical Religion and the Problem of Race in America* (Oxford: Oxford University Press, 2000), 46.

15 Martin Luther King Jr., *A Testament of Hope: The Essential Writings and Speeches of Martin Luther King, Jr.*, ed. James Melvin Washington (San Francisco: Harper Collins, 1986), 295.

16 Mark Noll, *Scandal of the Evangelical Mind* (Grand Rapids: Eerdmans, 1994), 156.

17 William Pannell, "The Religious Heritage of Blacks," in *The Evangelicals: What They Believe, Who They Are, Where They Are Changing*, ed. David F. Wells (Nashville: Abingdon, 1975), 102–6, 96–107.

18 Carl F.H. Henry, *A Plea for Evangelical Demonstration* (Grand Rapids: Baker Books, 1971), 13.

19 Ibid, 111–12.

20 Ibid, 112.

21 See John Perkins and Thomas A. Tarrants III, *He's My Brother: Former Racial Foes Offer Strategy for Reconciliation* (Grand Rapids: Chosen Books, 1994); John M. Perkins, ed., *Restoring At-Risk Communities: Doing It Together and Doing It Right* (Grand Rapids: Baker, 1995); George A. Yancey, *Beyond Black and White: Reflections on Racial Reconciliation* (Grand Rapids: Baker Books, 1996); Dennis L. Okholm, ed., *The Gospel in Black and White: Theological Resources for Racial Reconciliation* (Downers Grove, IL: InterVarsity Press, 1997); Michael O. Emerson and Christian Smith, *Divided by Faith: Evangelical Religion and the Problem of Race in America* (New York: Oxford University Press, 2000).

3

A Christian Politics of Vulnerability

Anna Mercedes

Official policy may separate church and state, but Christianity and government remain closely aligned in the United States. In recent decades, this alliance has rapidly grown more entangled. As Ray Suarez observed about George W. Bush's response to the death of Pope John Paul II, "in just over forty years we had gone from Senator John Kennedy, a Roman Catholic candidate for President, carefully distancing himself from one pope, to a 'born again' Protestant president ordering national, *public* recognition of the death of another."[1] In the contemporary United States, politicians win office by Christian votes; policies take hold due to the pressures of Christian constituencies.[2] Tremendous political power rests in the hands of (select) U.S. Christians, power that extends their reach around the globe.[3] This chapter challenges ways in which Christians handle that power.

Paul's letter to the Philippians gives a hint of how one might understand Christian power. It contains an admonition:

> Let the same mind be in you that was in Christ Jesus,
> who, though he was in the form of God,
> did not regard equality with God
> as something to be exploited,
> but emptied himself,
> taking the form of a slave,
> being born in human likeness. (2:5–7)[4]

Christians of the United States may not rival "equality with God," but they wield great political power and possess the opportunity to exploit it. Early Christian communities, singing these words in what was perhaps a baptismal hymn quoted by Paul,[5] urged the newly "born-again" to adopt the "emptying" mind-set of Christ. Paul in turn exhorts the Philippians to this Christlike ethic.

How might the ethics of the Philippians hymn shape contemporary Christian politics? At a time when the United States is involved in various degrees of destruction—from oil drilling in critical habitats, to consumption of goods made under exploitive labor, to major preemptive war— many U.S. Christians are in collusion with these destructive politics. Christian political power could surely support life-giving ends, but by colluding with destruction, Christians choose to exploit their power. The "emptying" Christ of Philippians intimates a more vulnerable politics.

There certainly are many kinds of Christians, and not all are counted among the politically powerful. As a Christian living in the United States, I argue for a Christianity that, when tempted by exploitive uses of its power, is confidently able to refuse such a use, opting instead to open its power-shares to others and to risk vulnerability. In this chapter I do so by exploring the theological concept of kenosis (*kenōsis*), which comes from the Greek word (*kenoō*) translated as "emptied" in Philippians; it denotes "self-emptying" or, more plainly, self-sacrificing or self-abnegating. The term "kenosis" also carries with it the themes of submission and humility that permeate much of Christian discourse. Here I present two contemporary and contrasting applications of kenosis: The first is in the work of Sarah Coakley, a British philosopher of religion, feminist theologian, and professor at Harvard Divinity School. The second is in the work of Gianni Vattimo, an Italian Nietzschean-Heideggerian philosopher increasingly open about his Christian faith. I draw on the insights of these two scholars to inform a Christian politics of vulnerability.

Sarah Coakley and Contemplative Kenosis

As Sarah Coakley is well aware, applying kenosis to Christian life can entail dangerous politics. Submission and humility heighten vulnerability; indeed, the Philippians hymn traces Jesus' kenosis to his crucifixion. Accordingly, feminist theologians have questioned the place of kenosis in Christian ethics, rightly emphasizing the ways in which Christian teaching has too often sanctified submission to domestic abuse.[6] Nonetheless, Sarah Coakley strives to articulate a feminist Christian understanding of kenosis. She is one of the few feminists who makes such a defense extensively.[7] Her work contrasts with feminist colleagues like Daphne Hampson, who concludes that kenosis may inform male ethics, but "for women, the theme of self-emptying and self-abnegation is far from helpful as a paradigm."[8] For Coakley, however, kenosis is "not only compatible with feminism, but [also] vital to a distinctively Christian manifestation of it."[9]

Coakley articulates "a vision of Christological *kenosis* uniting human 'vulnerability' with authentic divine power (as opposed to worldly or 'patriarchal' visions of power)," such that the human is "wholly translucent to the divine."[10] This "authentic divine power" comes from an omnipotent, or all-powerful, deity. Yet she is critical of the way in which Enlightenment understandings of the human person yield a correspondingly powerful idea of humanity: "a sovereign self-possession and autonomy that is capable of rising above the weaknesses and distractions of human desires and human tragedy."[11] For the Christ figure, in whom divine and human are said to coexist, Coakley finds Enlightenment assumptions about humanity to be particularly problematic. If God is potently self-possessed and so is the perfect human person, then in the person of Christ, his "two natures" are each consummately self-contained and unyielding. Coakley asks, "How can the natures of *two* such 'individuals' concur christologically?" She solves this conundrum by softening the human figure: "What, we may ask, if the frailty, vulnerability and 'self-effacement' of [the gospel] narratives *is* what shows us 'perfect humanity'?"[12]

Within Coakley's model, Christ "empties" himself in his human, but not his divine, nature. Coakley develops a theological approach to kenosis that makes vulnerability and submission before a stable, omnipotent God enlivening for humans (and empowering even for some feminists).[13] The kenotic Christ reveals perfected human state as willfully vulnerable. For Coakley, the practice of kenosis is particularly appropriate in contemplative prayer. Contemplative submission provides a safe space for the praying person to "empty" herself before a nonexploitive divine power. In this kenotic silent prayer, humans can find empowerment toward just action in the world.

An example of this empowerment appears in Coakley's work with prison inmates who experienced communal and personal strength through the practice of silent group prayer. This was true for them despite the risk that these men who have been silenced by imprisonment would feel further silenced under God in such prayer. Coakley reports:

> Many of the men new to the practice found it hard to relax or to bear the inner turmoil that the silence engendered. At such times I felt strongly the influence of my inner group of more experienced practitioners, whose gentleness and poise were the best advertisement for the long-term efficacy of the undertaking. Gentleness, poise, peace and solidarity were indeed manifest ways of "bucking the system," if only for a short and blessed interval in the prison day.[14]

Prayerful vulnerability need not mean the loss of all power. Paradoxically, the practice of vulnerability can be an empowering practice.

Gianni Vattimo and Kenotic Secularization

Gianni Vattimo's work is quite different from Coakley's.[15] He is primarily a philosopher, not a theologian. His work therefore does not offer a straightforward theological proposal; rather, Vattimo analyzes the Christian story of the incarnation and links it to his analysis of the present day. Interestingly, he does so through the theological trope of kenosis.

For Vattimo, kenosis refers to the weakening of God the Absolute, or of a God conceived as "Being" itself.[16] Vattimo understands the Christian incarnation as the beginning of such weakening and thus the catalyst of contemporary culture's increasing secularization.[17] By emptying Godself through the kenosis of the incarnation, God's Word, or Logos, takes flesh in the everyday mundane, secular world. Vattimo describes this process as the "nihilistic vocation" of hermeneutics,[18] set into flow by the incarnation of the Logos. The incarnation of the Logos initiates a proliferation of religious interpretations. Hermeneutics, the interpretation of biblical texts, becomes *productive*; new meanings of a text can be articulated and cherished.[19] Thus, rather than in contemplative prayer as in Coakley, Vattimo's sense of kenosis is enacted primarily in the hermeneutical mode. Many meanings are made possible by the emptying-out of (capitalized) Meaning. Because of the kenotic nature of the incarnation, Christian hermeneutics cannot maintain a stable, fixed Truth; instead, interpretation now forms the fluid through which Truth self-empties.

As the Logos empties into a Spirit-enabled hermeneutical proliferation, the understanding of God as "an ultimate foundation, as the absolute metaphysical structure of the real,"[20] empties out. Though Coakley certainly has no comparable nihilism, she too is wary of the power dynamics of the Omnipotent and its dependents. But while she maintains this strong power by theologizing a specifically noncoercive omnipotence, Vattimo in contrast advocates the weakening of such a strong theological absolute. For him, the theological doctrine of the incarnation of Christ declares "an announcement of an ontology of weakening."[21] The "death of God" entails the death of the concept of God as absolute truth. For Vattimo, that false truth lowers itself in the incarnation: "Being" empties itself out, becomes fluid, becomes an ongoing event.

Further, the fluidity of what was once a strong rigidity loosens the validity of dominating power. Kenosis, revealing the *nihil* (nothing) of an omnipotent God hovering over and providing dominating organization for human society, allows for the diffusion of metaphysical violence and the physical violence that often accompanies it.[22] Carrying out its nihilistic vocation, this secularizing kenosis empties out violent possibilities of the Transcendent, leading into a "consummation of objective truth in different manifestations of friendship."[23] "Friendship," or *caritas*, constitutes a new fidelity, replacing fidelity to absolute truth. Vattimo writes that "the death of the moral God marks the impossibility of preferring truth to friendship."[24] Friendship, not Truth, now carries the flow of meaning. There are still encounters of truth in friendship, but it is a weakened sense of truth: truth that one can believe as one believes things heard from a friend,[25] not any ontological truth that would trump friendship.[26] For Vattimo, the incarnation reveals that God's movement is not violent but rather is bound up in love (caritas), thus boundlessly kenotic. In the flow of such kenosis, a new age dawns in which metaphysical violence is diffused, an age "with charity taking the place of discipline."[27] In the incarnation and the continuing kenosis of the Logos, faithfulness to Truth, Text, and Transcendence is replaced by faithfulness to one another.

Kenosis and Vulnerable Politics

As proposed by Vattimo, the kenotic secularization of Christian doctrine could have profound impact on Christian politics today. The idea that Christians have one correct interpretation of cosmology, one that they must defend and spread to all nations, could be replaced by an ebullience of interpretations checked by the principles of friendship and community. A less-violent society could at least hypothetically follow.[28]

Likewise, Coakley gestures toward an alternative politics for Christians today. She asserts that Christians can find in the figure of Jesus their Christ a model of perfected humanity. From Jesus, Christians can learn humility rather than powerful assertion as the perfected human form. The humility she advocates is specifically a humility in encounters with the divine, as modeled by the human-divine confluence in the person of Christ. It is, however, a humility with ramifications for the public sphere, inviting the empowering Spirit of the omnipotent God, and from that Spirit, charisma to act for justice. Coakley urges Christian politics toward a posture of empowered vulnerability—even when such humility might seem to be a risky choice, as with minority prisoners or with women. Christian identity need not be reserved for the powerful majority.

The work of these two scholars informs a Christian politics of vulnerability. Yet their descriptions of kenosis still hazard exploitive uses of Christian power: Coakley in her insistence on an omnipotent God, and Vattimo in his use of the Christian incarnation as an essential societal catalyst. To counter this danger, one could read theologies of a vulnerable God alongside Coakley's depictions of the omnipotent.[29] Interpreting Vattimo, one could carefully distinguish his hermeneutical understanding of the *doctrine* of the incarnation from the precise incarnation recognized at the start of the Common Era.

Coakley distinguishes between "worldly" and divine power, yet her omnipotent divinity is as unyielding in its force as is contemporary U.S. government. In upholding an omnipotent God under whom humans find empowerment, she reiterates the same dichotomy of power and vulnerability that so often translates into patriarchy and other forms of subjugation.[30] Theologies of an omnipotent God inspire humans to toy with omnipotence in *imago dei*.[31] Coakley insists on an omnipotent God and a kenotic humanity: a humanity that, in contemplative prayer, can "cease to set the agenda" and "'make space' for God to be God."[32] Yet what precisely is God *being* here, and why does God require space for free rein in order to be so godlike? Coakley's formulation implies that the essence of God thrives when hovering over the disarmed, humble human. It is precisely this idea of God as an omnipotent absolute that we humans will have to empty from our minds in order for those imagining themselves intimates with God—whether marriage partners or corporate bosses or whole nations—to stop imitating unyielding omnipotence.[33]

Theologies asserting unyielding power too often reiterate a paradigm of violence. My critique here echoes Vattimo's insight that the depletion of the concept of an absolute metaphysical God lessens societal violence and enables charity or friendship.

Vattimo writes of Christianity as "the condition that paved the way for the dissolution of metaphysics,"[34] and it follows all too easily that the Christian incarnation itself stands as a metaphysical absolute. Vattimo may seek to counter this conclusion with the explanation that the incarnation cannot be absolute precisely because it is an event of caritas.[35] Yet lending pivotal importance to such a specifically Christian "truth" as the incarnation gives Christianity administration over a strong metaphysical and even violent truth claim, despite the intention to weaken such claims; for many, the caritas of the incarnation will seem too tough of a love. If the incarnation marks "God's decision to institute a relation of friendship with humanity,"[36] then it supersedes, among many historical experiences of divine friendship, the ancient covenant between God and the people of Israel, leaving that relationship in the dust of God's self-realization in the incarnation. Supersessionist interpretations of Christianity have fueled terrible violence, particularly against Jews. In contrast, if Christian doctrines of the incarnation (as opposed to a specific incarnation itself) increasingly disclose God's decision for friendship, then these theological discourses, rather than the embodied life of Jesus, provide the catalyst for weakened metaphysics.

If Christians are to be in continuity with the kenotic life of God (or, as Vattimo might have it, in continuity with an ontology of weakening), then we will have to empty ourselves even of our grasp on the one incarnation of Christ in Jesus. Our own doctrines will need to reflect an ontology of weakening; we will need to become comfortable with a loosened grasp on truth, on "the way, and the truth, and the life" (John 14:6). As a start, perhaps our own baptisms will help them with this. The Philippians baptismal hymn does not say, "Yield to the absolute mind of Christ Jesus," but rather, "Let the same mind be in you that was in Christ Jesus." Christians need not idolize one incarnation. Rather, we participate in an ongoing event: a continuing—not closed or canonized—incarnation, taking the mind of the Christ onto ourselves and ourselves becoming sites of incarnation, of way and truth and life. In Vattimo's reading of kenosis, and in my own, the motif of God's kenosis best serves to position or orient Christian identity in contemporary society, not to orient contemporary society around a specific Christian doctrine.[37]

In contrast, the kenotic decision of God can be seen not only in Jesus' life but also in the many stories of God's fierce love and covenant loyalty in the Hebrew Scriptures, and in God's tendency to be swayed by the Israelite people and drawn into the vulnerability of emotional response to them. Beyond individual biblical narratives, the whole body of sacred texts comprising Hebrew and Christian Scriptures itself testifies to a self-disclosing God, entwined by law and Logos with a beloved people. The incarnation comprises much more than the flesh of one Galilean. Vattimo already carries forward a wide incarnation that stretches into interpretive communities of contemporary times; perhaps, by the principle of caritas, he would not be opposed to extending the width of the incarnation backward in time, well before the time of Jesus, well before a time even of human knowing (John 1:1).

Within the currents of divine kenosis, "Christ" becomes a Logos with which Christians can articulate our own specific personhood as incorporated into the larger divine flow of life. The stories of Jesus, in and out of the canon, offer us Logoi with which to illustrate what this divine current might look like: oriented toward others, giving of itself in healing and restorative ways. If kenosis is a trait of the divine, then emulation of or participation in the divine flow, even by those whom the world threatens, can be an endeavor of strength. Said differently, vulnerability can be our strength, even for women and all traditionally subjugated people. Though my feminist convictions leave me mindful of abuse, those same convictions inform me that we must all have the right and the privilege to participate in self-giving love with divine dignity.

Among the many persistent themes of the story of Jesus, kenosis has been transcribed through myriad Christian liturgies, through the early church fathers, the medieval mystics, the Reformers, and through contemporary theological voices. Still, the vulnerability of kenosis has not been Christianity's most prevalent theme. Rather, themes of more obvious power have fueled the Constantinian era, the Crusades, the intolerance of the Reformers, and the crusades of our own time. A Christian politics of triumph allowed for the consolidation of Constantine's empire and the desecration of holy sites dedicated to the less-triumphant gods. It fueled the slaughter of Muslims and Jews in the Crusades. It encouraged Reformer Martin Luther, after abandoning his hope that Jews would convert, to advocate violence against them in preparation for the seemingly imminent triumph of Christ's return. A politics of triumph enabled the missionizing that lubricated the wheels of colonialism. And a politics of triumph helps the current understanding that America's "Christian" ideals should rule in the world.

The Philippians baptismal hymn initially describes Christian posture as humble, not triumphal. Yet it also sings that the humble will eventually be exalted. Indeed, the song indicates that "at the name of Jesus every knee should bow" (2:10). If the Christian community understands itself to be "body of Christ" today, then a triumphalist implication of the Scripture too easily follows: every knee around the globe should bow to Christians.

However, disturbed by the collusion of Christian power with destructive politics, I pray that the Christian exaltation of which the Philippians hymn sings is itself kenotic: a shared glory. History has taught that the greedy grasping of glory only leads to the exploitation of others by Christians. In "every knee" is to bow to the name of Jesus, may we find the Christians to whom others are to bow themselves bowing, not to a throne of God but to a divine throne itself inverted, with God's own self bowing. Thus may God and all God's people—Christians but also many others—bow, in high regard and with hope, love, and peace, toward all those who have felt themselves to be not-of-God, and toward the earth as it aches in degradation. May the Christians on their knees see that they bow to a heavy load of suffering, in human and nonhuman others. May they see that we have much work to do: too much work to let ourselves be tempted and distracted by the exploitive power and costly comfort that is offered to select Christians in today's United States.

In contrast to theologies of immutable omnipotence and the politics of triumph that follow, Christians immersed in a politics of vulnerability are never able to arrive at one permanent truth claim about God or faith, nor are they able to make one steadfast political claim based on their theology. Far from the revelation of one definitive immutable truth, Christianity can yield a posture of mutability and open-ended truth claims. The kenosis of God flows with such strength that its currents resist any pushing upstream to name or to define their source. The mysterious wellspring of kenosis flushes through human ideas of the divine, working to dissolve even our theological idols. The Christian concept of God stands unguarded, and Christian truth about God is diluted in the wonder of God's presence: Christians roll with sacred waters, into today, into the secular, into communities of friendship and prayer in which they continue to transcribe truth.[38]

Christian interpretation of divine kenosis, and Christians interpreting their own interpretations as located in that kenosis—all this entails a constant loosening of Christian grasp on truth. God empties out, and in our hermeneutics God continues to empty out, such that our interpretations bear an emptying gesture, releasing our determination to define God. Emptying themselves of that determination, Christian people can stand open toward others, with open-ended truth claims routed by friendship, and thus with the Christic mind of which the Philippians hymn sings, refusing to regard Christian power in the world as something to be exploited.

Christian politics have historically taken many forms: the politics of triumph discussed above, the similar politics of empire and of colonization, but also a politics of resistance to empire; the politics of slavery, but also a politics of resistance to slavery; a politics of genocide. Christians can find fuel in biblical narratives for most of these politics. Now, as the U.S. government feigns omnipotence and omnipresence, seeking to control global economy, global oil, and global discourse on "freedom" (while sweatshop labor provides our goods, war safeguards our oil, and our freedom does not even include free health care), and while this government is held in place by Christian votes—it is time for a Christian politics of vulnerability to be gleaned from our gospel heritage. As is always the case with Christian ethics, such a politics will have different ramifications for Christians in different social contexts, offering unique directives, for example, to the Christian inmate, the Christian senator, the Christian mother, and the Christian megachurch pastor.

For those Christians currently in friendly alliance with the U.S. administration, a politics of vulnerability might call for something like the following: Refuse to lend your power in support of exploitive politics. Refuse to call as "Christian" the politics that revel in our own glory alongside the demise of others. Instead, let your visible Christian presence demonstrate physical hospitality to the immigration of others and spiritual hospitality to the truth claims of other people around the world, even to their theological truth claims. Whatever power you have in our nation's governance, use it to demonstrate a power seen in the Christ of the Gospels: a power that "empties itself" in the pursuit of healing, feeding, and fostering communal hope in the shadows of imperial government. Demonstrate a Christic identity that in the course of such loving pursuits risks its own vulnerability, leaves itself open to the possibility of being wounded. The outcomes of a Christian politics of vulnerability could be devastating (a crucifixion, perhaps, by military attack or governmental collapse), or simply weakening (an economy with fewer commodities, a less-diverse food supply), or uplifting (more alliances around the world, less poverty within our own borders). Yet, under the mind-set of potent vulnerability that the Christ of our name offers us, the gospel claims of Easter speak to the vibrant potential of our unknown future.

Notes

1 Ray Suarez, *The Holy Vote: The Politics of Faith in America* (New York: Harper-Collins, 2006), 10.

2 See David E. Campbell, ed., *A Matter of Faith: Religion in the 2004 Presidential Election* (Washington, DC: Brookings Institution Press, 2007).

3 "The world's leading economic and military power is also—no one can misread the data—the world's leading Bible-reading crusader state, immersed in an Old Testament of stern prophets and bloody Middle Eastern battlefields," says Kevin P. Phillips, *American Theocracy: The Peril and Politics of Radical Religion, Oil, and Borrowed Money in the 21st Century* (New York: Viking, 2006), 101–3).

4 The word translated here as "emptied" is the verbal form of *kenōsis* in the Greek. Scholars debate what it could have meant for Jesus to be in the "form" of God. Distinction about the "two natures" of Christ, one divine and the other human—came centuries after the Pauline letters. "Form" may have conveyed that Jesus shared in the glory of the Holy One (see Stephen Fowl, *Philippians* [Grand Rapids: Eerdmans, 2005], 90–94).

5 Ralph P. Martin, *A Hymn of Christ: Philippians 2:5–11 in Recent Interpretation and in the Setting of Early Christian Worship* (Downers Grove, IL: InterVarsity Press, 1997), 42–54.

6 Valerie Saiving's classic article "The Human Situation: A Feminine View," *Journal of Religion* 40, no. 2 [April 1960]: 100–112, reprinted in *Womanspirit Rising: A Feminist Reader in Religion*, ed. Carol P. Christ and Judith Plaskow, 2nd ed. (San Francisco: HarperSanFrancisco, 1992), 25–42, does not explicitly discuss kenosis but clearly labels self-abnegating behavior, rather than pride, as a major female sin. Melinda Contreras-Byrd links the Christian motif of self-sacrifice to the ongoing abuse of women. Daphne Hampson criticizes kenosis in *Theology and Feminism* (Oxford: Blackwell, 1990), relegating it to "a counter-theme within male thought" (155). Carol Lakey Hess's *Caretakers of Our Common House: Women's Development in Communities of Faith* (Nashville: Abingdon, 1997) discusses self-effacing ethics more generally in Christian education, naming "prophetic torpor" as a symptom of unhealthy kenosis in women. Catherine Keller discusses the dangers and possibilities of self-sacrifice in "More on Feminism, Self-Sacrifice, and Time; or, Too Many Words for Emptiness," *Buddhist-Christian Studies* 13 (1993): 211–19.

7 In addition to Coakley's feminist appropriation of kenosis (see next note), Rosemary Radford Ruether's *Sexism and God Talk* (Boston: Beacon, 1993) imagines

the kenosis of Christ as the emptying of divine patriarchy. Marta Frascati-Lochhead (*Kenosis and Feminist Theology: The Challenge of Gianni Vattimo* [Albany: State University of New York, 1998) applies kenosis to the field of feminist theology itself, using the work of Gianni Vattimo. Marcella Althaus-Reid writes of kenosis as the coming-out of God in her *The Queer God* (New York: Routledge, 2003).

8 Sarah Coakley, *Powers and Submissions: Spirituality, Philosophy, and Gender* (Malden, MA: Blackwell, 2002), 3.

9 Ibid.

10 Ibid., 18.

11 Ibid, 25.

12 Ibid., 26.

13 Coakley's feminist assertion is that vulnerability as the perfect human (rather than female) state provides an erosion of gender stereotypes. Coakley explains: "If Jesus' 'vulnerability' is a primary narrative given, rather than a philosophical embarrassment to explain away, then precisely the question is raised whether 'vulnerability' *need* be seen as a 'female' weakness rather than a (special sort of) 'human' strength" (ibid., 26).

14 Sarah Coakley, "Jail Break," *Christian Century*, June 29, 2004, 19.

15 Different Christologies are at work in Coakley and Vattimo, with Vattimo focusing on notions of kenotic divinity and Coakley on kenotic humanity.

16 Gianni Vattimo writes: "The incarnation, that is, God's abasement to the level of humanity, what the New Testament calls God's *kenosis*, will be interpreted as the sign that the non-violent and non-absolute God of the post-metaphysical epoch has as its distinctive trait the very vocation for weakening of which Heideggerian philosophy speaks" (*Belief*, trans. Luca D'Isanto and David Webb [Stanford, CA: Stanford University Press, 1999], 39).

17 Because this new age of diffused or weakened truth is a product of the Christian incarnation, Vattimo's "secularization" is not to be understood as an abandonment of, or a liberation from, "the religion of the book," but rather as its hermeneutical continuation.

18 Gianni Vattimo, *Beyond Interpretation*, trans. David Webb (Oxford: Polity, 1996), ix.

19 On productive interpretation, see Gianni Vattimo, "History of Salvation, History of Interpretation," chap. 4 in *After Christianity*, trans. Luca D'Isanto (New York: Columbia University Press, 2002), 14–15.

20 Ibid., 6.

21 Vattimo, *Belief*, 36.

22 Vattimo explains: "Outside of an authentic opening of Being as event, the Lévinasian other is always exposed to the risk of being dethroned by the Other (with a capital letter)" (*After Christianity*, 111).

23 Ibid., 105–6.

24 Ibid., 105.

25 Ibid., 8.

26 Ibid., 105. When asked how to distinguish his kind of secularization from other forms, Vattimo answers: "It is precisely here that one should rediscover the "principle of charity" which, perhaps not by accident, constitutes the point of

convergence between nihilistic hermeneutics and the religious tradition of the West. . . . For dogmatic Christianity (that is, the substance of New Testament revelation), recognition of its relation with nihilistic hermeneutics means the emergence of charity as the single most decisive factor of the evangelical message" (*Beyond Interpretation*, 51). This "single most decisive factor" of caritas lends continuity to incarnational kenosis. This is why "friendship" and "charity" are for Vattimo far more than beatific words. "Community," and the love necessary for its communication, cannot be a foundational criterion unless the kenosis of the "foundation" of Truth, or Presence, is presupposed (cf. Vattimo, "History of Salvation, History of Interpretation," 20; *After Christianity*, 111). For Vattimo, "only friendship, explicitly recognized as the decisive truth factor, can prevent the thought of the end of metaphysics from lapsing into a reactive—and often reactionary—nihilism" (*After Christianity*, 111).

27 Vattimo, *Beyond Interpretation*, 49.

28 Vattimo understands the "silencing of all questioning" to be "the only possible philosophical definition of violence" (*Belief*, 65n).

29 The vulnerability of God is particularly explored by theologies of the cross and in a different manner by process theology. For contemporary applications of the former, see the work of Douglas John Hall, particularly *Lighten Our Darkness: Towards an Indigenous Theology of the Cross* (Lima, OH: Academic Renewal Press, 2001), and for contemporary applications of the latter, see the work of Catherine Keller, particularly *The Face of the Deep: A Theology of Becoming* (London: Routledge, 2003).

30 This dichotomized power imbalance confounds the power-*in*-vulnerabilty Coakley wants. Cf. *Powers and Submissions*, 5.

31 See Catherine Keller's *God and Power: Counter-Apocalyptic Journeys* (Minneapolis: Fortress, 2005).

32 Coakley, *Powers and Submissions*, 34.

33 Politics of omnipotence also yield masses of the less-powerful who rest their trust in the all-powerful government. Valerie Saiving saw this trend in the United States fifty years ago, emphasizing at the end of her landmark 1960 article that "there is no mistaking the fact that there is a strong similarity between theology's view that salvation lies in selfless love and contemporary man's growing tendency to avoid his strong assertion of the self as over against others and to merge his individual identity in the identities of others" ("The Human Situation," in *Womanspirit Rising*, 41).

34 Vattimo, *After Christianity*, 107.

35 Vattimo writes: "The interpretation given by Jesus Christ of Old Testament prophesies, or (better) the interpretation which he himself is, reveals its true and only meaning: God's love for his creatures. However, this 'ultimate' meaning precisely by virtue of its being caritas, is not really ultimate and does not possess the peremptoriness of the metaphysical principle, which cannot be transcended, and before which all questioning ceases." "Love, as the 'ultimate' meaning of revelation, is not truly ultimate" (*Belief*, 64–65).

36 Ibid., 53.

37 "Christianity recovered as the doctrine of salvation (namely, secularizing kenosis), is not a legacy of doctrines defined once and for all, to which one might appeal in seeking solid ground in the sea of uncertainty. . . . However, the critical principle it provides is sufficiently clear to allow one to orient oneself in relation to this world, above all to the Church, and to the process of secularization" (ibid., 62–63).

38 Transcription is Vattimo's term, his way of describing the continuing kenosis of the Logos in communities of interpretation.

4

Truthiness, Family Values, and Conservative Consumerism

Adam S. Miller

My claim is that real political action is always rooted in the creation of something common. The connection here between creativity and collectivity is not arbitrary but essential. What is common appears in the process of creation because the act of creation compels us to surpass our private interests in producing something public. Though consumption is private and centered in self-satisfaction, creation is public and shifts one's center of gravity beyond the self and into the space of what is shared.

In this light, much of what goes by the name of "politics" fails to be political. Rather, contemporary politics are dominated by special interests whose aims are to maximize profit and consumption. When assessing a political action, the crucial question is simply this: is it oriented by consumption and self-interest, or is it centered in the creation of a common good? The difficulty of politics is that any common action can without warning slip into the orbit of consumption. The hope that sustains the possibility of political action is that the pursuit of satisfaction may also, at any moment, be pressed beyond its limits by a collective commitment to creativity.

In American politics, the rise of the religious Right illustrates precisely this difficulty. At the heart of this movement is a real political aim that is continually subverted, both intentionally and unintentionally, by consumerism. The driving political aim of the religious Right is its intention to refuse the general commodification of sexuality, reproduction, and family relations for the sake of a committed sexuality that creatively produces a common good. What continually subverts this aim is its unfortunate identification as a "conservative" position. The irony is that conservatism effectively works to "conserve" the status quo of consumerism on behalf of big-business interests while simultaneously conserving the "traditional" family as a model for what is common when, in fact, this model tends to perpetuate the priority of economy and self-interest.

Truthiness and Consumption

We misapprehend the real political potential of our contemporary situation if, following the rhetoric of corporate interests, we read key political differences as differences *in* consumption. The key to opening new political possibilities is to refuse these self-serving distinctions and, instead, to redraw political lines in terms of the difference between political actions that reinforce the priority of self-satisfied consumption, and those that are committed to the creative production of something common. However, to make any progress in reshuffling the political deck, we need to begin by clarifying what makes our current misapprehension of the political situation possible. Why can we not see beyond the ends of our own political noses?

The problem is that politics are distorted by the "truthiness" of self-interest. *Truthiness* is a particularly apt word in this connection. Named by the American Dialect Society in 2005 as its Word of the Year and similarly honored by the *New York Times* as one of the nine words that best expressed the spirit of that same year, *truthiness* is a term introduced into contemporary circulation by *Comedy Central*'s Stephen Colbert. Though Colbert only recently reinvented the word for the October 17, 2005, premiere episode of his political satire, *The Colbert Report*, truthiness has always been politically decisive. Essentially, truthiness is a way of describing the pervasive disconnect between political interests and the real conditions that shape our lives. It involves a kind of willful disregard for the truth in favor of the truthiness we would prefer to believe. This disregard for facts in favor of feelings is made possible by the premium we place on preference. What tends to matter most to us, whatever our political persuasion, is simple self-interest. The truth, then, about truthiness is this: self-interest is the lens that warps our perception of truth, bends the facts to meet our preferences, and disconnects us from the possibility of creating a good that is genuinely shared in common. Only that which is shared in common can center us in a truth beyond truthiness.

Republicans and Democrats alike suffer from the malady of truthiness precisely to the extent that their political positions are expressions of self-interest. It is no secret that today, as always, politics boil down to economy, and that economy is driven by the motor of consumption. Commodities are peddled for our consumption, and they are peddled for the sake of earning their peddlers an even greater power to consume. We choose what commodities to consume on the basis of preference, and personal preference is itself primarily a function of self-interest. In this way, truthiness is built right into consumerism as one of its defining features. As the art of advertising demonstrates, truthiness and consumerism are two sides of the same coin.

In the eye of truthiness, everything shows up in terms of self-interest, and everything becomes reduced to a type of commodity: our work, our religions, our politics, our friendships, our families, and even our selves. We no longer see things as they are, and so we are no longer able to connect meaningfully with other people or truthfully with ourselves.

Politically, the result is that the differences between parties tend to cluster deceptively around distinctions in taste and consumption in a way that conceals the real political stakes. This is manifest particularly in the way that the differences between Republicans and Democrats are today most starkly drawn in terms of consumption. Geoffrey Nunberg's recent analysis of Republican rhetoric is an excellent example of how this works. The mammoth title of his book is itself sufficient to illustrate the issue: *Talking Right: How Conservatives Turned Liberalism into a Tax-Raising, Latte-Drinking, Sushi-Eating, Volvo-Driving, New York Times-Reading, Body-Piercing, Hollywood-Loving, Left-Wing Freak Show.*[1] Here the distinction between conservatives and liberals is drawn in terms of a faux-culture war and characterized as a matter of taste: liberals are liberals because they choose to eat, drink, drive, read, pierce, view, and consume different foods, products, and media than conservatives. Now, these differences in taste (even assuming their general accuracy) may be interesting, but they do not constitute real political differences. Instead, they simply serve to obscure, for the sake of preserving the hegemony of consumerism itself, the ways in which Republicans and Democrats alike are potentially motivated by a genuine desire to create something common.

By reducing political differences to differences in taste and culture, truthiness conceals the way that substantive political impulses are fundamentally *rejections* of the prevailing logic of commodification as such. For example, the core of the liberal agenda has traditionally involved both its refusal to allow the worker to be treated as an expendable commodity and its commitment to preserving the environment from irreparable consumption. In this way, liberals aim to preserve both the public space of work and the natural space of the environment as places genuinely common and oriented by creative engagement. Likewise, the core of the conservative agenda is its commitment to resisting both the bureaucratization of our personal lives and the commodification of sexuality, reproduction, and family relationships. This is especially apparent in its commitment to lowering taxes, limiting government programs, promoting marriage and personal responsibility, and resisting abortion.

Here, at root, liberalism and conservatism are motivated by the same desire to resist the reduction of life to consumption. Their shared intention is to preserve human creativity and its potential for collectivity. A real political difference would be constructed along entirely different lines than those that presently distinguish Republicans from Democrats: it would cut across party lines by organizing collective political efforts not in terms of differences in taste and consumption, but in terms of a difference between individualistic consumerism and the creative production of a common good.

The irony of our current situation is that the real political aims of both parties are swallowed up by the monster of self-interested consumerism. In this way, organizing resistance to consumerism under the banner of an interested conservatism works effectively to misdirect political intentions down nostalgic paths that are ultimately capable of doing nothing but reinforcing the disastrous commodification of work, religion, and sexuality. To seriously pursue "family values" that are neither corrupted nor co-opted by the political shell games perpetrated by truthiness, the religious Right must make a clean break with conservatism and recognize that the common good they aim at is something that must be newly created rather than nostalgically retrieved.

Nostalgia and the "Natural" Family

Nostalgia is part and parcel of the truthiness conjured by the inertia of self-interest, and it deeply impairs the power of the religious Right to create and advance "family values" that exceed self-interest and consumption. Though it is easy enough to project onto the past our hopes for the future, it is precisely this misidentification of "family values" with traditional patterns of marriage and family that overlooks the crucial differences between the past and the present and causes us to miss the possibilities unique to our own time.

To concretely explore how the conservation of the "traditional" family ironically undermines an attempt to resist its commodification, I want to examine in some detail the manifesto for the "The Natural Family" written by Allan C. Carlson and Paul T. Mero and offered by the influential World Congress of Families as a basic explanation of its political and social aims. The World Congress of Families is an international organization founded by Carlson in 1996 to address global issues that threaten the stability and autonomy of families. Since its organization, three successful World Congresses have convened (1997 in Prague, 1999 in Geneva, and 2004 in Mexico City), with a fourth meeting planned for 2007 in Warsaw, Poland. The first meeting alone was attended by over 700 delegates from 145 pro-family organizations and 45 nations. Participants have included Roman Catholics, evangelical and mainline Protestants, Latter-day Saints, Eastern Orthodox, Jews, and Sunni and Shiite Muslims. A detailed examination of the manifesto for "The Natural Family" is particularly useful here because it simultaneously illustrates the religious Right's grassroots refusal of consumerism for the sake of something common, and the subversion of this position by an unfortunate adherence to a conservative framework.

In the same way that truthiness is a subversion of truth by self-interest, the manifesto's emphasis on the "natural" family subverts its commitment to what is common. The whole text of the manifesto pivots on its use of the word "natural." The word works simultaneously as (1) a shorthand for the kind of common family values that would exceed consumerism, (2) a name for what the family once was before the rise of industrialism fractured its integrity by displacing it from the center of our productive lives, and (3) a way of indicating what God "naturally" intended the family to be. The difficulty is that the second and third connotations of "natural" undercut the first. An understanding of the natural or common family as what exceeds individuality, consumption, and self-interest is, first of all, diluted by a melancholic and conservative glamorization of preindustrial economies as in some way innocent of oppressive self-interest. Preindustrial hardship and unavoidably cramped quarters are mistaken for an idyllic lifestyle freely chosen by pastoral families. In turn, the initial description of the common family is also undermined by a kind of protobiological understanding of the family as naturally being something that humans instinctively crave by divine design. I will return to this latter point momentarily.

For all of its problems, the manifesto seems to have a remarkably clear sense of what a genuinely common family would entail. The family's home, the manifesto argues, must become "the focus of their common life."[2] Here, "enmeshed in the lives of others, family members craft acts of altruism, where they make gifts without thought of self. Kindness begets kindness, shaping an economy of love."[3] Within this common space of creative acts that exceed interest, the "family, not the individual, is the fundamental unit of society," and the marital union is a "social bond" in which both partners are oriented ex-centrically.[4]

But the story that the manifesto tells about where this notion comes from and why it should be pursued reentangles the common family with a web of conservative naturalism. By telling a story about the family that posits a kind of original (i.e., natural) perfection and innocence, it becomes extremely difficult to understand the rise of contemporary culture as anything other than a kind of corruption. In this story, the symbolic dimension of human culture itself comes to be actually identified with the core of what corrupts a naturally pristine human family. Nature is misidentified with what is public and collective, and culture with what is private and self-centered. This is extremely problematic because, whatever its difficulties, the hope for creating a common family is grounded in the inventive and collective dimension of human culture, the dimension of human existence that is alone capable of exceeding our natural desires for satisfaction and instincts for self-preservation.

From the first sentence of the manifesto, the tension introduced by this misunderstanding is obvious. The manifesto asks, "What is the natural family? The answer comes to the woman and the man who take the risk of turning their love into promises of lifelong devotion."[5] This sentence correctly correlates the notion of the common family with the risk that love takes in turning a native impulse for companionship and reproduction into an unconditional promise of lifelong devotion. The mistake here is to read this shift as "natural." Rather than being natural, a promise of lifelong commitment is supranatural and belongs entirely to the symbolic dimension of human culture. The risk entailed in promising an uncompromising fidelity is precisely what exceeds the safety of the natural world. Our capacity for symbolic promises that are uncoerced by instincts and native affections is what distinguishes us from the natural, animal world and makes us human. It is entirely possible for human culture to be nothing other than an extension of our natural instinct for self-preservation—hence the reign of truthiness and consumerism in contemporary culture and politics—but this is the result of human culture being *too* natural, rather than not natural enough.

To conceive the unconditionality of the common as a conservative return to the natural is to mire it in instinct and consumption rather than to creatively set it free from the conditionality of self-interest.

This misidentification is likewise obvious in a number of other striking passages from the manifesto. At one point, the manifesto advocates the creation of a new vision and then, in the same breath, withdraws this claim to creativity by characterizing the vision as a conservative restoration: "We advance here a new vision and a fresh statement of principles and goals appropriate for the 21st century and the third millennium. We would see a world restored in line with the intent of its Creator."[6] It shortly thereafter declares that "the natural family cannot change into some new shape; nor can it be re-defined by eager social engineers."[7] Or again, it argues that, because the idea of the common family "is imprinted on our natures as human beings, we know that the natural family can be grasped by all persons who open their minds to the evidence of their senses and their hearts to the promptings of their best instincts."[8]

Yet, despite this dogged adherence to the shape of the way things naturally are and were, the manifesto defiantly and resolutely affirms that "economic determinism is false. Ideas and religious faith can prevail over material forces."[9] With respect to this last passage in particular, I fail to see any other way to read it than an as a stirring repudiation of the natural, material, and economic conditions that threaten to rob us of any freedom from the preprogrammed patterns of instinct and interest. Ideas and promises and symbols *can* set us beyond the interested conditions that govern the natural, material world, it declares. Our lives *can* exceed the domination of consumption in the inventive work of thinking the world as other than it is. However, the force of these novel declarations is constantly undercut by the backflow of conservatism. For every step forward, the argument appears to take two steps backward.

This is particularly (and painfully) clear when the manifesto pauses to explicitly address these very difficulties. "Some will say," the manifesto explains, "that we want to turn back the clock to restore a mythical

American suburban world of the 1950s."[10] Yet, despite the fact that these manifesters "look with affection to earlier familial eras," the manifesto offers a scathing and insightful critique of the ways in which the suburban, consumerist model of family life fails to be common. "This new suburban model—featuring long commutes and tract homes without central places such as parks and nearby shops where mothers and youth might have found healthy community bonds—proved incomplete" and the "'companionship marriage' ideal of this time" proved "fragile."[11] In light of the fact that both the 1950s' marriage "ideal" and its suburban consumerism worked to splinter marriages and communities into isolated and prefabricated enclaves, what is to recommend it as a model that we should try to conserve or retrieve?

Further, the same irony is at work in the manifesto's assessment of economic conservatism. It examines the rising prominence of a "fusionist conservatism" in which "economic conservatives holding to free market capitalism" formed a political alliance with "social conservatives focused on 'life' and 'family' questions."[12] The manifesto begins by claiming that, "at times, this fusionist approach has worked well politically," but it then proceeds to develop in a way that is identical to the previous example, a devastating critique of the very logic that drives free-market capitalism. "We point to an inherent dilemma in capitalist economics: the short-term interests of individual corporations in weak homes (places focused on consumption rather than productive tasks) and universal adult employment (mothers and fathers alike) versus the long-term interests of national economies."[13] As a result, "the interests of 'big business' and of families are not always compatible" because the "whetting of appetites commonly takes precedence over family integrity."[14]

With great precision, the manifesto here diagnoses the source of its own lack of political efficacy: it is the false convergence of consumerism and family values in the figure of a "conservatism" that robs the religious Right of both a genuine creativity and collectivity. Corporate consumerism takes advantage of the religious Right's misidentification of itself as a conservative (rather than revolutionary) movement by bringing the religious Right's real political aims under the "protective" umbrella of its own antithetical interests and intentions. The ensuing distortion and powerlessness are predictable.

The Common Family

Truthiness drives this misunderstanding. The desire to apprehend the common family as something natural or innate is the result of interest and fear for our interests. Reading family values as conservative rather than creative is a way of hedging one's bets. If it is the case that family values need only to be recovered or recapitulated rather than invented, then the risk involved in pursuing them is mitigated, and our interests are protected. We do not need a brave new world: we need only the world that once was. Thinking this way, however, reties what is common to the very fears and interests that must be exceeded.

In this respect, the opening lines of the manifesto remain the most important: "What is the natural family? The answer comes to the woman and the man who take the risk of turning their love into promises of lifelong devotion."[15] The work of creating something common, as the manifesto so clearly indicates, is a risk: we must be willing to risk the natural satisfactions of our love in an inventive and supranatural declaration of unconditional fidelity. Real political actions have no safety net. To be common, they must be creative, and to be creative they must exceed the conditions of interest and inertia that would prevent their invention. The fact that promises are symbolic rather than natural necessitates this conjunction of risk, creativity, and collectivity.

Fearful of the risk involved in the creation of something common, the religious Rightists fall prey to a nostalgic truthiness that distorts the essence of their own political aims. Having been thus distorted, the religious Right's real political aims are easily co-opted by the entrenched "conservatism" of big-business interests, whose only real interest is in maintaining a profitable status quo. Moreover, the alignment of the common family with conservation and restoration regrettably makes room for a whole host of fears and interests to ironically come home and roost in its branches. Patriarchy and homophobia, for instance, make quick work of distorting family values when we try to retrieve these values from eras in which patriarchy and homophobia were the status quo. Whatever the common family will look like, it will have no room for fear, abuse, or oppression.

The religious Right's penchant for this kind of self-misunderstanding is not unrelated to the biblical narratives in which its hopes for a common family are grounded. The temptation of Eve, the fall of Adam, and the loss of Eden are themes readily adaptable as ciphers for interpreting the way our own lives and families are tempted and threatened by an unopposed consumerism. But even within this biblical framework, there is no call to understand the common family as something to be retrieved or conserved. The common family is something that has never yet belonged to this world. To aim at God's original intention for the world as a template for the kind of families to be created is not even remotely conservative; instead, it is profoundly revolutionary. To confuse the way things are and have been with the way God intends them to be is to forfeit the possibility of success in advance. The promise of the common family is precisely that: a promise of something to come, a promise that requires both the risk and fidelity constitutive of any creative, collective act.

Notes

1 Geoffrey Nunberg, *Talking Right: How Conservatives Turned Liberalism into a Tax-Raising, Latte-Drinking, Sushi-Eating, Volvo-Driving, New York Times-Reading, Body-Piercing, Hollywood-Loving, Left-Wing Freak Show* (New York: PublicAffairs, 2006).
2 Allan C. Carlson and Paul T. Mero, "The Natural Family: A Manifesto," http://www.familymanifesto.net/fm/manifesto.asp (accessed November 23, 2007), 3. The page numbers given refer to the downloadable pdf version of the manifesto, also available at this Internet address.
3 Ibid., 4.
4 Ibid., 15.
5 Ibid., 1.
6 Ibid., 13.
7 Ibid., 15.
8 Ibid., 26–27.
9 Ibid., 17.
10 Ibid., 24.
11 Ibid., 25.
12 Ibid., 30.
13 Ibid., 31.
14 Ibid., 30.
15 Ibid., 1.

5

The Cultural Logic of Evangelical Christianity

Christopher Haley and Creston Davis

December 13, 1999

Republican primary debate in Des Moines, Iowa, USA

Near the end of the debate, one of the moderators, John Bachman, asks George W. Bush: What political philosopher or thinker do you most identify with and why?

Bush: Christ, because he changed my heart.

Bachman: I think that the viewer would like to know more on how he has changed your heart.

Bush: Well, if they don't know, it's going to be hard to explain. When you turn your heart and your life over to Christ, when you accept Christ as a savior, it changes your heart, and changes your life and that's what happened to me.[1]

In light of the controversial elections of George W. Bush in 2000 and 2004, Bush's answer (delivered with a hostile stare at John Bachman) about his transformational experience of Christ's presence in his life signaled the dawning of a new power of evangelical Christianity and its ability to influence the future of the America's political system.[2] In both the 2000 and 2004 elections, members of the evangelical Right (sometimes referred to as the "Christian Right")[3] played a significant role in Bush's success in terms of their grassroots campaigning and highly mobilized efforts to sway public opinion and ultimately turn out voters.[4] In this chapter, we examine the ideological procedure of the hegemonic form of Protestant evangelicalism emerging in the context of the profound social, cultural, and economic changes ongoing in the United States over the past three decades. In particular, we are interested in how the Christian Right is intimately connected with what is often characterized as its exact opposite: (neo)liberalism and its supplement, multiculturalism.

On first blush, it seems categorically wrong to think that evangelicalism is somehow intimately relatable to its (im)moral opposite—secular atheism materialized in multiculturalism—the fantasy of a middle-class liberal. Yet because this evangelicalism versus multiculturalism deadlock seems to render the world unproblematic and stable, this is precisely the reason why we need to penetrate beyond this either/or structure. Indeed, does not this dialectical structure beg for its own overturning? Anytime we encounter such a pristine opposition from the point of view of the True and absolute doctrine of any system (religious, legal, political, and so forth), we must be courageous enough to embrace a core Hegelian principle: The opposite of one's ground of truth always contains within it an essential truth of its own essence. This analysis, however, need not arrive from the speculative margins of high-floating philosophers like Plato and Hegel and the like. On the contrary, this analysis whereby we seek to penetrate the static ground of opposite positions (which contain the truth of its opposite) surprisingly comes to us from countless stories in the Bible. Think of Jesus' (and later Paul's) entire mission, which can be distilled as follows: turn the knowledge (mind) of this world on its head, show how the weak are, in reality, strong; show how the poor are the ones who can lay claim to the earth; show how the prostitutes (and the socially marginalized) are, in themselves, the truth of the social condition.

A contemporary example of this biblical *inversion* takes place in the first *Matrix* film, when the hero (played by Keanu Reeves) confronts a choice offered by Morpheus: the red or the blue pill. The choice essentially is either to return to the stable world (the world of fantasy, the Matrix—blue pill), or else risk letting go of a stable and predictable reality and enter into the *real* world (red pill). Could it be that evangelicalism (insofar as their version of the world seems so squeaky clean and rationalized—not to mention corporatized) is a fantasy lived out in order to avoid—at all costs—the risking of the *real*? Analogously, is it not equally true that multiculturalism too is guilty of forgoing the risk of penetrating beyond its formal truth condition, a utopia in which all differences simply coexist without hierarchy and violence? Evangelical Christian doctrine is explicitly opposed to multiculturalism (as undermining the absolute superiority and singular truth of Christian teachings), and multiculturalism is highly suspicious of fundamentalist claims that seek to dominate and exclude other perspectives (ways of living, values, and so forth). Yet multinational capitalism is able to incorporate both social philosophies into its internal logic because of a key shortcoming of evangelicalism and multiculturalism.

Rejecting any sort of functionalist analysis whereby global capitalism produces ideologies and subjectivities in service to its needs, evangelicalism and multiculturalism are social philosophies built on assumptions and social analytics that necessarily exclude economic factors from their ideological constitution. This is not surprising in light of how marketing and consumerism overbears the composition of everyday life in late capitalism. The desire for the new, the self-transformative, the authentic expression of self—all attempts to find something *real* in our personal effects (houses, cars, clothes, vacations, toys, etc.)—displaces our attention from the social history of commodities and the long-range consequences of our purchasing power. However, not only is the postmodern form of desire for commodities suspect; the problem also is exacerbated by the way in which commodities are presented to the consumer in the marketplace. Consumers experience the marketplace as an ideal space, faceless, and free from history and strife, in which commodities are wholly decontextualized from their origins.[5] In place of knowledge about the conditions of commodity production in particular and the social, spatial, and temporal dimensions of global political economy in general, the void is filled with fantasy and self-serving ideology promulgated by economic elites.[6]

In the final analysis, evangelicalism and multiculturalism both seek (though in vastly different ways) to redress glaring deficiencies of the U.S. society and the world at large, yet without taking into account the social effects of late capitalism and the neoliberal revolution. The movements of both evangelicalism and multiculturalism are impotent and can only act as divergent temptations, keeping one's attention away from the *real*. What better way of doing this than by offering millions of busy consumers systems of beliefs that do not require one to think at all, much less to challenge the "knowledge of this world," that is, the prevailing set of coordinates that overcodes the *real* and renders it irrelevant.

The Rise of Radical Evangelicalism[7]

Evangelicalism is derived from *euangelion*, a Greek word meaning "the good news," and was associated with publishing the birth of a king's offspring to nearby kingdoms. Evangelicalism emerges on the world stage with the influence of both the Pietistic movement in Germany (late seventeenth century into the eighteenth) and then the movement associated with the Anglican missionary John Wesley in England. In the eighteenth century, American evangelicalism became increasingly associated with religious revivals taking place as the United States was born. A revival was a religious phenomenon or event in which masses of people would either convert to a pious form of Christian living (no lying, cheating, stealing, sleeping around, and fornicating) or else rededicate their lives to Jesus Christ by living out a morally astute life, again defined by what one should not do. Thus, the logic of evangelicalism operated on two different but interrelated levels. First, there is the level of the social—in the evangelical imagination, if everyone promises to not cheat, or kill one's neighbors, sleep around, and so forth, individuals' sinful and chaotic passions are held in check, thus stabilizing the social commonweal. Controlling the practices and habits of the social domain was imperative, especially for a young and unstable colony (and its anxiety of occupying "the new world," which was already the home of Native Americans). The first level thus reformulated the fundamental bonds of society in moralistic terms.

The second level revolved around a new metaphysics of the individual. With the Protestant turn in Christianity, which preceded and foreshadowed the dawning of political liberalism (democracy) and economic liberalism (capitalism),[8] emerged the individual subject constituted in spiritual, political, and economic terms. The ecclesial community in Protestant countries such as England, which formally controlled one's salvation and fused Christianity into the material conditions of everyday life, was eclipsed by a new individualistic faith, in which one's relationship to God is expressed in purely immaterial, nonsocially mediated terms. Consequently, Christian evangelical faith lost its communal (and hence material) coordinates: in its place appeared the radically discreet and moral configuration of the individual. The shift from a Christian material community to an immaterial individualism in terms of personal piety is signified by the new emphasis on the heart as the fountain of one's faith. The moral sphere for each individual comprises a fixed set of socially acceptable behaviors, underwritten by personal piety and immaterial faith. An important effect of evangelical immateriality is how this new faith intersects with the rise of bourgeois political-economic subjectivity. As we will show below, evangelicalism, from its origins in England and manifestation in the United States, has always supported the interests of economic elites.

According to Larry Eskridge's article "Defining Evangelicalism," "By the 1820s evangelical Protestantism was by far the dominant expression of Christianity in the United States. The concept of evangelism and the revival—codified, streamlined, and routinized by evangelists like Charles G. Finny (1792–1875)—became 'revivalism' as evangelicals set out to convert the nation."[9] In addition, "these revivals were particularly responsible for the rise of the Baptists and Methodists from obscure sects to their traditional position as America's two largest Protestant denominational families."[10] Indeed, the United States of America becomes known as the "Benevolent Empire" by the famous historian Martin Marty; it was "actively attempting to reshape American society through such reforms as temperance" and other socially acceptable but nonpolitical values.[11]

In its latest manifestation, the rise of the evangelical Right in contemporary U.S. politics is described frequently as a backlash against the 1960s and its profound social and cultural changes. In actuality, the "1960s" has become the metaphor for a range of social movements that emerged in the period between the late 1950s (exemplified by the liberal Warren Supreme Court)[12] and Ronald Reagan's presidential election in 1981 (which was ironic in that it ousted a professed evangelical, Jimmy Carter, though Reagan was neither an evangelical nor even a practicing Christian). These movements opened the possibility of new lifestyles and personal practices, critiqued American foreign and domestic policies, and examined the ways received categories of race, class, gender, and sexuality privilege certain individuals and groups while marginalizing others. These movements included civil rights, peace, feminism, gay and lesbian activism, environmentalism, anticapitalism, anti-imperialism/ war, antisexism, and antiracism.

Proponents of the evangelical Right argue that America lost its moral bearing when powerful liberal elites leading these movements tried to found a new political order in America, based on secular, multicultural, and socialist values. Liberal elites simultaneously denied the Judeo-Christian values that had traditionally underpinned and secured America's status as the earth's vanguard nation-state fomenting peace and prosperity and spreading the good news of God's truth throughout the world and American life. Thus, the backlash began in reaction to the perceived threat of these changes to an imagined golden age where white Protestant nationalism flourishes, absolute property rights reign, and unencumbered capitalism enriches us all to the exclusion of all other forms of identity and practice.

What foments the contemporary evangelical political movement are two interrelated forces in the evangelical worldview: moral and political. The first is the evangelical perception that America is in a crisis of moral and spiritual decline. Here we have the first instance of our dialectical either/or structure whereby a hard and fast polemic is not only perceivable but helps to divert our attention away from what is really at stake. Evangelicals are morally privileged and thus believe themselves to be defending America and its Christian legacy against an atheistic "culture of death" brought about by America's turn toward secular values.

The second is the rise of "dominionism," the theological position that Christians have an obligation to assume political control of society because of their exclusive access to the universal and absolute decree of God's will, dictating all facets of human experience from the individual psyche to the community of all nations. Something sets apart this newest manifestation of evangelical political movement from previous expressions, as Michelle Goldberg has observed: it is "qualitatively different from earlier religious revivals," all of which base their beliefs on an inerrant Bible. In this case, however, contemporary evangelicals are "extrapolating a total political program from that truth, and yoking that program to a political party."[13] Consequently, many evangelical Christians have consciously re-created the Republican party to promulgate their worldview framed by an either/or logic of the culture wars: abortion, evolution, homosexuality, multiculturalism, pornography, and separation of church and state. To combat a perceived threat by the "religion" of secular humanism espoused by liberal elites,[14] evangelicals seek to reinstitute a biblical foundation on which to base individual morality, public policy and law, and seek to envelop all of society within God's truth.

Jesus Is a Neoliberal

Not surprisingly, the rise of the evangelical Right in 1979, culminating with the emergence of Jerry Falwell's Moral Majority as a national political force in Ronald Reagan's successful election in 1980,[15] occurred simultaneously with the emergence of neoliberalism as a political-economic revolution to overturn Keynesian-style policies of the postwar era.[16] Both these movements (the evangelical Right and neoliberalism) arose from a notion of crisis—moral and economic—within American society and economy. America was in moral decline—its values trampled upon by a rampant hedonistic secularism—and must be reversed by cultural renewal through the guiding principles of traditional authority: God, family, and personal responsibility. America's economy, oil-shocked into debilitating stagflation and encumbered by self-defeating governmental interventions (to increase employment and spending), must again be turned over to the dynamic initiative of individuals operating in a free market. Around these two crises, these seemingly antipodal ideologies coalesce around a shared vision of a new economy free from the government's intervention and find a shared tent within the Republican party, whose platform comes to endorse both the agenda of moral conservatives and neoliberal agenda favored by corporate interests.[17]

The relationship of evangelical Christian doctrine to neoliberalism hinges on a shared understanding of the proper level of state interference in the economy. Unlike socialist command, liberal welfare, and Keynesian-model economies, the neoliberal vision demands almost total economy-state separation. Our use of the term "neoliberalism" to indicate the dominant logic of our age is a choice from several other related terms ("neoclassical economics," "globalization," "multinational capitalism") frequently used to describe the same phenomenon. We find "neoliberalism" to be the most comprehensive term because in each case the other terms capture only certain aspects of the total socioeconomic revolution under way. For instance, "neoclassical economics" designates the school of economic theory (propounded by F. A. Hayek, Milton Friedman, and the Chicago School of Economics) that supports neoliberal policies. "Multinational capitalism" describes the newest organizational manifestation (in terms of new production and marketing strategies) of capital in a transnational logic. "Globalization" focuses attention on the new global interconnections made possible by transportation and communication technologies. "Neoliberalism" has the benefit of capturing both the political and economic components of this global revolution while assuming neoclassical economic theory and presupposing both multinational capitalism and the determinations behind the elimination of spatial and temporal barriers that have brought about globalization.

In terms of general social and economic policy, evangelicalism and neoliberalism reject giving control of society and economy to a centralized position of power. In the absence of vanguard communist parties, monarchies, and other dead institutions, the viable, modern candidates for such control have been the state or a transnational institution such as the United Nations.[18] Evangelicals and neoliberals disdain centralized control because it places determinative responsibility of the collective well-being in the hands of "man." As central powers run by fallible human beings, states are susceptible to corruption; their policies are swayed by special interests; and with their massive resources, they are tempted to undertake grandiose and usually destructive projects of social engineering. Centralized control does not allow the *natural* outcome as dictated by God and/or the collective wisdom enthroned within a decentralized marketplace (formed by individuals in aggregate, each pursuing their own ends) to determine our current and future well-being—what proponents call real democracy. Furthermore, when a centralized power usurps responsibility for social welfare and economic growth away from individuals and the family unit, people do not make the best choices for themselves[19]; consequently, that central power undermines collective benefits that decentralized economic decision making and personal responsibility would entail.

Indeed, evangelicals and neoliberals more or less support dismantling the legacy of the two great state interventions into society and economy: Franklin Roosevelt's New Deal (Social Security, business and financial regulation, public works projects, forty-hour work week, minimum wage, and so forth) and Lyndon Johnson's Great Society (Medicare, Medicaid, food stamps, Head Start, PBS, NPR, affirmative action, environmental protection, and so forth). The wholesale removal of the state from socioeconomic affairs has the effect of lessening political control, hence democratic procedural control of the conditions of economic activity, and in general the social fabric of countries that accept neoliberal reforms. The profound transformation now under way, the increasing number of hours spent on the job, changing labor conditions, issues of economic justice, the well-being of the billions of people incorporated into the global economy, and how these changes affect our daily life and our children's future—all these are not issues that evangelicals evoke as proper for theological inquiry or moral concern. On the contrary, how society intersects with the economic sphere is above reproach. The tumultuous and antagonistic field of economic competition in the form of unlimited capital accumulation and multinational corporate growth, concomitant with private property rights, deregulation, free markets, and free trade—all this is effectively naturalized as outside the political domain.

America, as are most countries around the world, is undergoing profound and rapid changes to its social structure and values.[20] Whether we judge these changes as negative determines a political response in terms of grasping control and modifying the general trajectory of these changes. What is both interesting and troubling about the perceived crisis that evangelicals find in contemporary America is that their diagnoses of the causes of this crisis *cannot* include any reference to the profound socioeconomic transformations under way. Instead, what evangelicals identify as the fundamental cause of America's unfolding crisis is purely ideological in nature. As Thomas Frank argues in *What's the Matter with Kansas?*[21] evangelicals express hyperconcern to oppose an "elite liberal" set of values forced on the body politic (multiculturalism, cosmopolitism, feminism, overturning of traditional sources of authority—family and church, and so forth) as the exclusive source of "troubling" changes. By disregarding the logic of multinational capitalism unleashed by neoliberal revolution, the evangelical analysis of crisis fails to understand the conditions and consequences of this juncture in history. The omission follows from a total doctrinal acceptance of the basic tenets of neoliberalism.

Consequently, it is not true that economic elites hoodwinked evangelical conservatives into accepting multinational capitalism, that they have false consciousness, or that they have just not taken enough social science courses. Rather, deep within the ideological structure of the evangelical worldview, free-market capitalism must be part of God's plan and cannot conflict with biblical teachings. In addition, what appears at the surface as the recent syncretism of evangelical doctrine and free-market ideology (now manifesting itself in a multinational phase), is in fact a long-standing relationship of ideological support. This is the great irony of the evangelical Right that Slavoj Žižek puts forth in this book's postface: "What moral conservatives fail to perceive is thus how, to put it in Hegelese, in fighting the dissolute liberal permissive culture, they are fighting the necessary ideological consequences of the unbridled capitalist economy that they themselves fully and passionately support: their struggle against the external enemy is the struggle against the obverse of their own position."

Evangelicals believe that individual spiritual redemption is the purpose of life, and that the liberal "welfare state" and its cornucopia of tax-supported social programs interfere with the spiritual imperative to take personal responsibility for the material conditions of oneself (working for food, shelter, clothing: basic existential needs). The logic of total personal responsibility as it manifests in economic decision making, and the socioeconomic status that results from an individual's decisions—these are ultimately a question of personal morality, not sociology, anthropology, or any other social-scientific explanations that understand individual decision making within historical and/or social, cultural, or economic contexts. Because social science categories omit the spiritual element of human beings, by elevating categories such as race, class, and culture[22] as exclusive and fundamental to the constitution of individuals, the effect is to define human beings in purely materialist and secular terms, which ultimately subordinate the individual to a given set of impersonal forces and structures.[23] Evangelicals repudiate secular understanding because it does not situate complete and absolute responsibility for an individual's existential condition within one's own volition.[24]

As a case in point, the issue of poverty is highly instructive for understanding the dominant evangelical worldview. The question of wealth and poverty is a salient issue for Christians because of God's providential relationship to humankind. However, because human societies are stratified by individual differences in wealth and power—especially free-market societies, why some are poor and some are wealthy begs to be theologically justified. Clearly, Calvinist doctrine has significantly influenced evangelical Christianity in that poverty becomes a kind of epistemological marker of personal salvation. Consequently, evangelicals expressly reject both economic and cultural explanations (because of their smacking secularism, as noticed above) for the cause of poverty, placing the burden squarely on the shoulders of the afflicted. Poverty is a mark of personal moral failing, and its suffering becomes a constant reminder by God to motivate the poor to redeem themselves. The state is not responsible for alleviating poverty, and society is not culpable for its existence. State-sponsored social welfare programs to uplift the poor coupled with the redistribution of wealth through a progressive taxation regime[25]—these contravene the God-given system of self-knowledge that places spiritual and material well-being in a cause-and-effect relationship. State intervention can only temporally mollify the *effect* (being poor) without addressing the *cause* (moral failing, disavowal of God's truth). Furthermore, by not letting the poor suffer, they have no impetus to change their hearts and achieve self-understanding of the total responsibility they bear for their spiritual health and material sustenance.

Nonetheless, attempts to synthesize the capitalist socioeconomic order with evangelical doctrine are not a recent development. As Gordon Bigelow shows, the evangelical link to capitalism emerges almost simultaneously with the study of national political economy as a reflexive sphere of knowledge about the overarching economic health and direction of the British nation-state.[26] Two early classics of political economy, Adam Smith's *Wealth of Nations* (1776) and David Ricardo's *Principles of Political Economy and Taxation* (1817), both sought to theorize the newly emergent national-capitalist-industrial societies and offer policy prescriptions to enhance free enterprise by removing remnants of mercantilism and other irrationalities from the economic system.[27] For both thinkers, however, their analysis of the workings of capitalist economy found certain features intrinsic to its nature or logic, which were rejected by the powerful block of middle-class religious reformers in early nineteenth-century England, reformers whose theological outlook Bigelow likens to contemporary U.S. evangelicals.

In Adam Smith's economic model, the "invisible hand" might work to benefit the social totality, and therefore it would justify free trade and unencumbered economic agents, but Smith finds the intentions of self-interest are morally questionable. Ironically, while a rising "wealth of the nation" is collectively rational, at the level of the individual it is irrational. The foundation of and motivation for the pursuit of wealth beyond basic needs is problematic because it is based primarily on a desire for prestige (conspicuous consumption) and happiness (the belief that wealth brings satisfaction), both of which, Smith argues, are problematic but apparently necessary.

Like Smith, Ricardo unabashedly supports the system of free enterprise and individual initiative. From Ricardo's microstudy of the economics of land ownership, he drew out the larger structural features of the economy as a whole. Ricardo identified that an effect of this system, with which evangelicals found problems, is that the interests of differentially situated agents within the economy (owners, investors, renters, laborers) inherently conflict.[28] Unlike Smith, in this case Ricardo was not troubled by the moral implications of the capitalist order, bringing inherent class conflict, but rather, he accepted conflict as part of the natural order.

For middle-class evangelicals, however, inherent conflicts and irrationalities at the heart of the socioeconomic order were untenable. God would not create a world whose inextricable logic is flawed. Gordon Bigelow writes, "The evangelicals believed in a providential God, one who built a logical and orderly universe, and they saw the new industrial economy as a fulfillment of God's plan." However, "for evangelicals it was unthinkable that capitalism led to class conflict, for that would mean that God had created a world at war with itself." Not accepting the "pessimistic element of Smith and Ricardo," the evangelical ideological move was to incorporate both the irrational motivations of wealth accumulation and inherent class conflicts of capitalist societies into what Max Weber identified as the cultural logic of the "Protestant ethic." This ethic performs a remarkable short circuit by annihilating the seeming contradictions between the economic system as a whole (good) and the individual participation in it (bad). Against the problem of "capitalist intentions" elucidated by Adam Smith, evangelicals reexamined the notion of original sin in relation to the self-interest expressed through a free market. Evangelical understanding of original sin asserts that all human beings by virtue of the unending desires of the flesh are inherently sinful and hence need salvation. God's forgiveness of sin, in manifest Protestant terms of individual responsibility for salvation (in contrast to the Catholic Church's hierarchical mediation of access to God and salvation), becomes fused into the meaning and conduct of individual economic activity.

The homology between the individual pursuit of salvation (Protestantism) and the individual pursuit of wealth (capitalism) allows their seamless integration: an individual's strict focus on one's own character and the execution of one's earthly calling through hard work, frugality, delayed gratification, and profit (!) comes to signify spiritual redemption. The relationship of earthly success (now measured in terms appropriate to a free-market economy) to salvation has a significant consequence: in addition to promoting capital accumulation, success in religiomoral terms justifies the financial success of the emergent bourgeois class and consequently the newly configured hierarchical social order based on money. In the past, the ideological complex known as the "Great Chain of Being"—placing God, angels, kings, aristocrats, and commoners in a fixed hierarchy—consecrated the social orders. For the future of Western societies, the newfound power of the monied class would increasingly sweep aside the determinations of social rank, enabling individuals to pursue their self-interest and create wealth. Evangelicals could therefore accept the social stratification and conflicts of interest that Ricardo exposed because differentials of wealth—being well-off versus being poor—become markers of spiritual success, thus delegitimating class conflict as mere resentment and not intrinsic to the God-ordered social world.

In short, Christian doctrine, far from being an ahistorical truth claim, is rearticulated through the new social and economic order. The Protestant ethic removes conflicts between competing interests and creates a complementary religious subjectivity to undergird the logic of capital accumulation. The combined effect naturalizes capitalism in religious terms in two interlocking ways. First, the motivation for and ends of capitalist enterprise (pursuit of wealth) as an earthly calling become signs of spiritual well-being—granted that the individual's character, personal habits, and lifestyle tastes remain highly circum-scribed by both Christian morality and a wariness of materialism (ad-herence to spending limitations). Second, the inevitable social stratifica-tion of capitalist societies derived from the uneven attainment and/or distribution of income and political and cultural capital becomes justified in terms of a Christian's duty to submit to the existing social order (Rom 13). Christians must find and accept their place in the world and abide by various forms of subordination to and domination of the nation-state, church, family, gender roles, economic position, and so forth.

Multiculturalism—the Other against Evangelicals

Now that we have examined the basic ideological structure of evan-gelicalism, we can interrogate its oppositional stance, multiculturalism. As recognized above, evangelicalism posits its own identity precisely by placing it up to and against what it is *not*. Its identity is thus par-tially dependent on its negation, which follows from evangelicalism's immaterial moralism and accounts for its cultural war against abortion, stem-cell research, gay marriage, secularism, and so forth. The very act of staging this war with the ominous Other is the point—the construction of the moralist self (the evangelical) requires the construction of its immoral opposite (e.g., a secularist, multicultural abortionist).

Beginning in the 1970s, the impetus behind multiculturalism is to create a neutral political space that accommodates human differences without hierarchy and domination of one group by another in terms of identity markers, such as language, nationality, ethnicity, social mores, religion, race, and values. The utopian idea behind multiculturalism is simple: by leveling cultural differences on an equal playing field, society would be more tolerant and just in terms of access to political and economic resources—which is what multiculturalism is really about: distribution of power. Multiculturalism as a sociopolitical goal is in direct contrast to the melting-pot ideal, most notable in the United States, where the expectation is for peoples of different national and ethnic cultures to assimilate into the dominant culture's language, values, and so forth. Multiculturalism, in the form of identity politics, overturned the melting-pot ideal, claiming that (in anthropological terms) the "unmarked categories" of race (white), religion (Protestant Christianity), gender (male), class (middle to upper), sexuality (heterosexual), and national origin (for the most part, northwestern Europe) disadvantaged individuals with "marked categories" of identity.[29] Multiculturalism seeks to dismantle the informal system of identity subordination that privileges some while marginalizing others.

In addition, multiculturalism actively works to undo the ideological effects of placing cultural differences within a hierarchy of advancement or progress toward a universally recognized state of civilization.[30] Nonetheless, the ideology of multiculturalism is not simply a perspective *between* cultures in terms of equivalence, from one person situated within a culture, to another person of a different culture: "If you respect my cultural difference, I'll respect yours. . . ." Instead, as Slavoj Žižek points out, a *third* position is created by the location of the multicultural perspective (perhaps construed as cosmopolitan, urbane, nihilistic) completely outside the cultural plane of identity.[31] This third, acultural subjectivity is in effect the structural position of capitalist logic, freed from the boundaries of ethnic and national communities, their mutual antagonisms, and their constraining cultural values. Capital's global outlook produces a rainbow assortment of goods and services designed to appeal to every possible identity across ethnic, national, racial, gender, ideological terrains.[32]

Žižek is thus right to point out that "the ideal form of ideology of this global capitalism is multiculturalism, the attitude which formulates a kind of empty global position and treats *each* locale [and] culture the way the colonizer treats colonized people—as 'natives' whose mores are to be carefully studied and 'respected.'"[33] Furthermore, "the multiculturalist respect for the Other's specificity is the very form of asserting one's own superiority."[34] Consequently, marketing commodities without ethnocentric or any other forms of bias, while demonstrating sophisticated understanding of the cultural values of potential consumers, indicates that the logic of multiculturalism has expanded to its fullest potential. From this analysis, we can clearly see the two levels on which things work: on the first level there is this functioning utopia in which there is a celebration of differences expressed as a radical inclusivity. There is a deeper level, however, that exposes its surface truth: the inclusive logic of multiculturalism masks a power game that maintains a bourgeois, capitalist status quo.

With this analysis of multiculturalism in hand, we can now begin to see a fundamental connection to evangelicalism and the identical structural logic with it. Just as multiculturalism acts on the surface level as a utopian dream of an unthinking acceptance of cultural difference, so too evangelicalism creates a convenient and unthinking culture war against the immoral atheist. However, the surface expressions of inclusion and exclusion are thinly veiled disguises for a deeper and more dangerous ideological unfolding, which in the final analysis keep our attention away from existential problems facing humanity. The logic of both multiculturalism and evangelicalism assume a construction of community in which economic considerations are absent. In other words, both social ideologies reproduce the structural features of neoliberalism (the complete disembedding of the economy from society) in its multinational phase. In twenty-first-century America, both evangelicalism and multiculturalism diagnose problems of crisis, injustice, social decay, and so forth and offer prescriptions to rectify these failings. However, by failing to interrogate the socioeconomic conditions of their own (evangelical and multicultural) formation, they are blind to see that the very logic of their social philosophy is intimately bound up with the logic of neoliberalism.

Žižek argues that the recent emergence of these religious and ethnic fundamentalisms (what he calls "ethnic Things") are totally inflected by the socioeconomic conditions set by the spread of neoliberal policies. Consequently, at a fundamental level, the relationship between the economy and community is severed. "It is therefore only today, in contemporary 'fundamentalist' ethnic, religious, life-style communities, that the splitting between the abstract form of commerce and the relationship to the particular ethnic Thing, inaugurated by the Enlightenment project, is fully realized: today's postmodern ethnic or religious 'fundamentalism' and xenophobia are not only not 'regressive,' but, on the contrary, offer the supreme proof of the final emancipation of the economic logic of market from the attachment to the ethnic Thing."[35]

If Žižek is correct that "today's new 'fundamentalist' ethnic identifications involve a kind of 'desublimation,' a process of disintegration of this precarious unity of the 'national economy' into its two constituent parts, the transnational market-function and the relationship to the ethnic Thing," then the uncanny relationship of multiculturalism and evangelicalism to the ideology and policies of neoliberalism makes sense. Once issues of economy per se (jobs, wages, who receives the income and who controls its outcome, workplace safety, the right to work, and so forth) are removed from the fabric of community intrarelations and social reproduction, and hence from political control, *the possibilities for social integration outside of economic issues are limited to ideological constructs*. Ethnic things, in the form of religious fundamentalisms and the assorted identities under the multicultural umbrella, are an impoverished stand-in for the possibilities of economic integration, for a community grounded in its materialist conditions and with political control of those conditions. In the national moral community, an embedded economy integrates individuals into a shared community, with mutual responsibilities for each other, which ultimately entails political control of the necessities of well-being mediated by an economy.

For Žižek, such a materialist politics is essentially and certainly a politics of class because class is inherently about economic distribution of resources and control of labor. Without recourse to a materialist politics, modern Western societies have no other sources of the self except the ideological constructs of religious, national, ethnic/multicultural identities. This does not mean that for evangelical or multicultural societies, materialist and class divisions do not exist or do not exert an effect. It only means that class, which always potentially and historically has been a manifest part of subjectivity (in socialist and communist party movements, certain populist uprisings in the United States, and so forth), has become latent, submerged, and overcoded by other identity-ideological expressions because materialist and economic factors are deemed outside and ancillary to the formation of the community.

Conclusion

The consequences of never-ending sustainable economic development further enhanced by the neoliberal revolution appear to necessitate environmental destruction, the undermining of real democracy by economic interests, the undermining of legal institutions, global poverty, and disease in the first, second and third worlds, and the general lack of accountability on policy making, increased bureaucracy, and the fragmentation of time. As we forge a new political hope today, we need to keep one's belief structure from undercutting one's thoughts, desires, and actions that unceasingly address injustice on all levels of life. The core belief here must espouse the axiom that thought is action, and conversely, action is thought. Thinking must unfold as the social and political horizon of its own actualization—on this point, the apostle Paul was finally right! When thinking becomes self-referential (as in multicultural and evangelical frameworks) and hence inert and apolitical, thinking and being in the world only inevitably reinforce the status quo and the unjust logic of empire. This means too that a certain and almost exhilarating passage toward the infinite starts to emerge in us and in the whole world. It is this infinite desiring for justice, peace, and above all love that is able to resist resting in the passive critical stance and reincarnate itself in the Being-of-the-world as the true condition of the political.

Notes

1   A transcript of the entire debate can be found at http://www.renewamerica.us/ archives/transcript.php?id=109 (accessed November 23, 2007).
2   In the 2004 elections, by far the most important constituency for Bush was "Traditionalist Evangelical Protestants," giving Bush 88 percent of their vote and 27 percent of Bush's total vote count. For an in-depth statistical analysis of the 2004 election in terms of religious belief affecting voter preference for George Bush and Democratic candidate John Kerry, see http://pewforum.org/publications/surveys/ postelection.pdf (accessed November 23, 2007).

3 Using the term "Christian Right" or "evangelical Right" is somewhat problematic. These terms ascribe a monolithic political unity to what is empirically a loose set of concerns and values. Within the Christian Right are several factions, each of which has its leaders, organizations, media outlets, and different theological positions. Nonetheless, in relation to the wider spectrum of social-political philosophies found in American politics (social moderates, liberal Democrats, paleo-conservatives, and others), even with internal differences, the Christian Right is more or less a coherent marker of recognition, and we think it is fair to use this term with the aforementioned caveat in mind.

4 For background on the history of the evangelical Right and explanations of the terms "evangelical" and "fundamentalism," see the Web site for The Institute for the Study of American Evangelicals: http://www.wheaton.edu/isae/defining _evangelicalism.html (accessed November 23, 2007).

5 Tags indicating commodities are "Made in China" or "Made in Bulgaria" are not sufficient.

6 Lack of knowledge essentially constrains individuals from drawing these conditions into one's horizon of political-moral concern and being responsible for the consequences of one's consumerism.

7 Obviously this section cannot do justice to the complexities of the history of evangelicalism; nevertheless, the important part is to identify the movement from a political, materially embodied faith to an immaterial, apolitical faith metaphorically encased in the language of "the heart." It is important, in this regard, to understand that the image of "the heart" is the precise moment when evangelicalism becomes ideological.

8 Max Weber, *The Protestant Ethic and the Spirit of Capitalism* (London: Routledge, 2002).

9 See http://www.wheaton.edu/isae/defining_evangelicalism.html.

10 Ibid.

11 Ibid.

12 Cf. Robert Bork, *Tradition and Morality in Constitutional Law* (Washington, DC: American Enterprise Institute for Public Policy Research, 1984).

13 Michelle Goldberg, *Kingdom Coming: The Rise of Christian Nationalism* (New York: W. W. Norton, 2006), 6.

14 A recent and best-selling example of this line of reasoning is Ann Coulter's *Godless: The Church of Liberalism* (New York: Crown Forum, 2006).

15 Sara Diamond, *Roads to Dominion: Right-Wing Movements and Political Power in the United States* (New York: Guilford, 1995).

16 David Harvey, *A Brief History of Neoliberalism* (Oxford: Oxford University Press, 2005).

17 While the corporate world is ambivalent about the implementation of evangelical doctrine (most corporate leaders individually are fiscally conservative but socially moderate), evangelicals strongly support neoliberalism: private property rights, deregulation, tax decreases, free trade, dismantling of the welfare state, and so forth.

18 The fear of the United Nations as the likely precursor to a "one-world government" looms large in the evangelical mind. For example, a one-world government is led

by the antichrist in Tim LaHaye and Jerry G. Jenkin's Left Behind series, 15 vols. (Wheaton, IL: Tyndale House, 1995–2006) with 60 million copies sold.

19 Economists complain that state intervention in the economy inevitably deforms "price signals," the key information needed to make sound economic decisions. Evangelicals complain that state intervention in society deforms social and economic consequences of our moral decisions.

20 It is far beyond the scope of this essay to describe these changes, but an analysis would include several key domains: demographic changes (population aging, immigration, women in the workplace); the eclipse of small, independent family farms in favor of the mass-scale and more-efficient agribusiness model; the decline of industrial and manufacturing sectors of the U.S. economy as corporations, enabled by advancements in communication and transportation technologies, seek cheaper labor abroad; the complementary shift from manufacturing to a postindustrial or "new economy" of service sector labor and what Robert B. Reich in *The Work of Nations: Preparing Ourselves for 21st-Century Capitalism* (New York: A. A. Knopf, 1991) identifies as the dominant rise of "symbolic-analytic services," which include science and technology, financial services, and a broad spectrum of administrative work in the private and public sectors (see 177–180); and finally, the coarsening of expressive culture in movies, music lyrics, and the narratives of Internet porn, shock jocks, *Beavis and Butt-Head, Desperate Housewives*, and so forth, brought about by the democratization of taste and elimination of the distinction and hierarchy of high and low culture.

21 Thomas Frank, *What's the Matter with Kansas? How Conservatives Won the Heart of America* (New York: Henry Holt, 2004).

22 It is worth mentioning that the explanatory efficacy of race, class, and culture ebbs and flows according to fashion. Though race and class have receded for the moment as an explanatory model of human kind, culture is in ascension.

23 From a social science perspective, individuals are not totally determined by the cultural and historical circumstances in which they are born. The reconciliation of agency and sociocultural structure as mutually constitutive in so-called "practice theory" has been thoughtfully formulated in slightly different ways by Pierre Bourdieu (theory of *habitus*) and Anthony Giddens (structuration theory). See Pierre Bourdieu, *The Logic of Practice* (Stanford, CA: Stanford University Press, 1992); and Anthony Giddens, *The Constitution and Society: Outline of the Theory of Structuration* (New York: Polity Press, 1991).

24 Evangelicals link secularism in general with the dominance of the Darwinian worldview, where individuals are determined by impersonal forces, whether economic, cultural, or DNA.

25 In place of progressive taxation (tax rates increase as income levels rise), evangelicals frequently support a flat tax as a modern equivalent to tithing. From the evangelical viewpoint, a free-market system and a flat tax confront everybody with identical economic conditions, thereby allowing the epistemological effect of personal economic success or failure to operate unadulterated by the state, and they consequently can signify the "true" spiritual condition of each individual.

26 See Gordon Bigelow, "The Evangelical Roots of Economics," *Harpers Magazine* 310, no. 1860 (May 1, 2005), 33–38, http://www.mindfully.org/Industry/2005/Evangelical-Economics1may05.htm. All quotations were taken from the online version of this text.

27 Adam Smith classified "political economic inquiry" as a branch of moral philosophy, a far cry from the discipline of economics practiced today, which sees itself as "king of the social sciences" because, economists argue, it most closely approximates natural science models (especially physics) of cause and effect and universality.

28 Ricardo's conceptualization of inherent conflict within free-market societies later becomes a fundamental building block of Marx's conception of "class conflict" and "historical dialectics."

29 Consequently, the working-class black lesbian is the ultimate subaltern position in America.

30 This teleological framework constructs people, cultures, and countries as "premodern," "primitive," "undeveloped," "less-developed," "third-world," and so forth.

31 Slavoj Žižek, "Multiculturalism, or, the Cultural Logic of Multinational Capitalism," *New Left Review* 225 (September–October 1997): 28–51.

32 For example, products include cigarettes marketed to African Americans, McDonald's lamb burgers in India, cruises and movies for gay people, "green" products for the environmentally concerned, and ideological products for cultural conservatives (in an important sense, Rush Limbaugh, Ann Coulter, and Fox News are forms of political pornography designed to attract advertising dollars and sales). The search for new markets in terms of targeting smaller and smaller groups based on ethnic, racial, class, and ideological identities—this search contrasts with the previous model whereby monolithic products were advertised to appeal to a generic everyman consumer in the name of efficiency and quality.

33 Ibid., 44.

34 Ibid.

35 Žižek, "Multiculturalism," 43.

6

Jeb Stuart's Revenge

The Civil War, the Religious Right, and American Fascism

Clayton Crockett

According to the postmodern philosopher of religion Mark C. Taylor, "There is a religious dimension to *all* culture. In order to appreciate the far-reaching implications of religion, it is necessary to move beyond its manifest forms to examine the more subtle and complex ways in which it influences personal, social, and cultural development. Religion is often most intriguing and influential where it is least obvious."[1] I agree with this statement. I also propose that sometimes religion is least important where it is most obvious. That is, in order to understand the significance of the religious Right in the United States today, we need to see how it is not only obviously religious, but also and perhaps even more importantly, how it is driven by *other*—less obvious—political, economic, and cultural phenomena.

This chapter argues that the current situation of religion in American politics and the rise of the religious Right can be related to the aftermath of the U.S. Civil War, when the South lost its military and political attempt to secede from the Union and form a new nation. "Jeb" Stuart (James Ewell Brown Stuart, 1833–64), a general in the Confederate army, was killed late in the war. Along with Stonewall Jackson, he became an iconic figure in Southern culture, and his death was identified with the lost cause of the Southern defeat. I am using Jeb Stuart to stand for the defeat and revenge of Southern culture and religion in general. My claim is that though the South was defeated in the Civil War, the contemporary resurgence of conservative political religion represents a dangerous victory for the South.

The division over states' rights and the continued presence of slavery in the South were an obvious key in the conflict. Yet an often-overlooked, though equally if not more important issue, was how the extension of the practice of slavery to new territories and states as the Union expanded westward in search of its Manifest Destiny had certain economic and political effects. The rise of maritime capitalism in the Northeast in the early nineteenth century created an economic paradigm competing with Southern plantations, and free (nonslave) factory workers toiling (slaving) for low wages actually proved more efficient than the "free" labor of slaves. The Northern states, with the exception of a small but vocal group of radical abolitionists, were content to contain Southern plantation slavery, but would not allow its expansion to new Western territories. The Southern states recognized that their lifestyle could not flourish politically or economically if they were overshadowed by an industrial capitalist North and West, so they made a desperate attempt to dissolve the Union.

As we know, this attempt failed: slavery was eventually abolished, and the Union was reestablished. In a religious context, we need to recognize that religion was not necessarily as significant for the American South before the Civil War as it was elsewhere in the United States. The waves of religious revivalism that swept across the United States in the early nineteenth century occurred mostly along the frontiers of the original thirteen colonies, and also included upstate New York's so-called "burnt-over district." This movement was called the Second Great Awakening (1800–1830s), to distinguish it from the First Great Awakening of the 1740s (or 1730s–1750s).[2] Although whites sometimes used religion to justify slavery, religiosity in the South was not especially intense compared with other parts of the country, with the exception of the African Americans themselves: stripped of their African religions, they embraced Methodist and Baptist forms of Christianity.

After the Civil War, white Southerners took refuge in religion and created a nostalgic picture of antebellum life, ignoring or downplaying the brutal aspects of American plantation slavery. In many ways, this turn to religion constituted a repression of other and more explicitly political desires. Northern military power enforced this repression as well as the postwar Reconstruction. All of the major Protestant churches split before the Civil War, and some of them eventually reunited; but after the Civil

War, religion was split between North and South. As the historian of American religion George Marsden explains, the incredible emphasis upon Southern religion was "an integral part of the southern glorification of the lost cause in the half-century after the War Between the States. Although Southerners had lost the war on the battlefield, they were determined to win the war of ideas."[3]

The Southern postwar struggle was not just a war of ideas. The Southern states, overwhelmingly Democratic in opposition to the Northern Republicans, evolved a system of segregation between blacks and whites that allowed Southern whites to maintain their economic privileges and sense of cultural superiority. The rest of the country accommodated this system in the course of its ascent to the position of a dominant world power. After World War II, however, segregation was increasingly difficult to justify and to maintain, both politically and economically. In the 1950s and 1960s, desegregation and the civil rights movement functioned to dismantle the institutions of segregation and inflicted yet another defeat on white Southern pride. Southerners experienced the civil rights movement, starting with the Supreme Court decision of *Brown versus Board of Education* in 1954 and culminating with the Civil Rights Act of 1964, as a repetition of the Civil War.

From the ashes of this defeat emerged the movement that became known as the religious Right, which managed to co-opt most strands of evangelicalism and fundamentalism in postwar United States. During the civil rights movement, a more-liberal Christian evangelicalism prevailed, particularly among the major activists and leaders of the movement, including the Southern Christian Leadership Conference (SCLC) cofounded and led by Martin Luther King Jr. Democratic party politicians promoted and enforced civil rights, which led to a backlash on the part of white Southerners. Although Lyndon Baines Johnson won the 1964 presidential election over Barry Goldwater in a landslide, Johnson also allegedly remarked right after signing the Civil Rights Act: "We have lost the South for a generation."[4]

From the ashes of its political defeat in 1964, the Republican party, historically the party of big business and corporate interests, made an alliance with white Southerners that eventually propelled them back into power.[5] The Republicans cultivated Southern anger and frustration over perceived wounds to their culture and pride; they began to adopt Southern white Christian religious language, which culminated in 1980 with the Reagan Revolution, closely tied to Jerry Falwell's Moral Majority and

Pat Robertson's emergence as a national religious figure. The religious Right became visible in the 1980s, seemed to peak in 1988 with the failed presidential candidacy of Pat Robertson, but reemerged at the grassroots level in the 1994 congressional elections, and finally cemented its central place in American political and cultural life in the controversial election and reelection of George W. Bush.

This is not simply a history lesson. I am analyzing the history of religion in the United States in order to propose a mechanism for understanding the development of Southern religion as a response to the outcome of the Civil War. Southern religion is the place where repressed political and cultural aspirations are consolidated. The civil rights movement is experienced as a repetition of the Civil War, but this defeat is far less traumatic, and with the help of the Republican party as a catalyst, it produces the religious Right as a "return of the repressed," to apply a Freudian term usually understood in terms of individuals to a broader historical and social process. According to Freud, individuals repress traumatic experiences from consciousness, but they reemerge later and elsewhere, often in a destructive way, in what he calls the return of the repressed.[6] In this case, the vanquished South represses its cultural and political desires per se, conflates those desires with Southern Christianity, and today we are seeing a return of the repressed, touched off by the civil rights movement and its aftermath.

During the Reconstruction following the Civil War, as well as the early part of the twentieth century, religion provided a space separate from contemporary culture, and American fundamentalism in particular was a movement that set itself apart from and judged a sinful secular society. In many cases, Southern white Christianity rejected the entire social and political process and focused more on their own religious purity and salvation than on saving the country at large. What changed after the civil rights movement, however, is that now this Southern Christianity positively attempts to remake and reconstruct American society along its religious lines. In other words, rather than setting itself apart from sinful, secular society and remaining what was largely an apolitical religious movement primarily concerned with saving individual souls, Southern evangelical Christianity has become politicized.

For example, one of the most significant, if not very well-known, movements that emerged in the 1970s and 1980s is Christian Reconstruction(ism). Christian Reconstruction is a form of Calvinism that reaches back to eighteenth-century Puritan optimism for refashioning society, as well as its emphasis upon the Old Testament. Christian

Reconstruction, as expressed by Rousas John Rushdoony (1916–2001), asserts the universal applicability of the biblical law of Moses.[7] There is no suspension or revocation of Mosaic law by Jesus, and furthermore, Jesus will not return until all nations, led by the United States, institute and follow this biblical law. According to Rushdoony's son-in-law, Gary North, "Christian Reconstruction is the only Bible-affirming movement on earth that offers an uncompromisingly biblical alternative."[8] This emphasis on the Bible is not just a matter of belief, but also a practical and political blueprint for transforming society. Furthermore, the primary transformation of what I am calling Southern Christianity during the 1960s and 1970s is from a standpoint of pessimism to optimism in its attitude toward American society and its political and economic possibilities.

The transformation of white Southern Christianity from pessimism to optimism, from defeat and nostalgia to victory and patriotic American nationalism, and from an emphasis on personal piety to politics, coincides with its alliance with the Republican party in the late 1960s and early 1970s. In many ways, this alliance appears to be bizarre and unholy because American nationalism and free-market capitalism is wedded to Christian evangelicalism and fundamentalism. Even if Christianity and nationalism have always coexisted during the history of the United States, in the nineteenth and early twentieth centuries it was generally a more liberal form of Christianity that aligned itself with national and political American interests. This convergence between capitalism, nationalism, and Christian fundamentalism is also an anomaly in comparison with the rest of the world. The resurgence of conservative, traditionalist, and antimodern forms of religion all over the world is well established, and in some ways the rise of the religious Right in the United States mirrors the growth of conservative religion across the globe. On the other hand, as Mark C. Taylor points out, for most people outside the United States, "conservative or even fundamentalist religion often becomes a strategy to resist global capitalism and all it represents. In the United States, by contrast, conservative religion is commonly used to promote the spread of global capitalism."[9]

Thus the American religious Right, as opposed to radical Islam (e.g.), is unique in being aligned with, rather than opposed to, contemporary capitalism and free-market economics, even though both conservative Christianity and radical Islam oppose what they consider to be the secular aspects of modern law, science, and civil society. My argument is that ultimately this Southern Christianity is at least in part a façade behind which dangerous forms of authoritarianism, wealth consolidation, and militarism thrive and grow. At the same time, religion is a necessary catalyst for these processes, because religious passion allows a cultural and political legitimization for many of these forces, which would not have been as acceptable or as successful without this religious cloak. The forms of Southern Christianity that have become so pervasive are both powerful and sincere, but they have also been appropriated, enflamed, and directed by these other financial interests.[10] Furthermore, the linking of the passion of white Southern Christianity with authoritarian nationalism and global free-market capitalism creates a distinctively American form of fascism.

I realize that this label of fascism is highly evocative and controversial, but allow me to explain. What I am calling American fascism is the specific conjunction of three phenomena: (1) an intensely passionate, angry, and sometimes brutal form of Southern Christianity traumatized by the Civil War and civil rights; (2) a nationalism that increasingly resorts to military means to defend its economic security and financial interests; and (3) a virulent and unrestrained corporate capitalism that has decimated labor, unions, and many forms of workers' rights, largely by downsizing and relocating jobs overseas. Fascism, then, is the alignment of these three phenomena, religious passion, authoritarian nationalism, and corporate totalitarianism, but not in equal or even relationships. Religious passion serves and is used by nationalist forces, just as national organs and interests are used in turn by corporate interests for financial ends. My argument is that the Republican party, historically the party of big business, has co-opted white Southern Christianity and used its energy, anger, and pathos as a cover to advance its own interests, even as it has in turn been shaped by these religious ideas and beliefs.

At the same time, and this is more subtle, corporate capitalism in the form of multinational companies has used both nationalism and religion as a smokescreen to advance its own global and financial interests, which often are in conflict with both national and Christian interests and values. These three things are bundled together in an uneven and highly dangerous fashion. Together they threaten to bring about an apocalyptic catastrophe in the form of financial depression due to overextended debt and a weak dollar, environmental devastation due to irreversible climate change caused by emissions from burning hydrocarbons, economic collapse due to the increasing scarcity of fossil fuels, and/or a military conflagration due to conflicts driven by energy needs and other economic forces.[11]

Again, "fascism" is a complex and difficult term, and it is usually applied historically to Benito Mussolini's authoritarian regime in Italy in the 1930s, although it is also often associated with Hitler's National Socialism because Mussolini and Hitler were allies and shared similar beliefs and practices. The word "fascism" comes from the Latin *fasces*, which was a bundle of sticks (with an ax, showing the power of life and death) used as a symbol of power and authority in ancient Rome. Mussolini invoked Roman imperial power and the glory of strength and war in his understanding of fascism. He claimed that fascism opposes pacifism: "War alone brings up to its highest tension all human energy and puts the stamp of nobility upon the peoples who have courage to meet it. All other trials are substitutes, which never really put men into the position where they have to make the great decision—the alternative of life or death."[12] For Mussolini, the agent of war and the subject of greatness is the collective state, not the individual; hence, the modern state must be endowed with authority, power, and control over its subjects. "Fascism conceives of the State as an absolute, in comparison with which all individuals or groups are relative, only to be conceived of in their relation to the State."[13]

The people must be persuaded, by force if necessary, to believe in this collective and authoritarian state, which is where appeals to the grandeur of war, empire, and the invocation of ancient Rome played a part. Similarly, Hitler appealed to the greatness of the German Reich and the Teutonic people. Likewise, many Americans today celebrate American freedom, democracy, and Christianity by believing that the use of American military force is right and just, and that it is necessary to sacrifice the civil liberties of that freedom to preserve freedom as an ideal. Finally, in fascism this state, though appearing absolute, is actually superseded by corporate and economic interests, just as the state adopts, supersedes, controls, and directs religious passions for its own ends. A quote often attributed to Mussolini but actually written by an Italian theorist of fascism, Giovanni Gentile, claims: "Fascism should more properly be called corporatism, because it is the merger of state and corporate power."[14] Corporate power hides behind state power, which in turn stirs human passions and desires, directing them to its own ends, which generally includes war, restrictions on individual rights, and impoverishment of the working classes.

I see these same aspects of classical twentieth-century European fascism playing a significant role in a distinctively new relationship in the contemporary United States. Yet it also is important to recognize that the Roman fasces appear on the wall behind the speaker's podium in the chamber of the U.S. House of Representatives, and that powerful interests in the United States were attracted to fascism in the 1930s. In 1933, wealthy businessmen conspired to overthrow President Franklin D. Roosevelt, but they were thwarted by the retired Marine Corps general Smedley Butler; he was invited to join the plot but instead opposed it and later testified about the conspiracy to a congressional committee in 1934. The congressional investigation substantiated the truth of the conspiracy, but most of this information was not made public at the time.[15] More contemporary examples of the trend toward authoritarianism that, taken together, constitute a new American fascism include corporate (including mass media) mergers and consolidations, restrictions on civil liberties by the USA Patriot Act, domestic surveillance carried out by the National Security Agency without judicial authorization, broad monitoring of phone calls and financial transactions of Americans, violations of International Law and the Geneva Conventions in the context of detainees at Guantánamo, and sadistic abuse of prisoners at Abu Ghraib prison in Iraq.

Some people claim that these authoritarian phenomena are explained by or justified within the context of the Global War on Terrorism, touched off by the attacks of September 11, 2001. In that case, is not radical Islamic fundamentalism the enemy rather than the American fascism that I have just sketched out? Actually, just as in the case of Southern white Christianity, conflict with Islam is also driven by other nationalist and capitalist interests. Militant forms of Islam were cultivated and supported by the United States, for example the U.S. government armed and trained the mujahideen in Afghanistan in their jihad against the Soviet Union in the 1980s, and later supported the Taliban regime in the 1990s.[16] At the same time, intellectuals and policymakers assisted in creating extremist Islam as the new enemy of Western democracy, to replace the USSR.[17] Furthermore, the greater the distance from the shock of the 9/11 attacks, the clearer we can see that most of these phenomena preceded the event of September 11 itself, including the desire for military action against Iraq, as evidenced by the letter to then-President Clinton calling for regime change in Iraq by the signatories of the Project for the New American Century in 1998, many of whom later took positions in the Bush administration.[18]

Warnings about peak oil in the global market were just beginning to be made public in the late 1990s, and shortly after taking office in 2001, Vice President Cheney held a controversial meeting of the National Energy Policy Development Group. The administration has fought hard to keep the details of this meeting secret, despite a lawsuit brought by Judicial Watch. Among the few documents that have been made public were maps of Middle Eastern and Iraqi oil fields, including information about pipelines, refineries, and a list of "Foreign Suitors for Iraqi Oilfield Contracts."[19] This meeting should receive even more scrutiny due to the fact that the purported weapons of mass destruction were never found in Iraq, and that upon invasion the first building to be secured and occupied by U.S. troops was the Iraqi Oil Ministry.[20] Oil and energy are often officially dismissed as the "reason" the United States went to war against Iraq. But it is difficult to discount oil as a factor, especially when one considers the rise in oil prices that coincide with predictions of the peaking of global oil production even as oil demand continues to grow (along with the record profits of ExxonMobil), and also when one compares the lack of urgency by the Bush administration for military action against North Korea.[21]

Whether or not the United States has shaped the War on Terror to pursue its own militaristic and financial ends, at the very least other concerns such as oil, energy, the state of the dollar, geopolitical interests, and even the conflation of war and violence with biblical revelations and predictions of the Apocalypse and the second coming of Christ suggest that something is deeply wrong at the heart of the American Empire. In terms of Southern religion, the irony is that in U.S. politics and culture, Jeb Stuart, the slain Confederate Army general and close friend of Robert E. Lee, the Jeb who later became a popular icon for Southern Dixiecrats, gets his revenge: but this revenge will ultimately lead to national and perhaps also to global defeat and collapse. Because of the takeover of Southern Christianity by nationalist militarism and corporate capitalism, we lose due to an unsustainable economy and immoral way of life. This time, in a repetition of the Civil War, the whole country loses. The question is, How much of the rest of the world will we take with us?

We need a new abolition movement, if it is not too late. We must abolish corporate fascism and its ideological control, which enslaves us to infotainment and the consumption of cheap goods and shallow experiences. Meanwhile (mostly nonwhite) others suffer and die from starvation, disease, or increasingly, warfare, in order to sustain our way of life a little longer.[22] We must abolish American fascism. We need the insurrectional speech of a Martin Luther King Jr. (1929–68) and possibly even the radical action (though ideally in a nonviolent manner) of a John Brown (1800–1859).

In hindsight, it does not seem surprising that King opposed the war in Vietnam, but at the time his public opposition in the mid-1960s was rare and controversial. In a speech called "Beyond Vietnam: A Time to Break the Silence," King says: "Some of us who have already begun to break the silence of the night have found that the calling to speak is often a vocation of agony, but we must speak. We must speak with all the humility that is appropriate to our limited vision, but we must speak."[23] His commitment to civil rights and human dignity extends not only to the war in Vietnam, but also to struggles for liberation all over the globe, and this radicalization of King's position incurs FBI surveillance and is possibly connected with his assassination in 1968. "These are revolutionary times. All over the globe men are revolting against old systems of exploitation and oppression, and out of the wombs of a frail world new systems of justice and equality are being born," King optimistically proclaims. Whether he is right or wrong in this assessment, he claims that we must act: "We must move past indecision to action," before it is too late. "We are now faced with the fact that tomorrow is today. We are confronted with the fierce urgency of now. In this unfolding conundrum of life and history, there is such a thing as being too late."

If it is not too late, the abolition of fascism may require radical action. John Brown is not usually considered a hero, at least by whites, and even less so in the context of the resurgence of Southern culture and religion. In 1859, he led a raid on Harper's Ferry, (now West) Virginia, with the intention of starting a slave rebellion. When he was caught and executed, most Northerners, Republicans, and even abolitionists dissociated themselves from Brown and his actions, but those actions helped bring about the Civil War, which ended slavery in the United States. Many Northern soldiers sang "John Brown's Body" to the tune of "The Battle Hymn of the Republic." I am not advocating direct military action, but vigorous and sustained resistance to fascism could resurrect the memory of John Brown as a symbolic figure in order to consolidate opposition to fascism, which is tied to the hope for a future beyond slavery, beyond war, and beyond capitalism.

To conclude, I quote King quoting "The Battle Hymn of the Republic" in his 1968 sermon "I've Been to the Mountaintop": "Mine eyes have seen the glory of the coming of the Lord" (Julia Ward Howe, 1862).

Notes

1 Mark C. Taylor, *The Moment of Complexity: Emerging Network Culture* (Chicago: University of Chicago Press, 2001), 6.

2 A good survey of the history of religion in the United States is George M. Marsden, *Religion and American Culture*, 2nd ed. (Belmont, CA: Wadsworth, 2000).

3 George M. Marsden, *Understanding Fundamentalism and Evangelicalism* (Grand Rapids: Eerdmans, 1991), 172.

4 See Clay Risen, "How the South was Won," *Boston Globe*, March 5, 2006, http://www.boston.com/news/globe/ideas/articles/2006/03/05/how_the_south_was_won/?page=full.Johnson's own assessment notwithstanding, Risen's analysis suggests that the South's "burgeoning middle classes naturally tilted to the Republicans' fiscal conservatism, which promised tax cuts and smaller government programs."

5 See Kevin P. Phillips, *American Theocracy: The Perils and Politics of Radical Religion, Oil, and Borrowed Money in the 21st Century* (New York: Penguin, 2006), esp. chaps. 4–6. My reading of the rise of the religious Right accords with Phillips's to a great extent, although I differ from his interpretation of minor aspects of the religious history of the United States before the 1960s. Phillips does an excellent job of explaining the historical development of religious conservatism in the United States, and he ties these views to dangerous attitudes concerning disturbing financial and economic situations such as the peaking of world oil production and the weakened status of the U.S. dollar. For another source in addition to Phillips and Marsden that addresses this understanding of the religious Right in relation to the aftermath of the Civil War, see David Goldfield, *Still Fighting the Civil War: The American South and Southern History* (Baton Rouge: Louisiana State University Press, 2002).

6 See Sigmund Freud, *Moses and Monotheism*, trans. Katherine Jones (New York: Random House, 1967), 160–64, discussing the notion of how the repressed returns.

7 See Rousas John Rushdoony, *The Institutes of Biblical Law*, 3 vols. (Nutley, NJ: Craig, 1973–99).

8 Gary North and Gary DeMar, *Christian Reconstruction: What It Is, What It Isn't* (Tyler, TX: Institute for Christian Economics, 1993), xii.

9 Mark C. Taylor, *Confidence Games: Money and Markets in a World without Redemption* (Chicago: University of Chicago Press, 2004), 30.

10 See the ties between conservative Christianity and the Republican party as documented by Theocracy Watch, www.theocracywatch.org.

11 For more on some of these imminent dangers, particularly the peaking of global oil production, see Phillips, *American Theocracy*, chaps. 1–3, 8–10. Also see Kenneth S. Deffeyes, *Beyond Oil: The View From Hubbert's Peak* (New York: Hill and Wang, 2005), Michael T. Klare, *Blood and Oil: The Dangers and Consequences of America's Growing Dependency on Imported Petroleum* (New York: Metropolitan Books,

2004), and Michael C. Ruppert, *Crossing the Rubicon: The Decline of the American Empire at the End of the Age of Oil* (Gabriola Island, BC: New Society, 2004).

12 See Benito Mussolini, "Fascism," an entry for an Italian encyclopedia edited by Giovanni Gentile, published in 1932: http://www.fordham.edu/halsall/mod/mussolini-fascism.html.

13 Ibid.

14 See Edward R. Tennebaum, "The Goals of Italian Fascism," *American Historical Review* 74, no. 4 (April 1969): 1183–1204.

15 See Arthur M. Schlesinger Jr., *The Politics of Upheaval: 1935–1936*, vol. 3 of *The Age of Roosevelt* (New York: Mariner Books, 2003), 85.

16 See Ahmed Rashid, *Taliban: Militant Islam, Oil, and Fundamentalism in Central Asia* (New Haven: Yale University Press, 2001).

17 See, e.g., Samuel P. Huntington, *The Clash of Civilizations and the Remaking of World Order* (New York: Simon & Schuster, 1998).

18 See the letter on the Project for a New American Century's Web site, http://newamericancentury.org/iraqclintonletter.htm.

19 See Phillips, *American Theocracy*, 76–77.

20 Ibid., 75.

21 The most controversial and disturbing aspect of the entire scenario of the War on Terror involves questions raised but not explored by U.S. media or the 9/11 Commission about possible American government complicity in the 9/11 attacks. Specific issues include these: plans already drawn up for an invasion of Afghanistan in summer 2001; at least four or as many as six war-game exercises going on that day, so that in some cases FAA employees were unable to be sure which blips were actual hijacked planes and which were decoys; the massive purchase of puts on stocks for United and American Airlines, betting that their value would drastically decrease, which they did in the wake of the attacks; the scientific and engineering claims that even exploding jet fuel would not have led to the collapse of steel towers, which have never before collapsed in such a manner (including the collapse of the WTC 7 building much later in the afternoon, though not hit by an aircraft); the unprecedented delay in scrambling fighter jets to intercept the hijacked planes; and evidence suggesting that Flight 93 may have been shot down. There may be explanations of all of these phenomena that do not indict the U.S. government or the Bush administration for allowing or undertaking these 9/11 attacks to justify the War on Terror and the invasions of Afghanistan and Iraq. But the corporate news media's near silence about many of these questions leads to researchers' suspicions and proliferating conspiracy theories on the Internet. For a discussion of these and other issues on 9/11, see Ruppert, *Crossing the Rubicon*; and David Ray Griffin, *The New Pearl Harbor: Disturbing Questions about the Bush Administration and 9/11* (Northampton, MA: Olive Branch, 2004).

22 See Samir Amin, *The Liberal Virus: Permanent War and the Americanization of the World* (New York: Monthly Review, 2004).

23 Martin Luther King Jr., "Beyond Vietnam: A Time to Break the Silence," speech delivered April 4, 1967, at a meeting of Clergy and Laity Concerned at Riverside Church in New York City: http://www.hartford-hwp.com/archives/45a/058.html.

7

Theocratic America?

Christianity and the Structure of Political Discourse

Ben Stahlberg

The Problem of "Theocracy"

One of the most notable developments in recent U. S. political discourse is the increased use of the term "theocracy." Especially from those on the Left, the notion that the United States is on the verge of becoming— or has become—a Christian theocracy seems to have become widespread. What does such a complaint mean? Whence does it arise, and to what does it refer? Is the term "theocracy" helpful for describing the political influence that the evangelical Right exercises in the United States?

This essay argues that the term "theocracy" actually elides much of the influence that Christian thought has come to exercise over U.S. politics, and that the general character of Christian political thought is itself greatly misrepresented if considered strictly under this heading. I offer an inceptive account of Christian political thought by examining a few thinkers who have come to exemplify it. For a great majority of Christian thinkers, theocracy is far from a desirable state of political association. Indeed, what characterizes Christian political thought is not the unification of church and state but their clear distinction.

Curiously, then, the insistence on the division of life between private (or spiritual) and public (or political) realms actually unites many Christian theologians and politically liberal thinkers. Both locate the first (private) realm in the interior of the human individual, often called the conscience. Here the individual exercises an unqualified right to consider one's life in any way one sees fit, as long as one refrains from trying to interject that consideration into the public realm. The second (public) realm is in the empirical world of contingent, corporeal existence. Since this is a finite and transient realm, its goods are vastly inferior to those that comprise the private realm. Indeed, the goods of the material world are usually seen as means rather than as ends. We see this when the legitimacy of a form of government is open for discussion, and the debate focuses on what values and goods a certain state can make *available* rather than what values and goods a certain state might actual embody or *be*. As we will see below, the problem with theocracy, with conceiving of God as a supreme political authority, is that it refuses to recognize the fundamental difference between the personal and the political.

Consequently, this paper argues that if we are truly interested in gauging the extent to which Christianity has become or is becoming a political force in this country, we cannot merely appraise the explicit and often-disturbing instances in which Christianity seems to cross the boundary between church and state (such as posting the Ten Commandments in our courthouses or teaching intelligent-design creationism in our schools). We must also examine the more-tacit and assumed notions that we have all come to rely upon, such as the ways in which we tend to prioritize individual intentionality or belief when considering whether or not a given act or institution is religious. If we attend to this influence, I maintain, we will be inclined to consider church-versus-state issues from a less-polarized and more-critical position, as we recognize the extent to which these very concerns are defined along primarily Christian terms.

Three recent books give a sense of how the term "theocracy" has galvanized the current discussion of Christianity's political influence. In *American Theocracy*, Kevin Phillips describes theocracy as "some degree of rule by religion," which he argues "has been anathema in the modern United States."[1] Yet, in Phillips's opinion, much of America has become swept up by the "radical side of U.S. religion" and "has embraced cultural anitmodernism, war hawkishness, Armageddon prophecy, and in the case of conservative fundamentalists, a demand for government by literal biblical interpretation."[2] The result is a contemporary "American theocracy," as Phillips terms it, which springs from a foundation in popular opinion and is thus a distinct version of a theocracy. God has not been placed in charge of our country by a group of priests nor directly intervened to shape our government to divine liking. Rather, our theocratic state has been born of the hearts and minds of the American people.

Phillips's conception of theocracy is thus much more nuanced than the traditional idea of a government ruled by a God or God's servants. Concurring with this thesis, Michelle Goldberg in *Kingdom Coming* argues that the current state of Christian thought in America can only be called a form of Christian nationalism, a "conviction that true Christianity must govern every aspect of public and private life, and that all—government, science, history, culture, and relationships—must be understood according to the dictates of scripture."[3] "There are," for Christian nationalists, "biblically correct positions on every issue, from gay marriage to income tax rates, and only those with the right worldview can discern them."[4] Here the rights of the individual exist only to the extent that the one is encouraged to embrace the prevailing ideas of the society as well as the state; those who choose not to do so are marginalized and dismissed as "un-American." Thus, while America is not yet a theocracy in the traditional sense of the term, we must recognize that Christian nationalism exercises significant theocratic power.

Sam Harris articulates this point in *The End of Faith: Religion, Terror, and the Future of Reason*, arguing that the "degree to which religious ideas still determine government policies—especially those of the United States—presents a grave danger to everyone."[5] Harris provides numerous prominent examples to back up his argument, asserting (e.g.) that Ronald Reagan "interpreted Middle Eastern politics through the lens of biblical prophecy" and depicting the U.S. Congress as "not wanting to have an obvious hand in actually *separating* church and state."[6] The only logical conclusion that we can draw from all this, Harris argues, is that the current U.S. government has fallen under the de facto control of the Christian right.

Phillips, Goldberg, and Harris all find fault with religion mainly when it crosses the line separating private beliefs from the public good and assumes an authoritative role in the formation of government policy. Further, all three charge that the U.S. government has come under the sway of groups of individuals who claim to represent the will of God. Hence, while we may not have a theocracy in the classical sense, with priests or bishops applying specifically religious or ecclesiastical laws to our polity, our elected political officials claim to exist in a correlative relationship with the word of God as revealed in the Bible. That this unique type of government has arisen democratically does not ease the minds of our three thinkers. Indeed, all argue that it is precisely due to this democratic cover that our modern theocracy is as powerful and as cunning as it is. Since this new theocratic character takes shape without an explicit declaration of religiosity, it has remarkable power as it cloaks itself in the private religious beliefs of a collective of individuals (and is thus not classically political). In the end, we wind up not only with churches in de facto control of our country but, more important, an inability even to articulate their form of control.

Early Formulations

If we find the argument outlined above compelling (as I believe we should), we are faced with a dilemma: Is our new or emerging theocracy a perversion of Christianity, or does it find some foundation in the past? The earliest use of the term "theocracy"—a combination of the Greek words *theos* (God) and *kratein* (to rule)—seems to come from first-century Jewish historian Flavius Josephus (37–100 CE), a thinker who exercised no small influence on the development of Christian thought. In his *Against Apion,* Josephus comments that "some peoples have entrusted the supreme political power to monarchies, others to oligarchies, yet others to the masses."[7] Of this diversity, Josephus singles out the Jewish form of government, ideally conceived, as the best yet devised. He presents Moses as the paragon of a political leader, or "lawgiver," who chooses a form of government directed not by human authority but by the will of God. For Moses (and Josephus, also), since God is immutable, so too are God's rules and legislation. The best form of political organization recognizes this and agrees to live by God's law, which the Israelites did for a time.

However, with the fall of the Israelite monarchy and the destruction of the temple, a new political/religious force emerged: the Roman Emperor Vespasian (9–79), in whom God awoke "imperial ambitions," choosing him to rule over *all* the people of the world.[8] In *The Jewish War,* Josephus casts Vespasian as a new Moses, a divine legislator who would unite all peoples in peace and make the proper worship of God possible. Although theocracy under Moses meant delivering divine laws to the Israelites, Vespasian's theocracy means instituting divinely appointed and divinely inspired sovereignty. Though this ruling authority does not adhere to commandments, Josephus sees God's hand at work in it; he argues that God has decided to guide the Roman Empire in its political affairs while leaving religion to the people who live under Roman rule. Thus Josephus initially identifies Israel as a theocracy, yet he concludes that the empire is also a government explicitly endowed by God.

Josephus's conception of theocracy and his depiction of Moses as the archetype of proper political leadership had a great influence on one of the earliest Christian historians, Eusebius of Caesarea (ca. 260–ca. 339). In his "Speech on the Dedication of the Holy Sepulchre Church" in Jerusalem, Eusebius similarly emphasizes that the polities that had developed over the course of history had organized human beings such that they were "variously distributed" into many governments and were thus "subjected to kingdoms and principalities of many kinds."[9] The consequences of this diversity include "war and strife, depopulation and captivity," which have "raged . . . with unceasing fury."[10] To undo this ruinous state, God has employed a two-pronged approach. On the one hand, he sent an "instrument of our redemption, the thrice-holy body of Christ," who brought about the "abolition of ancient evils."[11] On the other hand, God brought forth the Holy Roman Empire, which has disassembled the various "tyrannies and republics" that had ceaselessly waged wars against each other and brought all manner of devastation; they "were now no more, and one God was proclaimed to all mankind."[12] For Eusebius, the "good news" of Christ and God's election of the Roman Empire were designed to bring humanity under God's single, universal governing authority, with the empire ruling over the material world and Christianity over the spiritual. Thus Eusebius, like Josephus, portrays *his* emperor, Constantine (ca. 274–337), as a Mosaic figure divinely endowed to instantiate God's order in this world. He depicts Constantine as a liberator who, like Moses, has delivered an oppressed people from a tyrant (Emperor Maxentius, 278–312) who was given to all manner of pagan magic and licentious acts.

The idea that Rome was a divinely elected government, the material complement of Christianity, was dramatically challenged by Visigoths invading the empire in 410. What were Christians to make of the destruction of Rome—their new, refined Jerusalem—by pagan forces? In his *City of God*, Augustine of Hippo (354–430) took on this question by both accentuating the division (already present in Josephus and Eusebius) between the domain of the world and the domain of God, while at the same time insisting upon God's control of the world. Also like

Josephus and Eusebius, Augustine's understanding of the empire took shape in response to theological principles, specifically that God as "the only true God" is ultimately "the author and giver of happiness," and thus he "Himself gives earthly kingdoms to both good men and bad."[13] We will certainly never understand the reasoning behind God's guidance, but because his very nature is perfection, we should have no problem in trusting his plan for the world.

Augustine's famous theory of the "two cities" results directly from the above distinction. The first is the "earthly city," Rome being for a time the great example, wherein "the whole use of temporal things is directed towards the enjoyment of earthly peace."[14] The second is the "heavenly city," wherein the use of God's gifts "is directed towards the enjoyment of eternal peace."[15] Whether we seek to order our lives in concert with others or not, we are still only citizens of the earthly city, since whatever peace we seek or may bring about is only of a temporary nature. Though Augustine attributes the rise and fall of all states and empires to the will of God, he thus is clear that the worth of these political institutions is limited and fleeting; in all instances, we must understand them merely as an earthly means rather then a divine end. For Augustine, in other words, the key to the proper Christian life lies in diligently partitioning the world from God, the good of the state from the good of the church.[16] Although Augustine holds that the church and the state may work in concert, and that they can even prompt the same virtues and dogmas, they are fundamentally separate enterprises.

Augustine's understanding of a fundamentally bifurcated (though interactive) conception of human experience—an experience where Christians live in the city of man but live for the city of God—finds an important interpretation in the thought of Thomas Aquinas (1225–74) and especially in his conception of the *civitas*. The *civitas* (often translated as "community" or "state") is the form of human government that seeks to establish a complete, natural community by organizing the rules of the state in concert with the laws of nature. Aquinas calls the latter laws the "laws of nations," and asserts that they are laws derived from the laws of nature "as conclusions from its principles."[17] The former (laws of nature) Aquinas calls "civil laws," which are only "specific applications" of legal principles "according to which each community decides what is convenient for itself."[18] Though every state must choose its own particular laws, it must derive them from the natural laws to which all human beings are subject. This means that, following Aristotle, Aquinas thinks that it is perfectly acceptable, and indeed necessary, for political rulers to enforce virtue and curtail vice, because the rulers are responsible for leading their citizens to their true nature. Since Aquinas holds that "all things participate in this eternal law . . . because it is imprinted upon them through their respective inclinations," we can see that the tasks of the political and the religious are in a strong sense united.[19]

If such a unity exists, it suggests that Aquinas diverges significantly from the Christian thought we have considered thus far, because this unity implies the necessary integration of religious and political elements that thinkers like Eusebius and Augustine distinguished. Yet even in Aquinas there is a distinction between two ultimately different types of good. "In human affairs," Aquinas writes, there is "a certain [type of] common good, the good of the *civitas* or people." Yet there is "also a [type of] human good which—[though it] benefits not merely one person alone but many people—does not consist in community but pertains to one [as an individual] in oneself."[20] Certain religious goods (like an especially devout faith) are of the latter sort, since they are ultimately concerned strictly with a special object (an individual's soul). At the same time, Aquinas argues that just because such goods are directed toward a distinct object, it does not mean that these goods compete with others for human attention and practice. Rather, these different senses of good ideally enable rather than challenge one another. Aquinas even argues that political authorities ought through their own policies to advance the Christian life, even though it is properly not an object of their rule.[21] In this fine distinction, Aquinas maintains that rulers may help their citizens in their pursuit, but they must remember that they have no (final) authority over the pursuit as such. This theological and political worldview is grounded in Augustine's distinction between the two cities: the two may promote the same virtues and forms of behavior, but they are fundamentally different types of authority and address different human territories.

Aquinas's ideal of a peaceful and harmonious coordination of political and religious realms was significantly called into question by the great church reformer Martin Luther (1483–1546). For Luther, human beings cannot do anything to merit salvation; there are simply no forms of behavior or virtues that we can perform that will make any qualitative difference in our sinful condition. Even faith, for Luther, is rooted in the recognition of inherent sinfulness, in the recognition that one is fundamentally unable to bring about anything truly good.

Throughout the writings of Martin Luther, we see an emphasis on how the sinfulness of the human being is a foundational principle of political order. Though Josephus celebrated the idea of a Jewish government that tried to accomplish God's law at every turn, Luther sees this endeavor as fundamentally misguided. He argues that while it is certainly true that God's laws are good, they also "show us what we ought to do but do not give us the power to do it."[22] That is, the commandments "are intended to teach man to know himself, that through them he may recognize his inability to do good and may despair of his own ability."[23] Far from giving human beings a way to live profitably, God's commandments are meant to demonstrate that there is no true profit to be had in this world, and one's only true hope is the reception of God's grace by way of individual faith. Such a view of God's law certainly makes the idea of a theocracy, in Josephus's sense, impossible. Divine laws are intrinsically above us, and the laws that humans devise to mimic God's laws are inherently flawed. Indeed, the mimicry of such human laws is even destructive. Luther calls such actions or "works" a "perverse leviathan" since they "are done under the false impression that through them one is justified," but in reality "faith and freedom [in God] are destroyed."[24] Political authority, then, must be a form of earthly authority that recognizes and respects the limitations of its own power: it must not intrude upon the individual soul or conscience.

Yet Luther hardly dismisses the necessity—or even the value—of political order. Much like Aquinas, he argues that the goods of political order are important to the cultivation of faith. God has seen fit to create all manner of earthly authorities to keep order throughout his creation. It is the character of good Christian subjects to submit themselves to those authorities, not to attempt to extricate themselves from them. While it is plain in Luther's eyes that a Christian has no *need* of seeing a certain order maintained and a specific enemy punished, it does not follow from this that a Christian can simply remove oneself from these earthly concerns. Indeed, to remove oneself thus would be trying to figure oneself "beyond" this world, and implying that one is free from sin. Christians, rather, should submit themselves to the world, to serve it, precisely because they oppose it. Thus Luther's political thought limits the realm of individual freedom to the confines of the private, thoughtful life of the individual soul. We are fundamentally free to believe what we like, according to Luther. In all other areas, we must recognize both the necessary and the superfluous character of political authorities: necessary because God has established them, and yet ultimately superfluous because they amount to nothing when considering the *next* life.

Luther's simultaneous insistence on the insufficient yet necessary character of state authority was deeply influential on the theology and political theory of John Calvin (1509–64). Like Luther, Calvin's larger theology was oriented around the notions of sin and freedom: the freedom a Christian has through faith in Christ, the freedom from one's sinful condition. Indeed, Calvin argues that Christian freedom "is a thing of prime necessity, and apart from it consciences dare undertake almost nothing without doubting."[25] Calvin, like Luther, takes it as a given that the individual is thoroughly helpless in oneself to enact anything of true worth, and also that through faith alone the Christian is freed from the rites and superstitions that can weigh all too heavily on a believer's conscience.[26] As we have seen, the conscience needs to be attuned to itself and specifically to its own sinfulness. If it is elsewhere occupied, it is in trouble.

Yet Calvin's sense of private, individual, *spiritual* freedom did not mean the dismissal of political authority. Although he held the rather radical position that those who have received Christ's gift have been "released from the power of men," he did simultaneously argue that such freedom applied to the "realm" of the conscience only, the spiritual realm.[27] He argues that attempts to render all forms of authority (aside from God) null and void are distortions not only of the legitimacy of earthly powers, but also of the true freedom a Christian has through Christ. The world in which we live, the world of nature and the world of society, is God's creation, and we cannot exchange it for another. What is essential for Calvin is not that we try to set ourselves free in respect to all authorities except God, but that we keep the two extant forms of authority distinct. For Calvin, "there is a twofold government in man: one aspect is spiritual, whereby the conscience is instructed in piety and in reverencing God; the second is political, whereby man is educated for the duties of humanity and citizenship that must be maintained among men."[28] These two types of authority are in charge of fundamentally distinct objects: "the former sort of government pertains to the life of the soul, while the later has to do with the concerns of the present life."[29] Moreover, these two authorities occur on fundamentally different planes: the spiritual authority "resides in the inner mind," while the political authority obviously "regulates only outward behavior."[30] The Christian is free to pursue good works not because "believers are the authors of their own salvation" but because they provide the Christian with a great way to "meditate upon eternal life."[31] Although the works of the "secular" government and the beliefs of the "spiritual and internal kingdom of Christ are quite distinct," we must also acknowledge that they are "in no way incompatible with each other"—as long as each respects the other's sphere of authority.[32] This means that a state can and should support a church—it should protect its teachings and those who worship in it—because it can never address the object of the church: the soul or conscience. Though certainly not advocating a strict separation of church and state, Calvin clearly believes that church and state are radically different types of authority, addressing radically different aspects of human life.

Modern Formulations

It is one thing to demonstrate a certain "unity of form" surrounding the political organization advocated by the Christian thinkers above, and yet another to show its presence in modern, liberal democratic theory. To accomplish the second, and most important, purpose of this essay we need to turn ourselves to some of the most influential theorists of the latter point of view. An obvious place to start here is the thought of John Locke (1632–1704), whose *Letter concerning Toleration* is widely considered one of the earliest modern delineations of the relationship between religion and politics. Toleration, Locke argues, "is the chief characteristical mark of the true church."[33] Although Locke acknowledges that the history of Christianity has, in many respects, been the history of "Christianities," he holds that the truth persisting through the variations is the church, which he interprets to be "a voluntary society of men, joining themselves together of their own accord, in order to the public worshiping of God, in such a manner as they judge acceptable to him, and effectual to the salvation of souls."[34] While such a church is obviously communal, the emphasis falls on the believing individual. Indeed, for Locke a specific church is only the sum result of the number of freethinking individuals. Religion, for Locke, is a matter not of tradition or culture but of personal belief or faith.[35]

From this conception of a church, Locke concludes that "there is absolutely no such thing, under the Gospel, as a Christian commonwealth."[36] Although he recognizes that there are many cities and states that have "embraced the faith of Christ" in their "laws and statutes," they have never made the perilous mistake of coming to confuse their own, "fulfillable" laws with those "unfulfillable" ones given by God and potentially absolved by Christ. The proper appreciation of the nature of a political body means discerning its contours and limitations, understanding how the teachings of Christ fall outside—and above—this body. Subsequently, Locke follows thinkers more customarily seen as Christian by arguing that there are two societies comprising our world: "religious and civil."[37] If religion is understood properly, the personal religious beliefs of an individual are one's business alone, for they go no further (in this world) than the borders of one's conscience and address no one in this world. Once we acknowledge this distinction, Locke argues, peace, security, and toleration tend to follow.

Although their philosophies differ considerably, there is a great deal of common ground between the thought of Locke and the great German philosopher Immanuel Kant (1724–1804). Kant is best known for what many call his "critical philosophy," his insistence that any philosophical undertaking has to proceed within the limitations of reason. Philosophy, for Kant, is as much an exploration of what we cannot know as much as it is of what we can know. Central among the former is God, since Kant argues that we cannot know with any certainty by virtue of our own reason (that is, objectively) whether or not God exists. Religion thus is "only a *problematic* assumption (hypothesis) concerning the supreme cause of things," and "this faith needs only *the idea of God*, which must occur to every morally earnest (and therefore religious) pursuit of the good, without pretending to be able to secure objective reality for it through cognition alone."[38] Religion is necessarily subjective, for Kant, because it comprises judgments that human beings make about the God and the world that do not claim to have any standing as objective fact.

If religion is an inherently subjective orientation to this world, then the religious behavior of individual believers must follow accordingly. Kant argues that proper religious behavior and belief will result from and correspond to the idea we have of God, while improper behavior and belief will become distracted from this definition and be preoccupied with falling in line behind the religious traditions and ideas other human beings have held in the past. Since God is, by definition, a universal entity—in no way limited or particular—we know that God cannot be properly worshipped through the rites and traditions of particular religions or communities. For Kant, every individual has a conscience, so that "each individual can recognize, through his own reason, the will of God, which lies as the basis of his relation."[39] Kant argues that if "we assume [the] statutory laws" of a particular religious tradition and structure our religious life around fulfilling them, "then cognition of these laws is possible not through our own mere reason but only through [a partic-ular] revelation," and we would then have to face up to the fact that our faith would then be "a *historical* and not a *purely rational faith.*"[40] In such a situation, we would find ourselves believing and worshipping in a fash-ion that completely contradicts the idea of God as we know it. Christianity is the most universal of all religions for Kant precisely because it recog-nizes that God is the God of all, and because its idea of God arises necessarily from the individual conscience.[41] Rather than conjuring up a set of particular, finite laws, Christianity recognizes that a truly religious response to God stems from the conscience, or put more traditionally, from the soul.

Kant's conception of the proper relationship between politics and re-ligion has a great deal in common with the thought of Thomas Jefferson (1743–1826). This symmetry is clear in Jefferson's 1784 treatise *Notes on Virginia*, a text laying out the principles of religious tolerance that came to have a great influence over the construction of the U.S. Constitution. We are all "well aware," Jefferson writes, "that Almighty God hath created the mind free" and, subsequently, "that all attempts to influence it by temporal punishments or burdens, or by civil incapacitations, tend to beget habits of hypocrisy and meanness."[42] Further, such attempts are, to Jefferson's mind, "a departure from the Holy Author of our religion, who being Lord both of body and mind, yet chose not to propagate it by coercions of either, as was in his Almighty power to do."[43] Again, like Kant, Jefferson argues that this maxim is evident if we understand the *idea* of God properly.[44] If we believe that God is omnipotent, we must conclude that it is within the power of our "Author" to make us believe in him just as he made us to breathe in oxygen. That God chose not to do so means that he thought it the wrong course of action. Consequently, we should certainly be wary of those "impious presumptions of legislators and rulers, civil as well as ecclesiastical, who, being themselves but fallible and uninspired men, have assumed dominion over the faith of others, setting up their own opinions and modes of thinking as the only true and infallible."[45] Since the omniscient and omnipotent Author of our lives did not require the coercion of conscience, mere mortals, no matter how powerful *on this earth*, ought not to attempt such persuasion.

From this theological position, paradoxically, Jefferson goes on to ar-gue that our rights as citizens, and especially our right to worship as we please, "have no dependence on our religious opinions, more than our opinions in physics or geometry."[46] Again, sounding much like Kant,

Jefferson argues that attempts to enforce religious belief and action by legislation tend "to corrupt the principles of that very religion it is meant to encourage, by bribing, with a monopoly of worldly honors and emoluments, those who will externally profess and conform to it."[47] Indeed, Jefferson is not inclined to think that the truth of any religion is something that will need the help of governmental or ecclesiastical powers, for "truth is great and will prevail if left to herself."[48] It is this confidence in the truth (specifically religious truth) that motivates Jefferson's argument for religious tolerance:

> Difference of opinion is advantageous in religion. The several sects perform the office of a *censor morum* over such other. . . . Let us reflect that [the world] is inhabited by a thousand different systems of religion. That ours is but one of that thousand. That if there be one right, and ours that one, we should wish to see the nine hundred and ninety-nine wandering sects gathered into the fold of truth.[49]

As seen here, Jefferson's argument clearly has less to do with tolerance than with uniformity. Or rather, it puts tolerance in service of uniformity, since tolerance is prompted to bring about uniformity. To bring about religious uniformity, we need to make use of "reason and persuasion," which are the "only practicable instruments" we have at our disposal if we wish to make some impact on the hearts and minds of the individuals we wish to convince. The only way to "make way for these" instruments is for "free inquiry is to be *indulged*."[50] In Jefferson's view, the idea of religious liberty is far from a simple good in itself or a strictly individual right; he sees it as the best way to bring about religious uniformity.

This point becomes especially clear later in his essay. When commenting on the state of religious tolerance in Pennsylvania and New York, Jefferson reports how "well supported" religion is there. Religion "flourishes infinitely" and is "of various kinds . . . but all [are] good enough." When it comes to pass that "a sect arises, whose tenets would subvert morals, good sense has fair play, and reasons and laughs it out of doors, without suffering the State to be troubled by it." Indeed, Jefferson goes so far as to write that in these areas "harmony is unparalleled," and that this "can be ascribed to nothing but their unbounded tolerance." These people, Jefferson concludes, "have made the happy discovery that the way to silence religious disputes is to take no notice of them."[51]

The Structure of Christian Political Discourse

What are we to make of Jefferson's comments? How do we understand Jefferson's seeming to see the ideal of religious liberty as a means to Christian homogeneity rather than as a protection of the right of an individual to be religiously heterogeneous? For those who think that our country should refrain from promoting a specific religious perspective, it is disconcerting that the man thought to have first articulated this policy was, himself, tendentiously committed to it at best. Jefferson, as a "founding father," is still a source of authority for us in our debates around these issues. Indeed, we often hear that America was specifically conceived by our founding fathers *not* to be a Christian nation. Indeed, there are a great many organizations—the American Civil Liberties Union, Americans United for the Separation of Church and State, Theocracy Watch—committed to making sure that "the founders'" ideal is maintained and that the line separating church and state is distinct.

It is easy concede that the United States is not a Christian nation in that we do not have an official national church or denomination. However, if we follow Phillips, Goldberg, and Harris, we see that the absence of official religion tells us little about the influence of Christian thought on our political ideology. That we have no explicit official church or national theology does not in itself constitute the exclusion of religion from politics. What it *does* constitute is a primary condition under which these supposedly distinct domains must interact. I call this the condition of formal separation. Put simply, religion and politics may interact with each other to any degree provided that they do not explicitly identify that they are doing so.

We can see how this condition affects the interaction between religion and politics in two senses. In the first sense, it means that Christianity is able to exercise itself as a political force provided it does not formulate its force as explicitly political. Only when Christianity presents itself as a political disposition (in addition to a religious one) does it violate the condition of formal separation and become unviable. The condition of formal separation is as basic and crucial to Christianity as it is to our seemingly secular political discourse. Indeed, all the Christian thinkers examined above see formal separation as foundational, since it enables the Christian religion to be distinguished from the Jewish political body. Further, *all* of the thinkers discussed above identify the infringement of this condition as theocracy.

In the second sense, the condition of separation enables Christianity to exercise a commanding political influence: it allows its political effects to occur under a cloak of individualism and personal preference. Thus, far from hindering the political power of Christianity in the United States, the formal appearance of the separation of church and state allows it to be exercised silently and on a large scale.

Given this understanding, I suggest an amendment to the largely persuasive accounts of Phillips, Goldberg, and Harris. Though these critics of theocracy show the subtle and powerful influence of Christian thought in America, they do not go quite far enough. To the extent that these critics insist on reinscribing the line between religion and politics, between personal belief and political authority, they fail to disrupt the logic upon which the power of Christian political thought is predicated. These critics of theocracy deftly show how the formal division between church and state actually allows the church to have significant influence over the state, yet their solution is simply to insist that the boundary between the two entities be drawn once again. The reason is clear: these critics stake out their position over and against religion, taking an antagonistic stance toward Christianity. They do not consider that their own position may actually reflect the logic of religion.

The real political power that Christianity exercises today turns less on whether or not the United States or its citizens believe in a specific God, or whether or not our founding fathers or our most important documents profess a belief in God. These issues have been rehearsed enough. What needs more critical consideration is why we tend to think of religion, in both our personal and political deliberations, as a distinct matter of individual belief or intention *at all*. Why do we look at the issue of belief before and above all others? Does not this tendency signal a Christian influence? Indeed, how can we truly account for the political effect of Christianity in our country if our analysis of religion is confined to the realm of belief? We need to recognize that Christian and secular ideals are not themselves as distinct as we often make them out to be, but are actually part of the same worldview. Talal Asad has recently emphasized this connection between Christianity and liberal political theory. He has persuasively demonstrated how secularism and Christianity exist in a symbiotic and mutually reinforcing relationship as they both put forward the idea that conscience is the authority for any individual's religious deliberations. We can see this relationship in the work of Phillips, Goldberg, and Harris: all of these thinkers attribute a priority to the individual conscience as the ultimate arbiter of values and beliefs. When we can recognize this concord between secularists and Christians, we can also see that the priority we extend to the conscience of every individual—a priority that we theorize, generally, as a right (as in the right to freedom of thought)—is not a neutral or disinterested form of organizing and administrating human life.

This essay therefore formulates the beginnings of what Foucault calls "a factual description" of a discourse, specifically here, the discourse of Christian political thought.[52] What does it mean to consider the thinkers described above as constitutive of a discourse? For Foucault, a discourse is different from a straightforward language because it is not governed solely by the rules and elements that govern a language. A language, Foucault writes, "is a finite ensemble of rules which authorizes an infinite number of performances."[53] By contrast, a discourse "is the always-finite and temporarily limited ensemble of those statements alone which were formulated."[54] When describing a language, one looks at how it is that a given conception or declaration is *possible*; a description of a discourse looks at how it is that a given conception or declaration came to be. While the former examines the rules that allow a thought to be constructed, the latter looks at the conditions of a thought's construction. Foucault, however, also distinguishes his conception of discourse from what we normally think of as an "analysis of thought." An analysis of thought is an attempt "to rediscover" beyond a given set of statements themselves, "the intention of the speaking subject." Such an analysis aims to identify "conscious activity" and intentions in "explicit utterances." An analysis of thought always looks beyond the words immediately presented to the state of mind that gave rise to them. In contrast, the description or analysis of a discourse is directed toward determining "the conditions of its existence, to fix its limits as accurately as possible, to establish its correlations with the other statements with which it may be linked, and to show what other forms of articulation it excludes." Discursive analysis does not look beyond the subject of its analysis to another location for its subject's meaning. Discursive analysis "must show why the discourse could not be other than it was, what makes it exclusive of other discourses, and how it takes up a position among other discourses and in relation to them which no other could occupy."[55]

What are the terms or conditions of the discourse of Christian political thought? Though it is obvious that such a question cannot be answered definitively here, we can glean from the short sketch of the thinkers above that Christian political thought cannot be predicated on a conflation of the religious and political domains. It is clear in the work of Phillips, Goldberg, and Harris, as in thinkers like Eusebius, Aquinas, and Calvin, that these two seemingly opposed discourses can be aligned; yet it also stands that they must be *theoretically* distinct. Consequently, while Christianity is undoubtedly a clear and powerful political force, it is usually not recognized as such—or rather, it is persistently identified as a stranger to politics. Conversely, when it does become explicitly political, Christianity is usually chastised as a perversion and is urged to reconnect with its true nature. Although critics of theocracy are quite right to point out the real power now being exercised by certain Christian Americans and institutions, their focus on a reformation of the private beliefs and consciences of individual Americans is insufficient. To respond to the problem in this fashion does not address how the terms and conditions of the debate have been organized according to the very discourse that critics of theocracy seem to oppose. The impulse to return religion to its proper place (the individual conscience) overlooks that it is precisely this formal location that grants Christian thought its political power. If we are truly interested in appreciating and questioning the political power Christianity exercises in America today, we must unsettle this discourse as much as possible, specifically by questioning (by describing and thereby destabilizing) the value and authority of individual belief and intention. To effectively question or challenge the force of Christian political discourse in our country, we must first identify the terms on which it functions. If we simply accept the terms of the debate as constituted, we close off all manner of possible solutions.

Notes

1 Kevin Phillips, *American Theocracy: The Peril and Politics of Radical Religion, Oil, and Borrowed Money in the 21st Century* (New York: Viking, 2006), 208.

2 Ibid., 100.

3 Michelle Goldberg, *Kingdom Coming: The Rise of Christian Nationalism* (New York: W. W. Norton, 2006), 5.

4 Ibid., 5–6.

5 Sam Harris, *The End of Faith: Religion, Terror, and the Future of Reason* (New York: W. W. Norton, 2005), 153.

6 Ibid., 154.

7 Flavius Josephus, *Against Apion*, trans. H. St. J. Thackeray (Cambridge, MA: Harvard University Press, 2004), 22; cf. http://www.gutenberg.org/etext/2849.

8 Flavius Josephus, *The Jewish War*, trans. G. A. Williamson (London: Penguin Books, 1981), 221; cf. http://www.gutenberg.org/etext/2850.

9 Eusebius of Caesarea, *Speech on the Dedication of the Holy Sepulchre Church* [= *Oration in Praise of Constantine*], in *From Irenaeus to Grotius: A Sourcebook in Christian Political Thought, 100–1625*, ed. Oliver O'Donovan and Joan Lockwood O'Donovan (Grand Rapids: Eerdmans, 1999), 58; cf. http://www.newadvent.org/fathers/2504.htm.

10 Ibid.

11 Ibid.

12 Ibid.

13 Augustine, *City of God*, ed. R.W. Dyson (Cambridge: Cambridge University Press, 1998), 184; cf. http://www.ncwadvent.org/fathers/1201.htm.

14 Ibid., 940.

15 Ibid.

16 The clear counterexample to the idea of the proper Christian state is, for Augustine, the nation of Israel. Like Josephus and Eusebius, Augustine argues that the downfall of Israel was due to a certain conceit that arose within it, embodied in its priestly caste, who began to emphasize their own powers (which lay in the execution of multiple laws and rituals over which they had authority) instead of God's power. The climax of this apostasy came in the priests' selfish crucifixion of the Christ, for they were too entranced by their own earthly powers to recognize the Messiah foretold in their own Scriptures; the Jews turned on the God with whom they had been in covenant and were forced to pay for this transgression with the dissolution of their nation and their dispersion throughout the world. The nation of Israel is thus a lesson to those who wish to see Rome as a holy city.

17 Thomas Aquinas, *On Politics and Ethics*, trans. and ed. Paul Sigmund (New York: W. W. Norton, 1988), 54.

18 Ibid.

19 Ibid., 58.

20 Thomas Aquinas, *Summa contra Gentiles*, in *Aquinas: Moral, Political and Legal Theory*, trans. John Finnis (Oxford: Oxford University Press, 1998), 226.

21 Ibid., 229.

22 Martin Luther, "The Freedom of a Christian," trans. W. A. Lambert, in *Martin Luther: Selections from His Writings*, ed. John Dillenberger (New York: Doubleday, 1961), 57.

23 Ibid.

24 Ibid., 72.

25 John Calvin, *Institutes of the Christian Religion*, ed. John T. McNeill, trans. Ford Lewis Battles, 2 vols. (Philadelphia: Westminster, 1960), 1:833.

26 As Calvin values individual belief or conscience so highly, he is concerned that it not "ensnare" itself with destructive trivialities of particular rites and actions and thereby "enter a long and inextricable maze, not easy to get out of" (ibid., 839).

27 Ibid., 846.

28 Ibid., 847.

29 Ibid.

30 Ibid. Again, some fail to grasp this distinction. Specifically, Calvin argues, "it is a Judaic folly to look for the kingdom of Christ among things that make up this world, and to shut it up among them" (cf. ibid., 2:1486). This is because the Jewish nation was, again, spiritually immature and even obtuse. Thus, the "Lord of old" attempted "to nourish them better" in the promise of eternal life, and so "he displayed it for them to see and, so to speak, taste, under earthly benefits" (ibid., 1:450). God's guidance was misinterpreted and Israel became preoccupied with the things of this world, both with acts and rites that they put faith in and in the goods and property they (thought) they received as a reward.

31 Ibid., 1:822.

32 Ibid., 2:1487.

33 John Locke, *Two Treatises of Government: And a Letter Concerning Toleration*, ed. Ian Shapiro (New Haven: Yale University Press, 2003), 215.

34 Ibid., 220.

35 Locke is well aware that religion has generally not been properly conceived and practiced. To Locke's mind, the paradigmatic example of such misuse seems to be, again, Judaism generally and the nation of Israel more specifically. In regard to the latter, Locke argues that such a theocracy is the hallmark of a rough and uncivilized people, for "if anyone can show me where there is a commonwealth, at this time, constituted upon that foundation, I will acknowledge that the ecclesiastical laws do there unavoidably become a part of the civil" (ibid., 239). For Locke, there is no chance that such a "commonwealth" could have continued to exist simply because it would inevitably trample upon the rights of the conscience, giving way to widespread fragmentation and impiety. Locke thus sees the political problems that plagued the Jewish *state* as logical outgrowths of its religious problems. Indeed, if the Israelites had recognized Jesus as the Messiah and heeded his teachings, they would have been properly able to interpret the domain of religion—being the private, inner life of the individual—and so understand the proper domain of the political against it.

36 Ibid., 239.

37 John Locke, *Civil and Ecclesiastical Power*, in *Locke: Political Essays*, ed. Mark Goldie (Cambridge: Cambridge University Press, 1997), 216.

38 Immanuel Kant, *Religion within the Boundaries of Mere Reason*, in *Religion and Rational Theology*, trans. and ed. Allen Wood and George di Giovanni (Cambridge: Cambridge University Press, 1996), 177.

39 Ibid., 137.

40 Ibid., 138.

41 Not surprisingly, Kant follows the now-familiar tradition of identifying Judaism, and specifically the nation of Israel, as the prime example of a purely statutory faith—a faith in what are in reality contingent, material actions developed by human beings over history. "The *Jewish faith*," Kant writes, was originally established as "only a collection of merely statutory laws supporting a political state" (ibid., 154). Rather than recognizing and reflecting the universal character of God, "the Jewish faith" designed laws for its own particular benefit: laws that could effectively govern their specific nation and construct their own *distinct* identity. Kant writes, "Strictly

speaking, Judaism is not a religion at all but simply the union of a number of individuals who, since they belonged to a particular stock, established themselves into a community under purely political laws, hence not into a church" (ibid.). In Christianity, Kant concludes, we see the "total abandonment of Judaism in which it originated, grounded on an entirely new principle, [which] effected a total revolution in doctrines of faith" (ibid., 156).

42 Thomas Jefferson, "An Act for Establishing Religious Freedom [1779], Passed in Assembly in the Beginning of the Year 1786," in *The Life and Selected Writings of Thomas Jefferson*, eds. Adrienne Koch and William Peden (New York: Modern Library, 1993), 289.

43 Ibid.

44 In his "Syllabus of an Estimate of the Merit of the Doctrine of Jesus, Compared with Those of Others," Jefferson states that the ethics of the Israelites "were not only imperfect, but often irreconcilable with the sound dictates of reason and morality, as they respect intercourse with those around us; and repulsive and anti-social, as respecting other nations" (ibid., 521). Like Kant, Jefferson sees the Jewish religion as sort of an anti-religion that furthers the interests and political goals of a particular people rather than cultivating the universal moral sense inscribed into each individual's conscience by the Creator. Observing that Jesus confronted a corrupt political order and a generally primitive populace, Jefferson argues that he still devised a "system of morals" that is "the most perfect and sublime that has ever been taught by man" (ibid., 522). These "moral doctrines" of Jesus are much more "pure and perfect than those of the most correct of the philosophers, and greatly more so than those of the Jews" since they "went far beyond both in inculcating universal philanthropy, not only to kindred and friends, to neighbors and countrymen, but [also] to all mankind, gathering all into one family, under the bonds of love, charity, peace, common wants and common aids" (ibid.). "The precepts of the Hebrew code," Jefferson wrote, "laid hold of actions only," and in this respect were more properly political than religious (ibid.). In contrast, Jesus "scrutinizes into the heart of man; [where he] erected his tribunal in the regions of his thoughts, and purified the waters at the fountainhead" (ibid.).

45 Ibid., 289.

46 Ibid., 290.

47 Ibid.

48 Ibid.

49 Thomas Jefferson, "Notes on Virginia," in *The Life and Selected Writings of Thomas Jefferson* (New York: Modern Library, 1993), 256.

50 Ibid.

51 Ibid.

52 Michel Foucault, "On the Archaeology of the Sciences," in *Michel Foucault: Aesthetics, Method, and Epistemology*, ed. James D. Faubion, trans. Robert Hurley (New York: New Press, 1998), 306.

53 Ibid.

54 Ibid., 307.

55 Ibid.

8

Christianity, Capitalism, and the Battle for the Soul of the Republic

Andrew Saldino

You must be the change you wish to see in the world.

Mohandas K. Gandhi

It is hardly an exaggeration to say to that the Western intellectual tradition begins with Plato's *Republic* (ca. 375 BCE). Using his teacher Socrates as the protagonist, Plato composes a breathtakingly broad and penetrating dialogue that investigates all of the central questions of human existence—from the best kind of political and economic organization, to marriage and family life, to education and the arts. On all of these subjects, Socrates is guided by a singular obsession to convincingly articulate the most just manner for arranging human affairs. One interesting aspect of this obsession with justice is the way Socrates connects the pursuit of personal justice with that of social justice. The first of these terms sounds a bit strange to our ears, and the second does not carry its standard meaning. We often say that an individual can be moral or virtuous or even righteous, but rarely do we go as far as Socrates when he declares that, "justice is virtue of soul" (353c)[1]; indeed, it is the very quality of existence that determines whether a person "will have a good life" (353c). And while "social justice" is often used to imply an interest in more-equitable distribution of resources, the Socratic conception of this term has far more to do with what allows society to function in a healthy manner, regardless of how "equitable" the distribution of power

might be. This connection between the healthy functioning of the individual and society is certainly an idea that we have all heard before. It is
not, however, an idea that speaks to many of us at a particularly deep
level, given the enormity of the republic in which we find ourselves,
whether that republic refers *merely* to a nation of 300 million inhabitants or expands to include the 6.75 billion citizens with whom we share
the planet Earth. On the surface of our lives, the healthy functioning
of one individual person seems to have so little to do with the fate of
our nation or our world. Not only does Socrates challenge this sentiment; he also does so by providing a powerful lens through which to see
this connection, and thus to see into ourselves and the republic for
which we stand.

For Book 1 and the first half of Book 2 of the *Republic*, Socrates is
content to consider the question of justice in terms of the individual. But
Socrates' interlocutors are not satisfied with this approach. At one point,
when Socrates' idealistic refutations of perceived inadequacies of others'
definitions of justice has carried on too long, Thrasymachus jumps to his
feet and accuses Socrates of the worst kind of conceit. "Forget all of your
pathetic hooey about justice," Thrasymachus says (slightly paraphrased),
when "in every city the same thing is just, the advantage of the established ruling body. It surely is master; so the man who reasons rightly
concludes that everywhere justice is the same thing, the advantage of the
stronger" (339a). Anticipating the critique offered by an iconoclast like
Nietzsche over two millennia later, Thrasymachus argues that justice is
merely what those in power do to protect and increase their personal
interests. What makes a police officer more just than anyone else, for
Thrasymachus, is that he wears a badge, carries a gun, and has an entire
institutional apparatus supporting his authority.

This argument is so compelling that Socrates' own companion
Glaucon presents it in a similar form moments later, after Socrates has
apparently succeeded in refuting it. Indeed, in a world where *Wikipedia*
is considered a legitimate source for truth, and anyone with the power of
an Internet connection can edit an encyclopedia entry, this is a position
that simply will not go away. It cannot be wished away any more than
tweedy-coated professors might wish away *Wikipedia*, or the United
Nations might wish away a powerful rogue nation that refuses to cede its
own interests to those of the world community. These are not simply
fundamental challenges to justice, but to truth itself, and the very

possibility of achieving consensus on any issue where competing interests are at stake.[2]

Faced with the seriousness of the challenge, Socrates changes tack and follows the lead of his questioners in considering the relationship between justice in the individual and justice in the republic. Since the individual is so small, and justice so hard to locate in him, perhaps we can achieve greater clarity about justice by looking for it in the whole:

> "I tell you," I [Socrates] said, "There is, we say, justice of one man; and there is, surely, justice of a whole city too?"
> "Certainly," he [Adeimantus] said.
> "Is the city bigger than one man?"
> "Yes, it is bigger," he said.
> "So then, perhaps there would be more justice in the bigger and it would be easier to observe closely. If you want, first we'll investigate what justice is like in the cities. Then, we'll go on to consider it in individuals, considering the likeness of the bigger in the idea of the littler?" (368e–369a)

And so Socrates moves to consider where justice emerges in the creation of a city.[3] What is the origin of a city? Socrates suggests that a city "comes into being because each of us isn't self-sufficient but is in need of much" (369b). This mutual need first creates bartering, then eventually develops into a more-complex division of labor where each individual specializes in the production of one thing, makes that thing in excess of his own needs, and then trades or buys (with the establishment of a currency) this excess for the other things that he needs.

Here Socrates provides a rather simple natural history for human civilization that recognizes the economic basis of the social order. But while mutually beneficial economic relations may provide the foundation for peaceful relations between peoples living in proximity to one another, Socrates ironically traces the origin of war to the continued development of this same process:

> "All right," I [Socrates] said, "I understand. We are, it seems, considering not only how a city, but also a luxurious city, comes into being. Perhaps that's not bad either. For in considering such a city we would probably see in what way justice and injustice naturally grow in cities. Now, the true city is in my opinion the one we just

described—a healthy city, as it were. But, if you want to, let's look at a feverish city, too. Nothing stands in the way. For these things, as it seems, won't satisfy some, or this way of life, but couches, tables, and other furniture will be added, and of course, relishes, perfumes, incense, courtesans and cakes—all sorts of all of them. And, in particular, we can't still postulate the more necessities we were talking about at first—houses, clothes, and shoes; but painting and embroidery must also be set in motion; and gold, ivory, and everything of the sort must be obtained. Isn't that so?"

"Yes," Glaucon said.

"Then the city must be made bigger again. The healthy one isn't adequate any more, but must already be gorged with a bulky mass of things, which are not in cities because of necessity—all the hunters and imitators, many concerned with figures and colors, many with music; and poets and their helpers, rhapsodes, actors, choral dancers, contractors, craftsmen of all sorts of equipment, for feminine adornment as well as other things. And so we'll need more servants too. Or doesn't it seem there will be need of teachers, wet nurses, governesses, beauticians, barbers, and further, relish-makers and cooks? And what's more, we're in addition going to need swineherds. This animal wasn't in the other city—there was no need—but in this one there will be need of it in addition. And there'll also be need of very many other fatted beasts if someone will eat them, won't there?"

"Of course."

"Won't we be in much greater need of doctors if we follow this way of life rather than the earlier one?"

"Much greater."

"And the land, of course, which was sufficient for feeding the men who were then, will now be small although it was sufficient. Or how should we say it?"

"Like that," Glaucon said.

"Then we must cut off a piece of our neighbors' land, if we are going to have sufficient for pasture and tillage, and they in turn from ours, if they themselves go to the unlimited acquisition of money, overstepping the boundary of the necessary."

"Quite necessarily, Socrates," he said.

"After that won't we go to war as a consequence, Glaucon? Or how will it be?"

"Like that," he said.

"And let's not yet say whether war works good or evil," I said, "but only this much, that we have in its turn found the origin of war—in those things whose presence in cities most of all produces evils both private and public." (372e–373e)

For Socrates, war is finally about land and all that can be found in the land (including water, oil, and precious minerals) to satisfy the continual expansion of the material desires of a growing population as it moves from satisfying the basic requirements of life to seeking a more and more luxuriant lifestyle. Today, with the exception of the part about necessarily leading to war, the entire neoclassical economic tradition that we inhabit simply calls this process "economic growth" and considers it a foundation for the health of our nation. That our society's growing appetite for material goods could contribute to war is not a position that gets much public consideration, not when our universities are busily training students how to produce more and more economic growth, often without the slightest reflection on whether this model makes any long-term sense;[4] not when such an idea is considered an "environmental issue" and relegated to the smallest segment of media coverage, if it gets covered at all; and not when we obsess over the growth of the GDP and the stock market as if they were the most essential measurements for the overall health of the republic.[5] Our society is so deeply invested in a model of continued economic growth that to call it a paradigm that leads to war and not peace, injustice and not justice, is as anathema as proclaiming that "God is dead."[6] But is it so shocking to believe that an ever-increasing consumption of material resources on a finite planet with a growing population will necessarily lead to conflict over those very resources? When success is measured in material terms, and material is limited, why is it so difficult to deduce that success is limited as well?[7] Are we ready even to consider the idea that our very model of success is implicated in violence and war?

If we take the radical step and grant, for a moment, that material greed leads to war, then we might also consider the equally radical corollary that a reduction of greed is a precondition for more peaceful relations with other societies. War and peace are not incidental to the overarching issue of justice. Socrates is not yet ready to pronounce all wars as evil, because there are surely justified, defensive wars for Socrates; yet in this passage he is still willing to suggest a deep correlation between peace and justice.[8] Without peace, it indeed makes no sense to even begin speaking about justice. The very conversation about justice is only possible within a context of peace. If words are being exchanged, then fists are not flying. We may punch and scream at the same time, but we cannot punch and listen. To really listen to another person requires a measure of peace in our heart that is impossible when we are enmeshed in war. Bombs dropping on a rural village from 30,000 feet do even less to plant the seeds of justice than does a well-armed militia terrorizing citizens of a different religion or skin color. Rarely do the victims of such violence feel that their suffering is righteous punishment for their own sins, and almost always does such violence fan the embers of humiliation, hatred, and future violence. Just as there can be no discourse about justice without peace, surely there can be no lasting peace without a sense of justice.

Though Socrates condemns our absorption with continued economic growth as contrary to our presumed goals of peace and justice, it is perhaps surprising that he would be equally critical of the political organization of the modern liberal state. Far from affirming our emphasis on individual rights and transparent representational government as the paragon of a just social order, he suggests a form of government that we might call an oligarchy. His republic is to be ruled not by popular vote but by a small group of elite guardians, carefully trained and chosen by the preceding generation of guardians, who exercise absolute authority over all aspects of society. These guardians rule over two other social classes—a middle class of auxiliaries and a lower class of moneymakers. The auxiliaries are a group of soldiers trained to defend the interests of the republic, and the moneymakers are all of those individuals who produce the goods that a society needs to live, including farmers, smiths, bankers, and tradesmen of all sorts. And further, this hierarchical social structure is justified to the two lower classes not by a rational appeal, but through a "noble lie," or a myth propagated by the elite to justify their natural superiority over the other citizens of the republic.[9]

In this model, perhaps we see Socrates compromising an ideal society for one that makes sense, given the weaknesses of individual humans and the inescapable power dynamics of the political order. Or perhaps Socrates does not really believe that what we call the modern liberal state really is the most just society, in the sense that it might not produce a healthy, well-functioning society that can stand the test of time. To be fair to Socrates, these class divisions are not hereditary, but a function of the natural talent and character demonstrated in youth (all children are raised and educated communally), and each ends up doing the job for which he is naturally most suited. And in a manner that is most consistent with our modern sensibility, and twenty-five hundred years ahead of its time, Socrates affirms that women have every right to an equal education and opportunity to achieve any position in society.[10] Socrates defines a just society in terms of equality of opportunity, not equally of result.[11] Each person does one's job, and each class performs its specific function to keep society humming along. Bakers are not suited to crafting foreign policy, and most of the "decision makers" in our society do not even know how to bake bread, much less bread worth eating.

Figuring out what occupation each person is "naturally" suited for is no easy task, and this very issue propels Socrates to guide the conversation back to a consideration of the individual. Without a conception of human nature, a theory of social justice has no foundation. And when justice is itself a function of humans fulfilling their own natures, this question carries with it inescapably important consequences. If the individual and society are microcosm and macrocosm, respectively, then Socrates asks rhetorically, "Isn't it quite necessary for us to agree that the very same forms and dispositions as are in the city are in each of us?" (435e). This observation immediately leads Socrates to consider whether the self is singular or composite:

> "But now this is hard," [said Socrates]. "Do we act in each of these ways as a result of the same part of ourselves, or are there three parts and with a different one we act in each of the different ways? Do we learn with one, become spirited with another of the parts within us, and desire the pleasures of nourishment and generation and all their kin with a third? Or do we act with the soul as a whole in each of them once we are started?" (435e–436b)

Here Socrates is asking whether the tripartite division of society is mirrored in the individual. Is it possible that the human being has three parts—a part that learns, another that is spirited, and a third that desires the pleasures of food and sex? The first of these parts is rational, calculative, and always considering the consequences. The second is our spirit, our *animus*, that impels us to act in one way or another, and that is sometimes called the "will." And the third part is the animal inside of us, seeking self-preservation, reproduction, and all of the associated pleasures of the flesh.

To demonstrate that the self is not singular but composite, Socrates produces a simple argument based on the law of noncontradiction: a thing cannot have one quality and its opposite quality at the same time in the same respect. Have you ever wanted a beer and not wanted a beer at the same time? "Then you understand," Socrates says (paraphrasing again), "that your identity is composite and not singular." We are quite familiar with dividing the self into two parts, a body and a soul. But Socrates nuances this distinction by adding a third part between the other two, or a "spirited" part, which can obey either the desires of the soul/mind or those of the body. When these three parts are not arranged properly, the inevitable conflict of desires will lead to unhealthy choices. Socrates thus argues that getting these parts arranged properly is the key to becoming both a just individual and a just state.

What is the proper ordering of the self? Socrates proposes this tripartite division of the self, and then appeals to our own experience to suggest their ideal alignment. When you are not overcome by animal need or desire, what do you want? What do you *really* want? What manner of organizing these faculties will lead to the most fulfilling life imaginable? For Socrates, the answer to this question is not preordained; it can only be approached through rigorous self-examination and cross-examination of those who are leading fulfilling lives and those who are not. Socrates (or Plato, at least) calls this inquiry "dialectical reasoning," and it finally is the best answer Socrates gives on how we will ever arrive at any consensus about what constitutes the goodness, beauty, truth, and justice of life. And when we engage in this activity, it is hard for any of us, except the most immature or demented, to deny that a good life depends upon our will obeying the higher part of our selves and not the lower. This very quality is what for Socrates defines true guardians, and this quality explains why they can be trusted to legislate for the common good. But this is also a task that each of us is called to undertake, for it is crucial to our own fulfillment that the spirited part of our self obeys the part that learns rationally and not the part that just wants food and sex. "Isn't it proper," Socrates asks, "for the calculating part to rule, since it is wise and has forethought about all of the soul, and for the spirited part to be obedient to it and its ally?" (441e). To this Glaucon agrees, and if he had not, Socrates would have to persuade him to do so. That is how dialectical inquiry works.

Socrates is not just talking about the individual here, but of the republic as a whole, and with regard to the discourse on justice, he is ultimately insisting on a seamless transition between the two:

> "But in truth justice was, as it seems, something of this sort," [said Socrates]; "however, not with respect to a man's minding his external business, but with respect to what is within, with respect to what truly concerns him and his own. He doesn't let each part in him mind other people's business or the three classes in his soul meddle with each other, but really sets his own house in good order and rules himself; he arranges himself, becomes his own friend, and harmonizes the three parts, exactly like three notes in a harmonic scale, lowest, highest, and middle. And if there are some parts in between, he binds them together and becomes entirely one from many, moderate and harmonized. Then, and only then, he acts, if he does act in some way—either concerning the acquisition of money, or the care of the body, or something political, or concerning private contracts. In all these actions he believes and names a just and fine action, one that preserves and helps produce this condition; and wisdom, the knowledge that supervises this action; while he believes and names an unjust action [as] one that undoes this condition, and lack of learning, in its turn, [as] the opinion that supervises this action." (443c–d)

Here Socrates does not disparage moneymaking or politics or the pleasures of the flesh, but simply seeks their value within the harmonious organization of an entity whose spirit is controlled by the desires of the mind and not the desires of the flesh.

When we lay this framework onto the three social classes, it is clear that for Socrates, a just society is defined as one in which the auxiliary class serves the guardians and not the moneymakers. The crucial difference is that because the guardians have harmonized themselves, they make decisions based on the rational/spiritual goals of community, whereas the moneymakers make decisions based on maximizing individual profit. *A society where the auxiliary class, or military, serves the moneymakers and not the guardians is a society that has completely subordinated the concerns of the common good to those of individual profits.* Publicly funded war is great business for those who profit on producing weapons and other accoutrements of war, and here Socrates is warning us not to let moneymaking interests gain control over the military. Such a society is corrupt and unjust *in the same way* that a person whose will obeys the desires of one's flesh and not those of the mind is unjust: the lesser has come to rule the higher.

When we turn to consider whether that has happened to our society, an interesting place to begin is Dwight D. Eisenhower's last speech as President of the United States in 1961. Eisenhower rose to political power through his military success as Supreme Commander of the Allied Forces in Europe during World War II, and thus he was particularly well-suited to understand the developing relationship between the military, politics, and economics in our nation. Eisenhower took the occasion of his final speech as President (a great speech, which I encourage you to read in full; see *Wikipedia*) to stress both the necessity of a permanent, publicly funded arms industry and the grave dangers presented by such an arrangement:

> Until the latest of our world conflicts, the United States had no armaments industry. American makers of plowshares could, with time and as required, make swords as well. But now we can no longer risk emergency improvisation of national defense. We have been compelled to create a permanent armaments industry of vast proportions. Added to this, three and a half million men and women are directly engaged in the defense establishment. We annually spend on military security alone more than the net income of all United States corporations.
>
> Now this conjunction of an immense military establishment and a large arms industry is new in the American experience. The total influence—economic, political, even spiritual—is felt in every city, every Statehouse, every office of the Federal government. We recognize the imperative need for this development. Yet we must not fail to comprehend its grave implications. Our toil, resources, and livelihood are all involved. So is the very structure of our society.
>
> In the councils of government, we must guard against the acquisition of unwarranted influence, whether sought or unsought, by the military-industrial complex. The potential for the disastrous rise of misplaced power exists and will persist. We must never let the weight of this combination endanger our liberties or democratic processes. We should take nothing for granted. Only an alert

and knowledgeable citizenry can compel the proper meshing of the huge industrial and military machinery of defense with our peaceful methods and goals, so that security and liberty may prosper together.[12]

Here Eisenhower warns us of the distinct possibility of becoming a society in which Socrates' insistence that the military serve the politicians and not the moneymakers is finally irrelevant because there is no real difference between politics and economics. When our country moved to create a permanent state-funded armaments industry, one that both sought continued economic growth and had great influence on the political establishment, it unintentionally created a leviathan that continued to demand more and more tax dollars to fund its own growth.[13] The danger Eisenhower foresaw is that the "military-industrial complex" might exert "undue influence" on policy decisions, or that the pursuit of monetary profit (in the name of national defense) would determine politics.

The underlining issue here is the relationship between economics and politics, and the way in which economic interests have come to dominate politics in our country.[14] One only has to recognize that over 90 percent of the congressional elections in this country are won by the candidate that spends the most money to see how economic interests determine both who gets elected and what laws they are able to pass (thus making reelection possible).[15] There is no discernible difference between the economic and political structure of our nation, and this is why a political analysis of our society necessarily bleeds into an economic one, because the very separation of the two disciplines is a recent and somewhat artificial phenomenon.[16]

Indeed, the power of money to influence politics is almost axiomatic among U.S. citizens; we seem to retain few delusions that politicians can really buck the interests that fund their elections and truly legislate for the common good. Though these special interests sometimes make competing claims on politicians, this is really a competition *between* moneyed interests, not a competition between ideas on how to rationally legislate for the common good. The belief that our society can achieve political justice through this competition between powerful economic interests is a grave defilement of democracy. Yet it is the system that we inhabit, a system that plays the powerful interests in the Republican and Democratic parties off against one another through checks and balances. These parties are only adversaries in a quite superficial sense. Republicans may get more funding from the construction industry and Democrats more from the media, but finally there is little real difference with regard to economic policy between the two parties because the basic economic interests of those who have money are structurally very similar.

This similarity is underscored by Al Gore's recent comment that the best thing George Bush has done as President is nominate Ben Bernanke for Chairman of the Federal Reserve Board.[17] Indeed, the Federal Reserve System serves the interests of both the construction industry and the media, and thus in one sense it does not matter who is elected President, for the same man (and men) will still control the flow of money in this country. And given the profound power that the Federal Reserve System has on our economy (primarily by determining how much money to print and how much money costs to borrow), it is more than plausible to suggest that the Federal Reserve Board is the most powerful institution in the country. Not only does its leadership reveal the basic confluence of the Republican and Democratic parties on fundamental economic questions, but the structure of the Board itself also reveals the deep consolidation of private and public interests in our political economy. Of the twelve voting members of the Federal Open Market Committee, five are private bankers, and the other seven public officials on this board, appointed by the President, all have strong personal and professional ties to the private banking system. The distinctions between public and private, as well as Republican and Democratic, are virtually meaningless in the current Federal Reserve System.[18]

If everyone is invested in the system, then how can the system be wrong? Even if politics are essentially a function of economics in this country, what is wrong with that? Even Socrates recognizes that civilization itself is a function of our desire for material improvement, and we all "know" that capitalism is better than socialism or communism for achieving this end. I will omit a discussion of whether our current form of corporate capitalism bears any real resemblance to Adam Smith's original vision of numerous small businesses in competition with one another so that I can consider a more fundamental question. Even if human society begins with the desire for material improvement, does this mean that material advancement is our highest end? *While having the basic necessities of life may be prerequisite for achieving higher goals, does the mere fulfillment of continually expanding material desires constitute the highest possibility of the human spirit, either individually or collectively?*

Most of us would deny this, and yet our manner of social organization implies this very goal. By reducing politics to economics, we have, according to Socrates, confused the higher and lower parts of our selves. We have taken the basest element of our animal nature and unconsciously elevated it to the highest intellectual and spiritual possibility of our republic.

How has this happened? How have we let capitalism dominate politics to the extent that a vast majority of American citizens seem not only to acknowledge this situation, but also to accept it as thoroughly as Thrasymachus accepts that "justice" will always mean the set of policies and regulations that favor the established ruling class? We know that "capitalists" run our country, even our world, and somewhere deep inside we might even acknowledge that a society cannot achieve justice when capitalism determines politics. So why do we fail to do anything about it? Why do we not exercise our political power and elect individuals that will represent the interests of the common good, individuals who will make decisions based on the proper ordering of spiritual and material concerns?

Simply put, from a Socratic perspective, because we live in cave. In an allegory that is extraordinarily prescient for a society whose primary source of information about the world is corporate-run television media, Socrates reveals that most human beings have spent their entire lives chained to the ground, deep in a cave, staring at shadows projected on the wall, and believing that those images are reality. A brave soul may break those chains, struggle out of the cave into the light, and experience reality for the first time, but when he returns to help those that he has left behind, his vision of the "truth" will be met with ridicule and scorn.[19]

When we ask why there is so little understanding of the way corporate capitalism is eviscerating the idea of the common good, and why there is little will to change it, we have to look no further than the very channels through which our citizens come to know the real. Television has the power to shape public conversation and frame the issues of our day, thus setting the parameters for what even counts as a legitimate political perspective. We all believe that we are smarter than our televisions, and yet we all buy the products that we would not even know we wanted if we had not seen them on commercials. And as a nation, we elect only those politicians whose images make it onto the walls of our caves. Is it possible that the political and economic interests of those who own and run media empires are not *exactly* the same as yours?[20]

The problem with this analysis, from a Socratic perspective, is that it forsakes the way that the institutions of the republic ultimately reflect the habits and desires of its constituents. I mean, Who are these capitalists? Who are these sinister people that prevent our society from achieving its higher ends? Do they sit in board rooms in skyscrapers and make enormously important decisions that impact the quality of life for the laboring masses? Do they call their friends in government, the very ones who are elected and reelected through their campaign contributions, and influence or even write public policy? Do they buy and sell stocks, and thus determine both the conditions under which work is performed and the effects of that production on the natural habitat, based primarily on short-term financial returns? Do they exert pressure to silence perspectives antithetical to their interests as an investor class? Yes, yes, and yes—to all of the above.

Nevertheless, we ignore the value of Socrates' analysis if we claim that these are the only capitalists. The rest of them, the vast majority or them, are people without significant economic or political power, people who go to work and buy the stuff that they need and want with the money they make. We are the capitalists, you and I, each one of us, and our decisions as consumers drive all of the market conditions to which fat-cat investor capitalists respond. Unless you do not believe in free will, and unless you claim that someone is forcing you to shop in the ways that you do, then the market is just giving you exactly what you want. The market, if operating effectively, is simply a reflection of our desires as consumers. When we watch reality television, we tell those who produce television shows to make more programs just like that. The media and the markets in general do not give us the society we *say* that we want, but the society that our actions reveal that we *do* want. Economists do not have to listen to what you say; they simply watch what you do and make decisions about what goods to produce, and how to produce them, based on that data.

The wisdom of the Socratic model is that the macro is only an illumination of the micro: thus, if we live in a society where politics are subservient to economics, then this structure is merely a reflection of our individual practices and interests as citizens. We may enter a world in which our initial desires are determined for us, and live in a world where billions of dollars are spent producing new desires, but these realities cannot obscure our ultimate responsibility for these desires and all of their consequences. The path of spiritual growth is one of coming to understand and then seeking to actualize one's true desires. This is both the blessing and curse that defines our lives as self-reflective beings. And as capitalists, this entails the recognition that we create the world we want, one purchase at a time.

To take one example, consider our societal addiction to oil. As a nation, we use approximately 21 million barrels of oil a day (one-fourth of the world's use) to fuel our private automobiles, fly across the country in jet planes, fertilize our crops, transport and store our food, supply medical technologies, and so forth.[21] Peak production of domestic oil in the United States occurred around 1970.[22] This means that as our use of oil increases, and right now this phenomenon is a precondition for continued economic growth, we become increasingly dependent on foreign sources for this commodity. Obviously, we would rather not pay more than we have to for this precious commodity, since it is the lifeblood of our economic "health." So now our national interest involves using all of our leverage to acquire this commodity as efficiently as possible. And when an extremely powerful country (politically, economically, and militarily) such as the United States seeks this end, it can profoundly influence the terms for negotiation involved in the acquisition of this commodity. Unlike many other commodities, oil is essentially owned by the government in many countries around the world, and thus the terms for exchange of this commodity are invariably political. Economic theory alone does not and cannot explain the exchange of oil around the world. If it did, we would not care about what kind of governments exist in countries rich in oil reserves, because these leaders would always sell this commodity to whoever would pay the highest price. But oil is too precious *not* to be used as a political weapon to maintain and expand power, and thus we care a great deal about who controls access to this resource.

We did not invade North Korea, even though we knew that they had (and still have) weapons of mass destruction. Nor did we invade our oil source of Saudi Arabia, even though fifteen of the nineteen hijackers on 9/11 were citizens of that country, and it has a record on human rights that is arguably worse than Iraq under Saddam Hussein. Instead, we invaded a country with a hostile leader that just happened to have one of the largest quantities of proved resources of the commodity that our economy needs to function and grow,[23] and the Oil Ministry was one of the first buildings we secured in Baghdad.[24] My point is not that invading Iraq was "all about oil," but rather that our pattern of consuming natural resources invariably affects our foreign policy in a real way. If tomorrow Iran, Saudi Arabia, and Venezuela declared that they would not sell oil to the United States, nor sell oil to countries that would in turn sell it to the United States, we would have to choose between a major economic depression and military action to wrest control of those natural resources from unfriendly "rogue" governments. And if our leaders chose economic depression, and the price of gas were consequently to jump to $6.00 a gallon tomorrow, the American public would, at the next opportunity, throw the bums out of Washington that "failed" to manage the economy productively. We are addicted to a drug, and those who make foreign policy are our drug dealers; this goes not just for oil, but also for cheap imported merchandise in general. Thus, if we live in a society in which the military is serving the capitalists, then we have to admit that the military is serving our own interests as well, whether we are aware of how this happens or not.

We love stuff, and we love that stuff as cheap as possible. Economically speaking, this makes perfect sense. Indeed, the pursuit of material self-interest is almost the founding principle of modern capitalism. But the question that we have to ask ourselves, even economically speaking, is whether this love of cheap stuff makes sense in the long run. Are these practices sustainable? *Is our model of success sustainable*? Does our very model of success mitigate the possibility of creating a more peaceful and just republic? Do our desires (for more cheap stuff as well as for a more just and peaceful world) conflict irreconcilably with one another? And further, does an economic orientation of the social order allow us to engage these questions meaningfully? Indeed, from an economic perspective, it is almost a natural law that success is limited, that some will succeed while others fail, since competition over scarce resources constitutes an irreducible component of the very struggle for survival that defines the nature of life for all animals, including humans.

No one denies that this is part of our nature, both as individuals and a society. The question is, Which part? Are these animal desires for infinite increase of the pleasures of the flesh the *highest* part of our nature, or the *lowest*? Should they *rule*, or find their proper place as *ruled* by our higher nature? This is where religion, or "Christianity," as I say in the title of this essay, comes into play. Not because religion is necessarily rational or calculative, in the way that a scientist is rational, but because religion, or anything worthy of the name, is concerned fundamentally with spirit. A religious worldview transforms the will if it has any meaning whatsoever. The religious question is always, What is my will working to serve? Is my will serving the higher or lower part of myself? For Socrates, along with Jesus, Buddha, Confucius, and all of the revered figures in the human wisdom tradition, allowing economics to define human nature would reduce us to beings concerned merely with our animal self-preservation and propagation. For creatures endowed with the possibility of being so much more, this is a miserable existence, a suffering in our soul that only our own experience can confirm or deny.

When all of the great wisdom traditions agree in defining the human being primarily in terms of soul and secondarily in terms of the flesh, they offer an alternative conception of human nature to the one that now shows itself in both the political and economic organization of society and the individual practices of our everyday lives. If the self is primarily soul and not flesh, then our task is one of *becoming just* by having the spirit or will to serve the mind/soul and not the flesh. We are then called to transform the way that we inhabit the world through our desire for what is truly good—not good for the animal within, but good for the part of our self that participates in the life of the spirit, in what is sometimes called a life dedicated to God. For Socrates, and perhaps all of his spiritual kin, this is not a denigration of the flesh, but simply the proper ordering of a human being.

While I have here marshaled the forces of religious traditions to buttress Socrates' argument, this is itself perhaps a dangerous conflation. Socrates values rational discourse above all and believes that the proper harmonizing of our selves, both individually and collectively, depends upon a deep engagement with others through dialectical reasoning. The New Testament as a whole, to take one religious example, does not believe that reason is the path to our salvation, but rather faith. To mark the contrast plainly, Socrates has faith in reason and the apostle Paul has faith in faith. Socrates defines the human being rationally, as a passionate lover of reason; Paul defines the human as a being capable of the deepest love through surrender to Christ. The common denominator here is love, defined by deep communion with other human beings, communion made possible by a higher power, whether that higher power is Reason or God. And perhaps, as the Christian tradition has argued, this is a false dichotomy since that higher power of which we speak goes by the name of Logos in both the Socratic and biblical traditions.[25] From a biblical perspective, Socrates is indeed right when he declares that civilization is founded on our lack of self-sufficiency, for the love that constitutes our highest potential as human beings signals precisely this inability to find satisfaction within, as well as the inability to find spiritual satisfaction through merely animal pursuits. There is only an antagonism between the Greek and biblical perspectives if we ignore the essential connection between the love of wisdom and the wisdom of love that infuses both traditions with the spirit of truth. Perhaps what we name this higher power is of far less significance than the manner in which the Word embodies and creates love. This is a difficult task, but perhaps the only one that justifies our existence.

Notes

1 *The Republic of Plato*, translated, with notes, an interpretative essay, and a new introduction, by Allan Bloom, 2nd ed. (New York: Basic Books, 1991). All parenthetical citations in this chapter refer to this translation of *The Republic*.

2 This is not meant as a denigration of *Wikipedia*, which this author uses quite regularly, nor as a blanket indictment of the way that any country might seek to have its own interests reflected in U.N. policy. Rather, both examples are indicative of a general malaise that has settled into our culture with regard to the ideas of truth and justice. A cynicism about the purity or authenticity of *any* perspective defines attitudes on college campuses today, a skepticism that is only fueled by the continuing proliferation of conflicting perspectives available on the Internet. An alternative reaction to this proliferation of "truths" is the intense and uncritical attachment to one's *own* perspective, which is the very definition of fundamentalism. In situating this issue, one might say that the greatest problem we face today in higher education is that students no longer believe in truth, and the second biggest problem is that those who do believe in truth believe in the wrong kind of truth (in an uncritically accepting style).

3 The Greek word for city is *polis*. Allan Bloom defines *polis* as "the community of men sharing a way of life and governing themselves, waging war and preserving the peace. The *polis* is the natural social group, containing all that is necessary for the development and exercise of human powers" (*Republic of Plato*, 439). As such, the *polis* might be a city, a state, a nation, or the world, and given the ties that bind us together in an increasingly globalized economy, perhaps our republic (the Greek word for republic, *politeia*, is derived from *polis*) is not the city-state of Athens, but the planet Earth.

4 A student can earn a degree in business from many institutions in this country without ever seriously engaging the idea of the "common good" in the classroom.

5 Recent estimates are that the wealthiest 1 percent of U.S. households own 44 percent of the stock market, the next 9 percent owns 40 percent, and the bottom 90 percent owns 15 percent. This number, and a compelling account of wealth distribution in the U.S., can be found in Edward N. Wolff's "Changes in Household Wealth in the 1980's and 1990's in the U.S." (Working Paper No. 407, The Levy Economics Institute and New York University, May 2004, http://www.levy.org/pubs/wp/407.pdf (accessed November 24, 2007).

6 A slogan made famous by Friedrich Nietzsche, particularly in Part 1 of *Thus Spoke Zarathustra: A Book for All and None*, trans. Walter Kaufman (New York: Modern

Library, 1995). The idea that continued economic growth will lead to peace is often considered a platform of so-called "free-market fundamentalism" (see Milton Friedman's *Capitalism and Freedom* [University of Chicago Press, 2002] for a classical statement of this perspective), but *that* continued economic growth is necessary (even if not sufficient) is also a foundational assumption of intellectuals that are more skeptical about the potential of the free market to solve social problems (see Jeffrey Sachs's *The End of Poverty: Economic Possibilities for Our Time* [New York: Penguin, 2005] as an example of the so-called liberal position on economic growth). Indeed, one has to go all the way outside of thinkers trained in the neoclassical economic tradition to find serious challenges to the model of economic growth (see Herman E. Daly's *Beyond Growth: The Economics of Sustainable Development* [Boston: Beacon Press, 1997] as an example of such a iconoclastic challenge).

7 It has been estimated that it would take the resources of five Earths for the world's population to live a Western lifestyle (see James Bruges's *The Little Earth Book* [New York: Disinformation Co., 2004] for one such estimate). Whether the estimate is accurate is less important than the basic idea that current Western consumption habits cannot be attained by all.

8 Socrates' provides one such account of a defensive war in Book 4 of *The Republic*.

9 Socrates' "noble lie" promotes both (1) patriotic attachment to the republic ("And now, as though the land they are in were a mother and nurse, they must plan for and defend it, if anyone attacks, and they must think of the other citizens as brothers and born of the earth" (414e); and (2) an acknowledgement that social hierarchy is really a natural law ("'All of you in the city are certainly brothers,' we shall say to them in telling the tale, 'but the god, in fashioning those of you who are competent to rule, mixed gold in at their birth; this is why they are most honored; in auxiliaries, silver; and iron and bronze in the farmers and other craftsmen'" [415a]).

10 Book 5 of *The Republic*.

11 The same position is often bandied about in discussions of affirmative action today, but it still presents us with a serious problem: if we believe that all persons are created equal, how can we determine equality of opportunity *except* by equality of result? If both genders and all races are fundamentally equal with regard to academic achievement, for example, then any differences in result *must* indicate inequality of opportunity. Here is a "conundrum of equality" that is not easily answered for a country that affirms Jeffersonian ideals.

12 Quoted from "Eisenhower's Farewell Address" at http://en.wikisource.org/wiki/Eisenhower%27s_farewell_address (accessed November 24, 2007).

13 For a succinct summary of U.S. military spending, see "Military Budget of the United States" at http://en.wikipedia.org/wiki/Military_budget_of_the_United_States (accessed November 24, 2007). The actual amount the U.S. spends on the military is a complex and controversial subject, however, depending on what exactly constitutes military spending.

14 Perhaps the "have come to" in this sentence is highly misleading, because it suggests that there was a time in which politics was not a function of economics. Whether this has ever been the case, in the United States or any other great power, is debat-

able. But even if this has "always" been the case, does that *justify* this state of affairs, or simply provide more reason to overcome it?

15 "In 95 percent of House races and 91 percent of Senate races that had been decided by mid-day today, the candidate who spent the most money won, according to a post-election analysis by the nonpartisan Center for Responsive Politics. . . . While the overwhelming majority of yesterday's races featured incumbents running for reelection, money was also decisive when two newcomers squared off in open seat races. The top spender in House open seat contests won 84 percent of the time. In the Senate, the candidate who spent the most in an open seat race did even better, winning 88 percent of the time" ("2004 Election Outcome: Money Wins." http://www.opensecrets.org/pressreleases/2004/04results.asp (accessed November 24, 2007).

16 Two hundred years ago, the emerging discipline of modern economics was known as the "political economy." When economics began to consider itself a science, the political component of economic analysis was thought extraneous to cold, hard economic methodology.

17 "Al Gore: Movie Star," interview by Lisa de Paulo, Men.Style.com, http://men.style.com/gq/features/full?id=content_5179&pageNum=4 (accessed November 24, 2007).

18 For a splendid and readable account of the Federal Reserve Board, see William Greider's *Secrets of the Temple: How the Federal Reserve Runs the Country* (New York: Simon & Schuster, 1989).

19 The "Allegory of the Cave" is told in Book 7 of *The Republic*.

20 This is not to suggest that there is *no* relationship between the economic interests of the wealthy investor class and those of ordinary citizens. If the stock market crashes tomorrow, it will affect everyone, and certainty those at the bottom of the economic spectrum would suffer the greatest material hardships. Continued investment (often generated through previous investment income) creates more jobs and ultimately puts food on the family table of the working class. But the confusion of the financial interests of the investor class with the economic prosperity of American society as a whole is one of the great tragedies of our era. It is what allows a "booming" economic expansion (meaning growth in GDP and stock values) to coincidence with a decrease in median income, and increases in both income inequality and rate of those in poverty. For a synopsis, see "U.S. Poverty Rate Was Up Last Year," http://www.nytimes.com/2005/08/31/national/31census.html? (accessed November 24, 2007); and for the original data, see http://www.census.gov/hhes/www/poverty/poverty.html. The latest data show a leveling of the poverty rate and an increase of 1.1 percent in median income, but a continued increase in wealth and income inequality during a time of astounding growth of GDP and stock values.

21 See http://www.solcomhouse.com/usenergy.htm (accessed November 24, 2007).

22 In 1956, geophysicist M. King Hubbert correctly predicted, against conventional scientific wisdom, that U.S. oil production would peak in the early 1970s. "Hubbert's Peak" is now being used as a term to describe the coming peak in world production of oil. Some are predicting that oil will peak as early as 2007, which would be catas-

trophic for the world economy. See Kenneth S. Deffeyes's *Hubbert's Peak: The Impending World Oil Shortage* (Princeton, NJ: Princeton University Press, 2003), for one example of the many books being written on this subject.

23 For a paper detailing the controversy over just how much oil Iraq has, see Gal Luft's "How Much Oil Does Iraq Have?" Iraq Memo #16, The Brookings Institution, May 12, 2003, http://www.brookings.edu/papers/2003/0512globalenvironment _luft.aspx (accessed November 24, 2007).

24 "Oil Ministry an Untouched Building in Ravaged Baghdad," *Sydney Morning Herald*, http://www.smh.com.au/articles/2003/04/16/1050172643895.html (accessed November 24, 2007).

25 "In the beginning was the Word [*Logos*], and the Word was with God, and the Word was God" (John 1.1).

9

Sovereignty and State-Form

Rocco Gangle

It is not, I repeat, the purpose of the state to transform men from rational beings into beasts or puppets, but rather to enable them to develop their mental and physical faculties in safety, to use their reason without restraint and to refrain from the strife and the vicious mutual abuse that are prompted by hatred, anger or deceit. Thus the purpose of the state is, in reality, freedom.

Spinoza, Theologico-Political Treatise (1670)

We must not allow our elected officials—many beholden to unaccountable corporate elites—to bastardize and pulverize the precious word *democracy* as they fail to respect and act on genuine democratic ideals.

Cornel West, Democracy Matters (2004)

All things excellent are as difficult as they are rare.

Spinoza, Ethics (1678)

In many ways the philosophical concerns of the present day recapitulate and renew the fundamental disputes over political and religious legitimacy that arose in the early modern European context of the seventeenth century. The religious conflicts that swept Europe then in the wake of the Protestant Reformation and which the Enlightenment notion of reason was meant to arbitrate are echoed today by conflicts over the enduring meaning of the Enlightenment itself and its global-historical effects through and after colonialism. The confrontations with other civilizations attendant upon the expanding trade networks of the seventeenth century and Europe's colonization of the so-called New World have culminated, in our age, in an uneasy balance of global economic interdependence and cross-cultural misunderstanding. As a critical response to modernity and the heritage of Enlightenment reason, postmodern philosophy has been marked by two dominant concerns: first, a prioritization of difference and plurality that challenges unity and identity as characteristic ideals of the Western tradition; and second, a critique of fundamentalisms of all kinds—philosophical, economic, religious—that would act or argue on the basis of univocal principles, methods, or sources of authority that are not themselves subject to interpretation. The interest of postmodern thought in politics has been refracted through these twin concerns, the former opening new ways of thinking about power as constituted through difference, the latter raising new questions about political authority and its legitimation.

In distinction from both classical and modern liberal political theory, postmodern philosophy has tended to view politics as a field whose limits are nowhere given in advance and whose extent is not restricted to the domain of governments and laws. Like the terms "culture" and "religion," the term "politics" for postmodern thinking, far from designating some definite region of human experience with its corresponding modes of inquiry and knowledge production, instead opens up an endlessly ramifying series of questions implying various methods and means of response. To deal adequately with such a complex field requires forms of thought that do not presuppose inherited ideas and conceptual distinctions as sufficient for the questions we face. Rather, our received patterns of thinking must themselves be critiqued, interpreted, and remade. We must ask not only familiar questions but must also question the very terms in which we frame our debates.

In the United States today we must question the meaning of democratic sovereignty. While the term "democracy" frames a good deal of current political discourse, the actual meaning of democracy often goes unquestioned. As attested by the epigraph above from Cornel West's *Democracy Matters*, the very sense of the word "democracy" may be threatened today in America at the same time that democratic political practices appear to fall into disrepair.[1] Democracy is generally understood as one form of political rule, a kind of sovereignty—sovereignty itself designating the free decision making and ruling power of a political authority. What, then, characterizes democratic sovereignty? It is *a form of power in which sovereignty is vested in the multitude of people themselves.* This formulation reveals a basic paradox at the heart of democracy: in democracy the distinction between ruler and ruled is meant to be overcome. In democratic practice the ruled rule: so how are we to think of this collective identity of sovereign and subject?

Why, if we Americans already live in a democratic state, would such thinking be necessary? Recent developments compel us. When we compare "democracy" as a rallying cry at Tiananmen Square in 1989 or in the Ukraine's Orange Revolution of 2004 with the current state of American political life, we apprehend an unsettling dissonance. At the demonstrations in Beijing or Kiev, "democracy" meant at once an ideal to be struggled and hoped for and a reality immanent to the desires and practices of resistance mobilizing the demonstrators themselves. Where in America today is such a democratic ideal evident in actual practice? At the level of governmental policy, contradictions are evident. On the one hand democracy is characterized by the Bush administration as a "gift from God," a universal ideal of human freedom that opposes tyranny and may legitimate the invasion and overturning of foreign states (as in Afghanistan and Iraq). Yet domestically no administration in recent memory has done more to centralize authority in the executive branch of government and specifically in the person of the President. Since 9/11 the democratic notion of human rights has been severely curtailed as a consequence of the ambiguous and in principle unending War on Terror(ism), with certain individuals—such as "noncombatant" detainees at Guantánamo Prison—explicitly designated as beyond the reach of both civil protections and international conventions regarding prisoners of war. Overwhelming statements of public opinion such as that expressed in the global Valentine's Day 2003 protests against a U.S.-led invasion of Iraq appear powerless to affect policy decisions.[2] Though individuals remain free to express their political opinions (within certain limits, such as the designated free-speech zones held apart from public gatherings and access to the press), charges of "treason" seem increasingly to mark political disputes.[3] What is the status of *democracy* under these conditions?

First and foremost, the idea of democracy risks being reduced to the mere privilege of choosing among pregiven possibilities offered by those already in power. Only by voting for a different set of representatives does it appear that citizens have any political efficacy. And then individual citizens are "represented" by official individuals who, as political scandals have recently shown, may serve highly circumscribed interests. Hence, democracy under such conditions appears at best as a form of largely despairing political shopping. The store shelves provide a spectrum of choices, and political freedom consists in affirming this and denying that. Indeed, this model of democracy tends more generally to reduce political freedom to the merely economic freedom of unregulated markets. This commodified image of freedom need not exhaust the meaning of democracy. We must ask: How can democratic political activity be creative and not merely responsive? be productive and not simply consumerist? Where would we look for a model of democratic sovereignty that would do justice to the creative potential of society and not merely to individual choice?

We must find a way to distinguish democracy as a generic form of practice from democracy as a species of the nation-state. As we know it today, the nation-state is a contingent product of a definite history, developing especially in seventeenth-century Europe. From childhood, we become accustomed to seeing the Earth represented on maps and globes as a kind of patchwork of distinct countries, the great continental land masses divided unevenly but exactly into discrete nation-states. Thus it takes an effort of thought to recall that this image of the human habitat is a political invention of relatively recent origin. The parceling of all human territory into nonoverlapping blocks of land—each corresponding to a single people, flag, government, unified economy, and often a common language—follows a definite history that has brought us to the current political organization of the Earth's peoples, and our notion of democratic sovereignty has been caught up with this history.

The creation of the nation-state model of government was a response to particular problems of the time, especially the religious factionalism and violence that spread across Europe after the Protestant Reformation. It anticipated the colonization of Africa, Asia, and the Americas, which spread the nation-state model across the globe. Two major events in the history of the modern nation-state were the 1648 Treaty of Westphalia and the English Civil War of 1642–51. The Treaty of Westphalia brought the widespread devastation of the Thirty Years' War to a close and determined the concept of nation-state sovereignty as a projected solution to the religious factionalism plaguing Europe. While confined to the Holy Roman Empire at the time, the treaty in principle established a model of nation-state sovereignty that over the next century would become more generally applicable throughout Europe and eventually the entire world. In the terms of the treaty, the disputed religious claims of Lutherans, Calvinists, and Catholics shifted from an unbounded terrain of war between nations to an internal affair of nations themselves, each nation taking the responsibility for such decisions upon itself. This power to guarantee both self-identity and self-responsibility at the level of the nation-state became the dominant concept of political sovereignty that emerged from the treaty. Thereafter, sovereignty would invest the nation-state itself as its very essence, regardless of the specific form in which it appeared in any particular state.

The Civil War in England—with the beheading of King Charles I, the subsequent rule of Cromwell and his armies, and the Restoration of Charles II to the throne in 1660—raised questions of kingly authority and the legitimacy of popular revolution. These questions would in turn make the American and French Revolutions of the late eighteenth century possible and would affect the Central and South American anticolonial struggles of the nineteenth and twentieth centuries. These struggles would eventually lead to the idea of national self-determination, which has become globally dominant since World War I.

In other words, beginning in the seventeenth century, philosophers were forced to reflect on politics in a new way, tying political sovereignty to the nation-state itself. Sovereignty had originally been an attribute of God and through analogy applicable to human rulers. The Jewish, Christian, and Muslim traditions, which had formed the basic religious matrix of European history since the demise of pagan Rome, had agreed in viewing God as a kind of king. In the half century following the Treaty of Westphalia and the English Civil War, this political model—which had endured for a thousand years or more—began to unravel. What distinguished the new modern political philosophy from its ancient and medieval predecessors was the correlation of the object of political thought (for the moderns, the new nation-state form of sovereignty) with the forms of reasoning that characterized the Enlightenment era more generally. Political authority was no longer guaranteed by divine providence or intervention; human involvement in struggles of power had to be understood on its own terms.

The very idea of sovereignty implied and expressed in the Treaty of Westphalia made the modern notion of democracy possible by identifying sovereignty as such with a formal entity—the state—without reference to an external and universal authority in which sovereignty would be grounded. In this regard, a shift in political organization at the level of interstate relations reflected a new conception of power as immanent to the world itself and an eclipse of divine authority as a source and guarantee of order. At the same time, a clear delimitation of internal and external domains—like the distinction between self and world in Descartes's invention of modern subjectivity—marked out the territories of political propriety. Yet questions remained: How shall we understand the state itself? And above all, how are the sovereign laws and decisions of the state to be identified with the conflicting wills and decisions of individuals? Everything hinges on the concept of sovereignty and on the account we give of how the sovereign power of the state is related to the powers of the individuals who compose it.

To invent or even to see the possibility of alternatives to our current state-based model of politics requires that we look to alternate figures in the history of political thought. One such figure with potential relevance for the questions raised here is the early modern philosopher Benedict Spinoza. Perhaps due to Spinoza's insistent and important differences from the philosophical and political mainstream of his day, the seventeenth-century Dutch Jewish thinker's ideas have enjoyed something of a resurgence in recent philosophy. By examining the stakes of these differences in what follows, we will see how Spinoza's notion of democracy offers a positive alternative to the consumerist model that dominates much contemporary political discourse. In this way Spinoza's political philosophy may point toward the needed creativity that will alleviate, if not resolve, the religiopolitical crisis that the United States faces today.

Spinoza's *Theological-Political Treatise*

The seventeenth-century philosopher Benedict(us) de Spinoza's very name reflects a cosmopolitan identity. His first name, Benedictus, or "blessed" in Latin, may be rendered alternately Baruch (Hebrew) or Bento (Portuguese). At various points of his life and under separate circumstances, Spinoza would have been called by all three of these forms of his given name. The son and grandson of Jewish merchants who had emigrated from Portugal to the United Provinces of the Netherlands, Spinoza had grown up in the economically and culturally flourishing Dutch Jewish community of Amsterdam. The United Provinces had declared their independence from the Spanish crown in 1579 and had begun to accept

Jewish émigrés in the early 1600s. Hence, the political atmosphere of the Amsterdam where Spinoza was raised was one of religious toleration and a much-greater freedom to speak and publish innovative ideas than in the rest of Europe. In this environment of cultural and intellectual exchange, Spinoza studied the new philosophy of Descartes as it raised disputes across the universities of Europe, and he associated with philosophers and political radicals such as Franciscus van den Enden, Adriaan Koerbagh, and Lodewijk Meyer. He was excommunicated from the Amsterdam synagogue in 1656 for his heterodox ideas and devoted the rest of his life to the craft of lens-grinding and the art of philosophy.

In his *Theological-Political Treatise* (*Tractatus Theologico-Politicus*; here, *TTP*),[4] Spinoza gives his vision of the democratic state and its relation to individual freedom. In that work, Spinoza's argument emphasizes the constructed and contingent aspect of the state's power and, beyond the state itself, the excess power of individuals and groups. The *TTP* was published in Amsterdam in 1670 and was soon recognized as a radical critique of traditional conceptions of religious and political authority. The *TTP* was quickly banned, but a large underground readership continued to print and distribute illegal copies, and it became one of the most influential philosophical texts of the early Enlightenment. The *TTP* itself combines three components: (1) a theory of biblical interpretation, (2) a defense of free speech, and (3) a theory of the state. Holding these three components together is a unified inquiry into the relationships between authority, interpretation, action, and meaning at the individual and collective levels.

The European discovery of the New World and the subsequent explorer's reports of native peoples that became widely read by a curious European public had spurred general interest in the *origins* of the forms of human government. For this way of thinking, it appeared that the essence of government should be located in its founding act, which was then understood as the transition from a natural to a civil state. Like other thinkers in this vein, Spinoza recognizes a contract entered into by individuals in a "state of nature." Together they agree to give (up) their right to an authority—who thus becomes sovereign over the individuals themselves—in order to preserve peace and the common welfare. In this respect, Spinoza's doctrine of the state can appear somewhat conventional in the context of other seventeenth-century theorists. But as in all serious political writing, the importance is in the details. What makes Spinoza's ideas relevant to our time is not the general contractual model of government, which he shares with many of his contemporaries, but the particular elements of Spinoza's model that differ uniquely from theirs.

One important feature of Spinoza's thought is his rejection of final causes. In his *Physics*, Aristotle distinguishes four kinds of causes: material, formal, efficient, and final. A material cause is the matter or stuff of which something is composed. A formal cause is the essential shape and structure that makes a thing what it is. Efficient causes are causes in the usual, everyday sense, events and processes consequent to which a determinate effect is produced. And final causes are the uses or purposes to which a thing is put. As a common example, in building a boat, the wood and nails are material causes; the blueprint of the boat represents the formal cause; the work of sawing, hammering, and nailing constitutes the boat's efficient cause; and the purpose of seafaring is its final cause. In Spinoza's second major philosophical work, the *Ethics*, he denies final causes as mere illusions of human desire: "Nature has no end set before it." "All final causes are nothing but human fictions."[5] Spinoza's notion of politics follows this model: democracy is not an end but a means, as is the democratic state.

Spinoza's notion of the state is notable for at least two other reasons. On one hand, he eschews an idealist interpretation of the state as truly possessing all political power; instead, the political activity within a state is never limited to the official laws and apparatus of the state itself. This means two things: (1) Individuals and groups within the state possess powers that are not exhausted in political representation. (2) The political processes do not necessarily stop at the boundaries of the nation-state. Economic trade between nations, emigration, and cultural exchange across national boundaries may contain political powers that are not limited by the state. On the other hand, Spinoza links human political activity directly to nature. The strength of Spinoza's theory of government is the way that, while couched in the language of his day including the "transfer of rights," Spinoza never falls into the trap of conceiving of this transfer as an actual event that would be simultaneously real and ideal, a solution conjured up out of theory that would somehow be adequate in practice. Spinoza gives concrete content to the notion of "inalienable rights" that figures in the American Declaration of Independence, rights that would be natural and not merely conventional. Spinoza's innovation is to put the sovereign on the same plane as the subjects insofar as both parties possess rights equal to their natural powers.

For Spinoza, politics concerns the formation of a state, which is an ideal entity. But the ideality of the state is itself nothing other than the real relations it establishes between individuals, groups, and institutions and the concrete effects it produces through those relations. To appreciate the importance of this view and its difference from more-common conceptions of politics and the state, we may contrast Spinoza's conception with two of his near contemporaries, Thomas Hobbes and John Locke. Two Englishmen profoundly affected by the events of the English Civil War, Hobbes and Locke remain poles apart on the political spectrum. Hobbes represents the conservative defense of the absolute sovereignty of the monarch; Locke is a proponent of limited, liberal government and the separation of powers. For both thinkers, however, the very being of the state depends upon a decisive break with the state of nature. The state only functions insofar as it subsists on a level that transcends the mundane interactions of the individuals within it. The sovereignty of state authority depends on its transcendence—its separateness in kind—relative to the relations of power and exchange among the state's subjects. For Spinoza, on the contrary, the sovereignty of the state is situated as merely one component of natural power on the same plane as all others—albeit the most powerful in any given situation. Situated in relation to these two thinkers, then, Spinoza does not stand out as common to either or as a mediating middle way between them both, but as thinking on a different basis from either. It is this separate basis, incorporating and synthesizing an essential pluralism and a thoroughgoing naturalism, that we will examine as Spinoza's *realism*, a realism that speaks most strongly to our conception and practice of democracy today.

Spinoza and Hobbes: Plurality and Unity

Medieval theologians in the Jewish, Christian, and Muslim traditions, drawing on scriptural authority, made frequent use of the metaphor of God as king, the Creator of the universe as a sovereign ruler with absolute power over creation and its creatures. While this metaphor of God's power was used in turn as a justification for the sovereign power of worldly kings, the metaphor itself was preserved always as a mere analogy: God's authority was understood always to be infinitely greater (in kind and not just in degree) than even the greatest human power; and conversely, human authority remained subject always to divine law. With the emergence of early modern European science and politics, and the notions of divine sovereignty and political monarchy coming under question at more or less the same time, Hobbes took the traditional theological image of God's sovereignty and transposed it directly into the human political sphere. He thereby became the inventor and champion of a uniquely modern political conception of absolute sovereignty.

Hobbes was the first thinker in Europe to apply the Galilean view of the world as subject to universal and scientifically knowable laws to the study of human politics. For Hobbes, political philosophy is rightly political science, and the knowable structures of social order are as eternal, predictable, and universal as the laws of physical nature. In contrast to the ancient notion of human beings as naturally social, Hobbes proposed a new, modern anthropology consisting of atomic and thoroughly selfish human individuals. Motivating these individuals to form social relations is nothing positive or creative in itself, but solely the fear of pain and death. Taking this pessimistic notion of humanity as a basic axiom, Hobbes thought it possible to derive the various and complex laws of human politics, which he set forth in his major work *Leviathan*, written in the midst of the English Civil War and published in 1651.[6]

For medieval theology, God's absolute power was a function of God's unity and uniqueness. The divine command "You shall have no other gods before me" (Exod 20:3) expressed the powerlessness of all competitors to divinity as well as the essential oneness of the true God. For Hobbes, in taking this theological notion and converting it to the sphere of worldly power, human political sovereignty becomes necessarily the unity of a single will. The sovereignty of a multitude, or disunited plurality, would be a contradiction in terms. The very transition from the state of nature to the civil state is the passage from multiplicity to unity. This provides Hobbes's basic image of the formation of a commonwealth. As Hobbes insists, in distinction from the animal collectivities of nature (beehives, flocks of birds, herds of antelope), human collectivities are formed only through an artificial "covenant," to which an authoritative supplement is necessary "to make [human individuals'] Agreement constant and lasting; which is a Common Power, to keep them in awe, and to direct their actions to the Common Benefit" (chap. 17). Hobbes's famous image of the formation of the commonwealth ensues:

> The only way [for individuals in the state of nature] to erect such
> a Common Power . . . is, to conferre all their power and strength

upon one Man, or upon one Assembly of men, that may reduce all their Wills, by plurality of voices, unto one Will. . . . This is more than Consent, or Concord; it is a reall Unitie of them all, in one and the same Person, made by Covenant of every man with every man, in such manner, as if every man should say to every man, *I Authorise and give up my Right of Governing my selfe, to this Man, or to this Assembly of men, on this condition, that thou give up thy Right to him, and Authorise all his Actions in like manner.* (Ibid.)

Only if the "Common Power" exceeds the power of any particular individual does the possibility of political authority emerge. Yet Hobbes goes further and requires that the individuals involved transfer "*all* their power and strength" (emphasis added) to the sovereign. For Hobbes, the unity of plurality thus constitutes "the Generation of that great LEVIATHAN, or rather (to speak more reverently) of that *Mortall God*, to which wee owe under the *Immortall God*, our peace and defence" (ibid.). Hobbes is unable to conceive of a plural form of sovereignty that would not dissolve sovereignty as such: "For what is it to divide the Power of a Common-wealth, but to Dissolve it; for Powers divided mutually destroy each other" (chap. 29).

In many respects Spinoza's philosophy appears remarkably close to Hobbes's. They share many common terms, and a superficial reading might easily conflate the two thinkers. But even at the points of greatest proximity, Spinoza's thought reveals important differences from Hobbes's. In Hobbes, human energies are egoistic and can only be so. The striving for self-preservation is mere selfishness, and for this reason sovereignty is granted to the monarch only at the expense of his subjects. Spinoza is scarcely less pessimistic about basic human nature than Hobbes, but he is far more hopeful. More important, the arguments presented in his philosophy provide reasonable grounds for hope. For Spinoza, the construction of social relations is motivated not only by fear, but may also be based in mutual benefit and shared creativity. Spinozist thinking, far from foreclosing the possibility of a sovereign multitude, as does Hobbes, actually entails a concept of sovereignty that is intrinsically plural.

In contrast to Hobbes, Spinoza writes in the *TTP*: "Nobody can so completely transfer to another all his right, and consequently his power, as to cease to be a human being, nor will there ever be a sovereign power that can do all it pleases" (chap. 17). Here, Spinoza does not say that a complete transfer of individual right to a sovereign authority is a bad or wrong idea; he says such a transfer is *impossible*. A basic limit to state sovereignty—whether housed in a monarch, a parliament, or in a balance of separate legislative, executive, and judicial branches—is always actually realized in the varied and multiple powers of individuals composing the state. The multitude of individuals exceed in power the powers of the state since the state's power consists only in what those individuals themselves have granted to it. For Spinoza, the sovereignty of the state cannot annul the sovereignty of the individual since "the individual reserves to himself a considerable part of his right, which therefore depends on nobody's decision but his own" (ibid.).

In this way Spinoza's thought runs counter to the dominant early modern tendency to presuppose the boundary of a state as clearly distinguishing inside from outside. Spinoza situates the entire political field, *including* the cultural and rhetorical distinctions that delimit the boundaries of states, in an all-embracing dynamic category of nature. Thus for Spinoza, the political map is never presupposed as already drawn but is posited in and through power relations that have produced it in its particular form. Hobbes takes the traditional theological model of sovereignty as an undivided unity and transplants it in the human sphere according to the doctrine of the absolute sovereign as head of the state; but Spinoza opens up the possibility of plural forms of power, of which the state would be only one among many. In the organization of this plurality, no single center necessarily holds absolute control. Indeed, no such center is even possible for any length of time, since it forms a structure that is inherently unbalanced. For a Spinozist view, not one but many forms of equilibrium among the different powers in a state are possible and are in fact constantly being renegotiated and spontaneously reordered in any actual society. On this model, the dynamics of social power, including those of the state, are inherently in flux, a flux that does not cancel out the stability of the state but rather ensures the state's flexibility and continuance in the face of inevitable change.

Spinoza and Locke: Nature and Right

Like Spinoza, John Locke disagreed with Hobbes's defense of the absolute sovereign. But while Locke's conception of the civil state and the enforceable rights it implies involves a definite break with the state of nature, Spinoza conceives of rights on the basis of an ultimate continuity of nature and culture. At stake is the status of political action itself, affecting especially our ideas of individual rights as in continuity with collective power.

Locke's *Two Treatises of Government*[7] appeared in 1690, nearly four decades after Hobbes's *Leviathan*, twenty years after the publication of Spinoza's *Treatise*, and more than a decade after Spinoza's death. The first of Locke's two treatises is devoted to attacking a now otherwise forgotten defense of absolute monarchy: Robert Filmer's *Patriarcha* (1680). Though Filmer claims that human beings are unfree by nature and hence naturally subject politically to an absolute sovereign whose prototype would be Adam's "patriarchy" in Eden, Locke maintains that humans are free by nature. Where Filmer reads God's blessing in Gen 1:28 ("Be fruitful, and multiply, and fill the earth and subdue it; and have dominion over the fish of the sea and over the fowl of the air and over every living thing that moves upon the earth") as the establishment of a supreme monarch over all humanity, Locke understands simply the natural "dominion over the other creatures" (par. 40).

In the more-important second treatise, Locke presents his own view of political authority. For Locke, an individual human being enjoys two powers in the state of nature: (1) a power "to do whatsoever he thinks fit for the preservation of himself and others within the permission of the law of nature"; and (2) "the power to punish the crimes committed against that law" (chap. 9). A strange confusion is already apparent here. Locke refers to a "law of nature," but unlike the scientific notion of law as not able to be broken (a *descriptive* rather than *juridical* notion of law), Locke conflates the law of nature with the moral dictates of natural reason. Thus nature for Locke appears as already divided against itself, a natural *is* opposed to a natural *ought*. It is possible for nature (including human beings) to act other than as it/they *should*. The second power listed by Locke, the power to punish, in this way becomes necessary due to "the corruption and viciousness of degenerate men" (ibid.). Nonetheless, when individuals join any "particular politic society," both these natural powers are given up: "Whenever therefore any number of men are so united into one society, as to quit every one his executive power of the law of nature, and to resign it to the public, there and there only is a political or civil society" (par. 89). Thus political or civil society is constituted first in an abrogation of natural power.

Locke understands his view to be opposed to the idea of absolute monarchy since only a collectively organized decision both constitutes and maintains civil society as such. In other words, government is intrinsically plural in its constitution. In this respect Locke and Spinoza agree. They also agree in the essentially productive character of politics. Locke's notion of political right is derived from that of property, and property in turn is analyzed as the "ownness" implicit in the action of productive labor. If I make or do something intentionally, with a definite end (purpose), the result of my action becomes mine. In the state of nature, the products of labor become immediately the objects of property: "All that his industry could extend to, to alter from the state nature had put it in, was his" (par. 46). This accounts for Locke's famous claim that "in the beginning all the world was America," that is, available for appropriation (par. 49). The need for protecting property accounts for the formation of society and civil government: "The reason why men enter into society is the preservation of their property; and the end why they choose and authorize a legislative [assembly] is, that there may be laws made, and rules set, as guards and fences to the properties of all the members of society" (par. 222). Locke is careful to define property as the "lives, liberties, and estates" of individuals (par. 123), thus avoiding a vulgar reduction of property to material commodities. Yet he still conceives "lives" and "liberties" on the basis of individual ownership; and it is ultimately the desire to protect one's own that underlies all political activity.

Where Locke might have made the explicit connection here between productive labor and political right such that rights would be realized in the actual production and practices of their owners, he instead chose to retreat to a formal notion: he defined rights as the abstract property of individuals, with no enforceability of their own outside of the formation of a political state. For Locke, the original or natural (prepolitical) state of humanity is one of equality before the natural law, or reason. According to this law of nature—which "teaches all mankind, who will but consult it"—the equality of human beings before God as his "workmanship" and "property" implies a natural democracy (sec. 6). Yet since this ideal law of nature seems nowhere to have been practiced in fact, Locke must have recourse to the Christian doctrine of Adam's fall to distinguish the genuine state of nature (Adamic) from the only nature we know (postlapsarian) (par. 57). The problem consequently arises of the enforcement of political rights. If rights exist independently of their enforcement, who or what will enforce legitimate rights, and why? The question for Locke can only be answered in terms of the sovereign state, whose sovereignty, ideally, would transcend the fallen state of nature.

For Spinoza, in contrast to Locke, the civil state remains always in continuity with the state of nature. Yet this signifies primarily a difference in their respective interpretations of *nature*, rather than their understandings of the civil state. For Locke, nature plays the role of a myth from which we as both fallen and civilized remain doubly alienated. Indeed, we cannot even conceive of a nature that would not already be fallen and in need of sovereign remedy. For Spinoza, on the other hand, nature is not divided against itself but is simply everything real, not excluding the myths, interpretations, and obfuscations that we produce and dissimulate concerning the real.

According to Spinoza, then, the democratic state is "the most natural form of state, approaching most closely to that freedom which nature grants to every man" (*TTP*, chap. 16). Democracy for Spinoza is the reasonable social form in which individual self-creation and self-expression is not intrinsically at odds with collective well-being and political authority. Such a condition is not given a priori as a definite ideal, but must be invented and constructed piece by piece, part by part. Thus there is no general form of democracy for Spinoza but always singular expressions of productive democratic desiring unique to contingent situations. This invention is the work of subjects, not slaves, and what distinguishes the subject from the slave is the use of reason for the common good (ibid.). For Spinoza, reason is never mere rationality but rather the powerful effect of common and productive activity. This important difference shifts the problem of the enforceability of rights from the ideal to the practical sphere.

Spinoza radically reconfigures the idea of natural right, identifying natural right and natural power (ibid.). For Spinoza, right is essentially natural since it necessarily expresses and involves nature's intrinsic creativity. This implies that rights for Spinoza are not formal attributes of independent subjects but rather concrete relations between reciprocally determined centers of power. Rights do not simply belong to individuals such that external authorities must subsequently enforce them. Rather, rights are collectively constructed in and through their enforceability and are inherently relational. For a Spinozist conception, for example, the human right to basic health care is inseparable from, and indeed identical to, the actual institutions and practices that embody relations between sick and healthy bodies, scientific knowledge and training, hospital funding, and so forth—in short, the entire complex field of relations embodying this particular "right." Considered in this way, it is clear that the domain of a right to health care extends into the farthest reaches of social production. The notion that every human being deserves basic health care is undoubtedly a humane and noble judgment, but intellectual assent to the idea "Health care is a basic human right" remains a merely formal gesture without the construction of social habits and institutions that produce such a right as actual. And since the infinite variety of concrete relations that affect this right in any particular society are constantly changing, the right itself is not a static thing but a dynamic process that must be continually reinvented. Thus the Spinozist conception folds the Lockean problem of enforcement directly into the meaning and constitution of right itself.

Spinoza's Democratic Realism

Like Niccolò Machiavelli (1469–1527) before him, Spinoza is a realist in his conception of political power: both thinkers demand an account of how power is actually won, held, and administered in concrete situations rather than a definition or stipulation of what authority is (or ought to be). Such an account treats power as relational, as actually constituted between and among the individuals and groups that power affects (insofar as and how in fact they are affected by one another through authority and obedience). According to a realist conception, for someone to say that a king is sovereign because kingship is divine is to say nothing. What is required instead is to ask: King over whom? Expressing kingship in what way? Implying and producing what kind of subjects? King and subject are reciprocally produced, and so what is required is an account of how the relations of power expressed by a given king (or president, or worker's collective) become possible in terms of concrete connections to other individuals, institutions, systems of discourse, productive fields of labor, and physical energies.

In this sense, realism is not anti-idealist. It does not deny the important—in many cases, central—role of mental representations, habits of thought, regulative norms, and other immaterial entities. Rather than denying such entities, a realist political view seeks to understand the actual functioning of such ideas. This is as true of the general ideas of democracy itself and our conception of the nation-state as of the specific issues that become sites of contention in the public sphere. Seeking to understand how such ideas have developed and have come to play such a key role in today's world does not imply that one would explain their meaning away. Rather, one would know them in and through the history of their interpretations and their real effects.

For both Hobbes and Locke, the political or civil state is a milieu rather than a means. Despite their quite different conceptions of what a state is, Hobbes and Locke basically agree that a state is constituted in order to guarantee a peaceful and ordered "place" for the exchange of goods and services and the pursuit of individual goals. In neither case do the relations established within the state contribute to the form of the state itself. Indeed, a distinction between matter and form is built into the way both Hobbes and Locke conceive of the state as such. Once constituted, the state fulfills its role by remaining fixed and neutral; a dynamic state would be a contradiction in terms. For Spinoza, on the contrary—at least for his vision of the democratic state—the private goals and interactions of individuals are not just contained in the state, but are always constitutive of the relations that compose the state. On this model, the state is as dynamic as the forces that convene and interact within it. The state therefore is not a form but a process, and it is not the sole political process. Set among the infinitely diverse interacting powers of nature, the state is just one human construction among many. The state does not circumscribe a totalizing domain within which all civilized human activity would take place, but participates instead as merely one factor among others, the particular locus of certain relationships of control and obedience. Human activity—always and everywhere an expression of power, but power understood as constructive activity, not dominance—exceeds the state on all sides. Democracy is that conception of political power that includes these untotalizable forces as genuine political expression.

Spinozist Democracy Today

Contemporary American ideas about democracy tend to oscillate between Hobbesian pessimism and a neutered Lockean defense of intrinsic, formal rights. The former may find expression equally as a paranoid statism in which "democracy" may verge toward fascism or toward a libertarianism, denying any positive collective or constructive nature to the state entirely. The latter characterizes the forms of liberalism that affirm democratic ideals such as social and worker protections *in principle* but are often unable to make those principles immanent in political

practice. Both these poles, Right and Left—despite their important differences—take the form of the nation-state to be the primary subject of
democracy. Neither a Hobbesian nor a Lockean view can comprehend
the real power of diverse social relations as at once constitutive of the
state and in excess of the state's structure. In this respect both views remain inescapably individualistic and caught in the consumerist logic that
in large measure dominates politics today. Precisely because of this shared
individualism, neither Hobbes nor Locke is able to conceive of a truly
plural form of sovereignty. Both thinkers remain bound to a centralized
model of authority in which power is regionalized or housed in a discrete
part of the social body, and thus alienated or subtracted from the
remainder.

Nation-state sovereignty was a useful myth invented in the mid-
seventeenth century to address the interminable resurrections of religious conflict in Europe over the previous 130 years; it was meant
especially as a way to moderate and clarify the war-making powers of
states. Yet as a political myth it was never fully adequate to the actual
structures of power it was meant to explain. Today, challenges to the
nation-state model of sovereignty include multinational corporations
and globalized financial markets; trade blocs such as NAFTA, ASEAN,
and the EEU; the World Bank and World Trade Organization; and groups
such as the World Economic Forum and World Social Forum. In quite
different ways, each of which would deserve careful study, these organizations produce relations that cross nation-state boundaries. Whether
for good or for ill, the nation-state does not determine all political activity
in today's world. On a Hobbesian or Lockean model of government, it is
difficult to know how to conceive of these new developments or of the
possibilities they harbor for democratic action since the state itself is the
very form of politics. Because government has a fixed form, structural
innovations must either support this form or contest it. There is no third
alternative. On a Spinozist model, the construction of new kinds of institutions and effective exchange is to be expected as human societies
develop and interact. Rather than occurring necessarily either inside or
outside the state, they may develop autonomously (and relationally) according to the new forms of power they instantiate and create.

The model of the nation-state did not abolish previous political forms
but recontextualized them by theorizing them from a more general
framework. So, too, the political formations emerging on our twenty-
first-century horizons are likely to develop from within existing forms as

mutations, supplements, and hybrids rather than as ex nihilo substitutes for the nation-state. For a Spinozist conception, freedom is made, not born. Sovereign authority is housed not in a transcendent body but in collective and reciprocal relations. In terms of recent American history, we should remember that the rights and freedoms won by American blacks, women, gays, and other groups in the period from the 1950s through the early 1980s were produced by a variety of methods of political action. The United States government—whether understood institutionally as the American legislative-judicial-executive triad or more generally as the American people's will—did not simply grant out of sovereign benevolence the freedoms enacted by judicial decisions such as *Brown versus Board of Education* or legislation such as the Voting Rights Act. The freedoms expressed in these acts were built by the creative languages and bodies of marchers and activists: writers, artists, and demonstrators who brought political issues to light and demanded their resolution in the public sphere. In this regard, we may see why Spinoza chose to link a defense, or rather a project of democracy, to the question of freedom of speech and religious expression. Democratic action and freedom of speech are inseparable to the point of identity. To speak freely as individuals provides the best possible model of a powerful society in the creative potential of complex yet common relations: religious and secular festivals celebrated and shared; the traditions and innovations of art; the disciplines of collective inquiry and the dissemination of knowledge.

Who says "democracy" in America today? Under what conditions and for what motivations? What smoke screens might be set by the skillful use of a word attended by ubiquitous and frequently thoughtless applause? Spinoza's conception of democratic power enables us to include the dynamic contentions over the very term "democracy" in both the theoretical analysis and the constructive synthesis of actual democratic practices. In light of contemporary concerns, what does Spinoza's conception of democracy say to us today?

Concluding Imperatives

In a contemporary context, Spinoza's *Theological-Political Treatise* enjoins us with three democratic imperatives:

   1. *To rethink the meaning of the politicization of religion.* According to a Spinozist conception, religion is always already politicized by virtue of the collective habits of action and thought cultivated by religious

practice. Since the sphere of the political is not limited to the structure of the state, it is not always necessary to enter into the logic of state power in order to be politically meaningful or effective. A vision of politics in which all individual (and group) power is necessarily mediated through the apparatus of the state can only conceive of the constitutional separation of church and state as a forcible exclusion of religion from politics. Such a view seems to lie behind the resentment and anger evident in the Christian Right's recent self-assertion in American politics. Yet the most powerful effects constructed by religion are the bonds of friendship and community that form in churches, synagogues, and mosques and spread outward to society at large. Spinoza himself points to the dominant effects of justice and charity created by and within religion, regardless of sectarian difference. These effects are immediately political insofar as they affect our everyday lives and our educational and business practices in light of a relation to the infinite that cannot be captured by the logic of the state. In this regard, the separation of church and state may be understood as *preserving* the unique political possibilities of religion. For a Spinozist conception, the nation-state is finite while the extent and variety of democratic practices remains in principle unlimited. This is a view of human political relations consonant with the traditional Christian understanding of the church, or *ecclesia*, as irreducible to finite, worldly political projects. From this standpoint, the political mobilization of churches for the purpose of harnessing state power appears as profoundly antidemocratic as well as anti-Christian.

2. *To conceive of democracy not only as possible but also as already actual beyond the schema of the nation-state.* Understanding the sphere of democratic practice to extend beyond the logic of nation-state unity does not imply a rejection of the nation-state but rather a mitigation of its idolatry and the forgetfulness such idolatry entails. Spinoza's conception of democracy is equally theoretical and concretely practical, something thought and something made incarnate in action. When democracy is understood as a simple predicate or category of nation-states rather than as a complex web of individual and collective activities, it becomes easier to shirk the political responsibilities inherent in all aspects of our lives. Increasingly, our actions and decisions as individuals take place on a terrain that is globally connected. Eating lunch at a fast-food restaurant, shopping at Wal-Mart or Prada, or riding a bike to work—our basic activities in everyday life have ramifications that extend like lines of latitude and longitude to parts of the globe we are unlikely ever to encounter

directly. And the consequences of our acts are not only distributed geographically but also extend into the future in ways that only increase our responsibilities. Spinoza's ideas of power (in contrast to those of Hobbes and Locke) allow us to understand these everyday global connections as political in themselves, both opening creative possibilities and producing political responsibilities.

3. *To practice democracy through continually reinvented means, and to affirm the essential belonging-together of democratic means and ends.* Recall Aristotle's distinctions among the four kinds of causality: material, efficient, formal, and final. In a Spinozist conception, it becomes not only possible but also necessary to think of democracy according to material and efficient causality, not simply formal and final causality. Whenever democracy is understood simply as an ideal essence or preestablished structure, formal and final causes are dominant. If, on the other hand, democracy is understood rightly as a creative project, material and efficient causality come to the fore. Means then take precedence over ends, and there can be no question of justifying antidemocratic methods such as torture or political assassination as *ways* to democracy. In this regard, one of the most pressing issues for contemporary political practice is the development of creative and powerful forms of resistance to violent and antidemocratic governance and foreign policy, forms of resistance that themselves demonstrate positive democratic alternatives. To demonstrate for democracy in this sense would consist equally of speaking out against authoritarian injustice and of showing how democratically cooperative action actually works: such action serves at once as critical interlocutor with the state and creative model for its transformation. The African-American civil rights struggle is still perhaps the best example in recent American history of such performative practice. Today we must reinvent the transformative and exemplary power of Claudette Colvin, Rosa Parks, Martin Luther King Jr., and countless others, just as King reinvented Gandhi's *satyagraha* (the practice of truth), and as Gandhi himself reinterpreted the religious vision of Leo Tolstoy and Hindu tradition.

Political modernity was born of religious contentions that destabilized earlier ideas of authority, reason, and sovereign right in sixteenth- and seventeenth-century Europe. Today, political postmodernity faces conflicts similar to those that inaugurated the modern period: religious disputes, debates over political legitimacy, and questions of the rights and limits of resistance to established power. As inheritors of the theories and practices of early modernity, it is incumbent upon us to revisit the texts of the early modern political theorists so we can better understand ourselves and our political drives. We must look to thinkers such as Hobbes, Spinoza, and Locke not only to know the ideas that have shaped us historically, but also to seek alternative political possibilities and paths not taken. As witnesses to a steady erosion of the American democratic ideal in favor of reactionary values and simple greed, we cannot afford not to do so. Among the thinkers of early European modernity, Spinoza stands out as uniquely comprehending the constitutively plural and naturally creative dimensions of democratic society that America needs today. The challenge of Spinoza's democratic realism remains our contemporary challenge: to seek democracy in practice as a collective, rare, and difficult task, and to know democracy's historical roots as an inheritance of global scope, more as responsibility than as privilege.

Notes

1 Cornel West, *Democracy Matters: Winning the Fight against Imperialism* (New York: Penguin, 2004), 3.

2 In these worldwide protests—which involved, conservatively, tens of millions of individuals from over a hundred different countries—the citizens of Rome, London, Sydney, and other major cities filled the streets with a sense of possession, expressing their views clearly. Only in New York City were demonstrators forced to "march" in secure, wire cages guarded by police forces, which prevented free movement and mass association. We can only raise the question here if such containment and control of public expression is compatible with a democratic polity.

3 As witness, see the Bush administration's response to the *New York Times*'s decision to publish stories revealing secret wiretapping of American citizens and a prominent Belgian bank's sharing private financial data with U.S. authorities.

4 Benedict de Spinoza, *Theological-Political Treatise*, ed. Carl Gebhardt, trans. Samuel Shirley, 2nd ed. (1925; Indianapolis: Hackett, 2001).

5 Benedict de Spinoza, *Ethics*, ed. and trans. Edwin Curley (London: Penguin, 1996), Part 1, appendix.

6 For the most accessible modern edition of this work, see Hobbes, *Leviathan*, trans. A. P. Martinich (Calgary: Broadview Press, 2002).

7 For the new revised version of the standard edition of this text, see Locke, *Two Treatises of Government*, ed. Peter Caslett (Cambridge: Cambridge University Press, 1988).

10

The Politics of Immanence

J. Heath Atchley

We should be indifferent to good and evil but, when we are indifferent, that is to say when we project the light of our attention to both, the good gains the day.

Simone Weil

It may be that believing in this world, in this life, becomes our most difficult task, or the task of a mode of existence still to be discovered on our plane of immanence today.

Gilles Deleuze and Félix Guattari

Any thoughtful person who finds herself in the United States is likely to think that we live in troubled times. Thoughtfulness, however, should cause one to question the very notion of "troubled times." Because when has there ever been times that have not been troubled? Simply consider the twentieth century, the object of so much utopian hope from its predecessor century and the cause of so much disappointment to its residents. Any decade before the 1970s would be characterized by systemic and often legalized forms of racism, along with a general lack of recognition of significant rights for women (not to mention that these decades were home to two world wars, two unresolved military conflicts in Asia, an international economic depression, the genesis of the nuclear age, and the consequent Cold War). In addition, the 1970s brought a disgraced

President, an energy crisis, and intense inflation. The 1980s witnessed the deification of materialistic greed, the reemergence of bloody conflicts in the Middle East, and secret wars in Central America. The 1990s began with the First Gulf War and continued with U.S. ineffectiveness in the face of genocide in Rwanda, Somalia, Bosnia, and Kosovo. These descriptions are made with broad strokes, but they should make the case that no time within memory (and indeed within history) has lacked significant trouble.

Characterizing the current times as troubled, however, is not so much incorrect as it is cliché, and cliché is language lacking thought. Hence, succumbing to the exasperation (even if it is heartfelt) that we live in troubled times is a way of avoiding thought. Such avoidance approaches cynicism, because thought compels language to change and open onto unknown futures. Cynicism closes off the future by imagining it as another form of the present. The avoidance of thought is understandable, however, because so often it appears powerless. How do one's thoughtfulness and intellectual acumen and concern change the world? This problem is relevant for anyone troubled by the times. For despite my criticism of cliché, these times (like all others) are indeed troubled.

Before this essay winds itself into confusing places, something should be said about the act (or practice) of reading, especially if one is new to texts with philosophical (not to mention spiritual) ambitions. The most common manner of reading is to dig through a text, looking for its meaning as if one were hunting for a precious gem. Once this gem is discovered, the rest of the text—its dross—can be satisfactorily put aside. Such a method, I suppose, has practical importance when one has the responsibility of a long reading list. But if we presuppose that an author has a discrete message that is separable from the text and whose delivery is its sole purpose, that puts a reader into a state of mind like that of a consumer: words can be disposed of once their value is calculated and spent. I do not mean to suggest that texts cannot be summarized. But as an alternative approach, one could entertain the thought that words themselves have some agency; that is to say, they are not simply the instruments of a writer but also influences upon a writer; as words emerge they shape thinking as it is ongoing, as it moves into new territories of consciousness and reality. Taking such a perspective, then, would cause the act of reading to become an open attention rather than a search. The former poses the promise of surprised interest (noninstrumental value), while the latter houses the possibility of frustrated disappointment. These observations are relevant to this essay not only because I desire generosity from its readers but especially because one of its central themes is the critique of transcendence, the pervasive habit of overlooking what is emerging in one's own proximity—the value that grows out of a reality extending horizontally beyond complete comprehension but not into the beyond of another realm corresponding to our conscious needs. So when encountering a philosophical text, the most pertinent question is not always, "What does this mean?" Instead, more promising ones are, "Where does the interest lie? What can that turn into?" Maybe it will turn into nothing, maybe a laugh, maybe revolution.

At least since Plato, it has been a dream of much philosophy to produce a new and better world, one more in accordance with truth and, perhaps, justice. In times perceived by thoughtful people as especially troubled, this dream acquires such an intensity that it appears on the verge of becoming a reality, and troubled reality itself feels like a nightmare. Many of us, people who find ourselves thinking about the world, experience the current times this way. In short, since the horror of 9/11 (a well-worn phrase that itself needs critical examination),[1] the ascendance in American culture of conservative political thought, buttressed by conservative religious thought, has become starkly clear.[2] And the sheer effectiveness of this marriage between a politics that clings to defense, suspicion, and security on one hand, and religious views that cling to dogma, certainty, and self-righteousness on the other hand—this wedding has created an environment of despair for those of us who long for a politics based on an ethics that exceeds national self-protection. The question now becomes, What kind of philosophical thinking, especially a thinking that takes religion seriously, might support or even satisfy this type of political longing?

A typical urge in this situation, as the very word *progressive* suggests, is to dream a hero into the future, a new candidate or leader (or even a thinker), one with not only the right thoughts but also with the power to directly implement those thoughts. But this urge, I suggest, is precisely the problem. Establishing a fulfilled future as the promise of value and imagining thought as having a controlled and direct effect within the world is a pattern of thinking all too similar to the conservative religious mind-set that progressives seek to combat: salvation lies in the future, if only we believe the right things. Call this, if you will, transcendence—a pattern of thought in which value is placed in an imagined remove, like the future or another world. For the evangelical Christianity that so dominates our current politics, that remove is an afterlife, where god rewards the righteous and punishes the wicked. For consumer capitalism, it is a future where one can take satisfaction and security from the profits of one's investments. For the progressive reformer, it is a utopian state in which the selfish errors of humankind are overcome by the human capacity to think critically about those errors—a capacity often called rationality.

Transcendence works; it gives power to evangelical Christianity and consumer capitalism because the results of these two phenomena cannot be disputed. There is no way to demonstrate the falsity of the claim that god will gather the righteous into a holy, postmortem existence, and such a thought proves to be consoling for many troubled by life. And the fruits of capitalism are readily available to anyone with the means and intention to invest; profits are collected all the time. For the progressive reformer, however, transcendence impedes success, because success never completely happens. With each correction within society, there is always more to do, some condition left untreated, and down the line a specific correction itself might need to be rethought and reformed. Thus, progressive reform never comes to fulfillment. It always disappoints, and such disappointment can easily transform itself into a cynicism that negates the urge to reform altogether. So for those who are genuinely troubled by the times and want to avoid the Scylla of cliché and the Charybdis of cynicism, transcendence must be confronted in acts of thought. Such acts could be called criticism; I prefer to call them philosophy, because doing so suggests that they are not merely instances of intellectual acumen but also practices embedded within life.

The pervasiveness of transcendence, however, indicates that it is not simply a pattern of thought, one that can be willfully chosen or not chosen, like a garment that can be put on and taken off with ease. We can characterize transcendence as the longing for a fulfilled future or the desire to be in a better, more ultimate place; yet it is more. Modern consciousness (forgive this unwieldy generalization) is structured transcendently. When the world appears to us as a collection of discrete objects with names and descriptions that serve as cognitive handles for control, we have already moved beyond it, using what we know for our needs and waiting for a time and place when those needs will be no more. A static object standing before me is already a transcended object emptied of its own value by the urge toward comprehension and the consequent (if only potential) ability to control it.[3] So within modernity (however it be dated or defined), transcendence as a pattern of thought or mode of existence is, more or less, the given, because the tools of modernity (e.g., technology, democracy, revolution) transcend the immanent existence of things and make of them objects that find their places in the multitude of human schemata. Hence, this mode of attention gives more people more power to control more life—not always a bad thing. But neither is it inevitable, natural, or essential, and one of the more noble things that philosophy can do is to confront the pattern of transcendence in ways that expose the immanent value masked by neurotic consciousness. This exposure (or attention) is not the purely private affair it may seem; because it cuts against such a pervasive fold in the fabric of modern consciousness, it is a political (and perhaps even spiritual) act.

To get a feel for how the practice of philosophy can criticize transcendence and articulate an alternative, one with political and spiritual ramifications, consider Henry David Thoreau. Thoreau is a likely candidate for the concerns expressed here because he is already an icon. His nature writings are a canonical part of American environmentalism, and his essay "On Civil Disobedience" inspired the political strategies of Mohandas Gandhi and Martin Luther King Jr. His ideas have had noticeable effects (something so often demanded of ideas).[4] But there is a texture to this thought that is typically overlooked. Thoreau's most familiar and cherished ideas, such as civil resistance to government and the preservation of wildness, spin out of a spiritual attention that moves horizontally rather than vertically: God and value are life as it is encountered through patient perception. I am not interested in providing a scholarly answer to the complexity of Thoreau as a thinker. (What good would such an answer be if one could give it?) Thus, what follows is not a full account of a particular theme within a philosopher's oeuvre. It is a continuation of the concerns that began this inquiry: transcendence and the troubled times.

We can call slavery the most extreme, if not ultimate, form of transcendence. This might sound perverse or downright offensive, because transcendence is most often associated with the goodness of religion. The transcendent sacred, which is not of the world but is responsible for the world, saves and justifies us in one manner or another (if we are believers). Even without a metaphysical or traditionally religious component, ultimate goodness is often conceived in terms of vertical extension. What is good is beyond what we normally do or experience. But in the quest for goodness, salvation, or the sacred, what do we step on and climb over in the reach for the heights? Sometimes it is other people. After all, humans are the perfect tools. With our opposable thumbs, upright posture, stereoscopic vision, and ability to complete complex tasks, we are more capable and efficient than most devices we create. Using what are called natural resources as a means for survival and prosperity is something so common and necessary that it hardly stimulates thought. But when other humans become natural resources (or are deemed inhuman so as to be viewed that way), a line has been crossed, and thought demands an inquiry. Such inquiry, however, does not always go far because we can dismiss slavery as something that we have (painfully) overcome and no longer count as a source of moral perplexity: Of course, slavery *was* an evil. But if the pattern of slavery matches the way value typically becomes rendered (as a form of transcendence), then we are not yet done with this moral monstrosity.

Hence, one can say that slavery exists even when it does not exist (in the old style); slavery does not always appear clearly before the eyes but can take subtle shapes, which frustrate all efforts toward justice. This is Thoreau's insight in his essay "Slavery in Massachusetts." Read at an antislavery meeting in 1854, the essay surely expresses Thoreau's thoughts in a time when actual human slavery exists in the United States. But the slavery that structures the plantation economies of the Southern states is not the primary target of his criticism, as the essay's ironic title indicates. Thoreau wants to talk about slavery in Massachusetts, but there is none—at least, no large-scale, state-sanctioned human enslavement that fuels economic production. Yet through the Fugitive Slave Law the tendrils of slavery cross the line drawn by Mason and Dixon, thereby directly affecting Massachusetts; therefore, there is slavery in this northern commonwealth in the sense that there are within its borders escaped slaves, people helping them, and people hunting them. But additionally, the essay suggests something even less obvious: "Much has been said about American slavery, but I think that we do not even yet realize what slavery is."[5] Despite the boldness of this assertion, it is not simply the case that Thoreau seeks to give us the ontological scoop on a phenomenon that seems straightforward enough. He has no curtains he pulls back to reveal the real thing. But the suggestion that there *is* slavery in Massachusetts means that within all of the struggle against this social evil, there is something not seen, something close that has yet to be given attention.

Often when we read something like an essay, we give less attention to the opening lines. This introductory material sets the stage for the real argument, the main point designed to elicit agreement or disagreement from the reader, the genuine core of the work. Skilled (and hurried) readers frequently look (or jump) past the initial sentences in order to grab the essence of the work and do something with it. The introductory lines are most in front of the reader, closest to one. Hence, if the title of Thoreau's essay implies that there is something about slavery that we do not see but is right in front of us, then an optimum strategy for taking on the essay itself would be to give uncommon attention to its opening.

In the essay's first paragraph Thoreau reports that he went to a citizens' meeting in his hometown of Concord, prepared to discuss the topic of slavery in Massachusetts, but his fellow citizens were only interested in talking about the expansion of slavery into Nebraska: "It was only the disposition of some wild lands a thousand miles off which appeared to concern them. The inhabitants of Concord are not prepared to stand by one of their own bridges, but talk only of taking up a position on the highlands beyond the Yellowstone River. . . . There is not one slave in Nebraska; there are perhaps a million slaves in Massachusetts." This concern for a far-off territory coupled with the lack of concern for one's own bridges constitutes a transcendent longing, a casting of an activist gaze into a land essentially unaffected by one's concern. These lines sound cold because, as Thoreau no doubt knows, showing concern or demonstrating outrage over Nebraska could very well affect (for the better) the lives of people living there. For this reason, the dark humor of the paragraph's final line is important. The literal falsity of that line introduces to the reader a pattern of thought imperceptibly welded to the social condition he detests. In other words, it implies that what is not seen somehow causes the disturbing condition one knows to exist but can only imagine. So it would seem that the treatment of such condition would be to see (more truly) what lies before one.

Hence, there is the first line of the second paragraph: "Those who have been bred in the school of politics fail now and always to face the facts." Since there are no clear facts to speak of, the emphasis of this line falls on the act of facing. Facing can be understood as not overlooking (literally, *looking over*, as in passing over) what is always overlooked. It is a turning toward something true that is close but as yet unacknowledged, like an old intimacy regained. There is the feeling of conversion and revolution in this verb, as when we speak of making an about-face, a complete turn in the opposite direction, allowing one to see what was previously invisible. When Thoreau condemns the politically schooled for not facing facts, he is not diagnosing an ignorance. He claims, rather, that the active political class fails to engage in the act of facing, which is a way of repeating the message of the first paragraph: Because of their transcendent gaze, Massachusetts abolitionists fail to see the slavery in their midst.

Before this exegesis sounds overly sophisticated (or even mystical), one should consider the essay's practical observations and suggestions. At the most ostensible level, the Northern form of slavery is Massachusetts's compliance with the Fugitive Slave Law. Thoreau observes that his fellow citizens are eager to celebrate their own liberty and to commemorate the historical sacrifices that made it possible, but they do not do enough to secure the liberty of others. He thus advises his readers that government policy is not the equivalent of morality, and that concerned citizens should withdraw their support from the commonwealth until the commonwealth withdraws its support of the Union that supports slavery.[6] These thoughts constitute the essay's most straightforward advice. But its philosophical and spiritual import lies elsewhere—in life.

In the last six paragraphs, life emerges as a topic, beginning with this line: "The effect of good government is to make life more valuable—of a bad one, to make it less valuable."[7] He finishes with these lines: "Slavery and servility have produced no sweet-scented flower annually, to charm the senses of men, for they have no real life: they are merely a decaying and a death, offensive to all healthy nostrils. We do not complain that they *live*, but that they do not *get buried*. Let the living bury them: even they are good for manure."[8] Slavery offends life. This is the ethical core of Thoreau's argument, but its surface simplicity can be misleading. Being Yankee abolitionists, Thoreau's original readers already object to slavery, and most of his subsequent readers do as well. So simply telling them that slavery is wrong constitutes something of a truism. But claiming that slavery is wrong because it has no life in it raises the issue of life itself: life becomes the justification for efforts at reform. There is no appeal here to god as a source of morality or to a principle that transcends existence in order to determine right action. The appeal to life might not immediately catch one's eye, because this word finds its way so easily into our speech. Its use here, however, warrants thought.

First of all, life cannot be an object of knowledge. How could Thoreau possess knowledge of life as a whole and then use this knowledge as a basis for moral reform? To do so would require him to occupy an impossible perspective of grandiosity, where all of life could come within his view. In other words, he would have to stand outside of life in order to know it. So any sort of moral imperative Thoreau gains by invoking life must come by a way other than knowledge. Notice also that life is not an object of belief. Thoreau does not *believe* in life in order to object to slavery. Though often we contrast belief with knowledge (the former being uncertain, the latter being certain), it is common for us to act on our beliefs as if they were knowledge. The uncertainty endemic to belief is not so much a barrier to specific action as it is an enhancement to such action. Thus, belief and knowledge function in a similar, almost identical, manner. Thoreau, then, neither believes in life nor has knowledge of life. Yet he still speaks of life, and it is this speaking (in part) that makes the difference in his objection to slavery.

Think of life, in the way Thoreau invokes it, as a concept. Normally we consider a concept to be a generalization that houses particulars, a form within the mind that actual experience fills with content, an intellectual template: thus the concept of an apple contains within it all of one's particular experiences of apples. And a mastery of concepts multiplies the mastery one can have over individual experiences: the concept of an apple might not enhance the experience of eating apples, but it does help one to recognize that the fist-sized red things growing on certain trees are tasty. Certain concepts, however, function quite differently. Because it is one of the biggest generalizations one could make, the idea of life is virtually meaningless as such; it is a container in which nearly everything fits (even death, as when one says, "Death is a part of life"). So the concept of life must have a different function than the cognitive mastery that most other concepts seem to give.

When Thoreau calls out life, this utterance creates an opening in a consciousness that seeks to clasp around things, because the concept is not itself an object that can be clasped. What would it mean to grasp life? Possibly the possession of an absolute wisdom, but that is laughable. When life is invoked, its importance is obvious (though its meaning is not). Life signals importance (for nothing could be more serious), but it signifies nothing in particular. When Thoreau introduces this concept, he gives no real information to the reader. Instead, he raises the issue of value, and life's value can be enhanced or diminished by the quality of government. It is not the case, however, that life stands beyond signification, like a radically transcendent deity. It is the case, rather, that this concept (of life) disrupts human attempts at control that such radically divine transcendence would allow. If god belongs to another world, what is to keep us from doing what we will to this one? Possibly an intervention from god. But these days, who is willing to lay serious claim to such an event? Would one want to be such a person? It makes sense, then, that the concept of life opposes slavery because slavery is an extreme form of control, violently controlling a human for the specific desires of another.

Now is the time to draw the connection between life and the critique of transcendence. Indeed, these two notions form the bookends of Thoreau's essay. With irony and a little mockery, the essay begins by criticizing the tendency of abolitionist activists to overlook what is in their midst in favor of more-dramatic (but no more important) events in a distant place—a tendency that I have called a transcendent gaze. It finishes with an invocation of life as that which opposes slavery and servility. I suggest that such a finish is a version of the essay's opening. Raising the concept of life acts as another critique of transcendence. For what could be more immanent than life? We participate in it; it surrounds us at every turn; we can hope some form of it exists after death, but that hope testifies to the value it holds here. One could attribute a transcendent source or a transcendent end to life. But to speak, think, or act is to acknowledge (if not to attend to) the presence (at the very least) of life. So life not only opposes slavery; it also opposes transcendence. Life must, therefore, possess or enact an immanence of value. Put more simply: If life matters to you, that mattering is a response to a value that does not reside beyond anything; the attachment to life occurs before one can project life's source into a transcendent sphere. Before one can interpret life as a gift from god, one must experience life as a good thing. And because such immanent value serves as a prod to moral reform, it cannot be equated with personal satisfaction. Immanent value is not for or of one's self, because it trips the transcendent tendencies of a self that will step on (and over) anything to be satisfied.

More needs to be said about the nature of this concept. It is common to oppose an idea or concept with experience. An idea is something to be thought, and an experience is something lived; thinking and living are not the same, or thinking is an emaciated version of living. So along these lines one might claim that life is an experience rather than a concept, that Thoreau calls his readers to a more intense experience instead of a refined intellectual practice: carpe diem. To say that one experiences life, however, suggests that there is something else to experience. One might say that there is death, but is death something that is to be experienced, or is it the final cessation of experience?[9] Furthermore, as I wrote earlier, it is commonly acknowledged (in a range of tones, from trite to profound) that death is a part of life; life is the larger term. And if death is a part of life, then life is not simply the organic process of genetic self-replication; dead things have a life to them as well: inert matter, as contemporary physics teaches, is not that inert; it is always moving, pulsating, changing. So if life is not merely an object of experience among other such objects, then the dichotomy between a concept and experience does not hold so well. A concept, then, is part of experience and has effects within it.

One significant effect of raising the concept of life is to stimulate a turn of attention away from transcendence and toward immanence. Such an effect can be seen vividly in these lines from Thoreau's masterwork *Walden* (so oft-quoted that they can seem ordinary):

> I went to the woods because I wished to live deliberately, to front only the essential facts of life, and see if I could not learn what it had to teach, and not when I came to die, discover that I had not lived, living is so dear; nor did I wish to practice resignation, unless it was quite necessary. I wanted to live deep and suck out all the marrow of life, to live so sturdily and Spartan-like as to put to rout all that was not life, to cut a broad swath and shave close, to drive life into a corner, and reduce it to its lowest terms, and if it proved to be mean, why then to get the whole and genuine meanness out if it, and publish its meanness to the world; or if it were sublime, to know it by experience, and be able to give a true account of it in my next excursion. For most men, it appears to me, are in strange uncertainty about it, whether is it of the devil or of God, and have *somewhat hastily* concluded that it is the chief end of man here to "glorify God and enjoy him forever."[10]

The first thing worth noting here is how life stimulates a practice. In "Slavery in Massachusetts," life provokes moral reform, specifically, the resistance to slavery because slavery has no life in it. In this text, the concept stimulates Thoreau's two-year experiment in living alone on Walden pond, an experiment that Thoreau consistently describes as a spiritual and philosophical practice. The chief end of such practice is a turning of attention toward immanence.

Living deliberately implies focus, casting attention in a specific (and perhaps necessary) direction. Life's facts, its most significant realities, are to be fronted; one is to place oneself in front of them, not below and not above them. This fronting is akin to the facing called for in "Slavery in Massachusetts," and just as in that instance, the facts are of a nonepistemological sort; this is not detective work or accounting but a seeing. What is seen is life, and this is accomplished through an ascetic-like reduction, reducing life to its lowest terms, which means getting rid of what is not life, putting it to rout: philosophy as economy. This includes, most significantly, god. Those who are uncertain of life's worth might make the (common) mistake that the purpose of life is to glorify god: something outside and above life. The mockery within this passage's final lines directly criticizes the transcendence that fails to acknowledge the marrow of life, much less suck it out.

I have been insisting that Thoreau uses life as a philosophical concept and that a concept of this sort does not oppose experience. Such a concept also does not stand in opposition to a reality. Indeed, life is not a concept that stands apart from a reality it describes; instead, it evokes a reality of which it is a name. The concept of life, especially as it is encountered in Thoreau's texts, stimulates thoughtful practice (i.e., moral reform, philosophy) by turning one's gaze toward the immanent reality called, in certain instances, life. In other words, life is not *merely* an idea; it is a reality deserving attention. In the previous passage life maintains its conceptual character because it is clearly a thoughtful stimulant to action, but it is also a presence all its own, something that can be driven into a corner. So the concept and the reality interchange, slip into one another; but the concept cannot fully contain the reality. This is the case because, as was said earlier, life is not an epistemological object, something to be known. Furthermore, in Thoreau's writings the concept of life drifts into other concepts, including (not without some irony) god. Another passage from the same chapter of *Walden* illustrates this sort of drift:

Men esteem truth remote, in the outskirts of the system, behind the farthest star, before Adam and after the last man. In eternity there is indeed something true and sublime. But all these times and places and occasions are now and here. God himself culminates in the present moment, and will never be more divine in the lapse of all the ages. And we are enabled to apprehend at all what is sublime and noble only by the perpetual instilling and drenching of the reality that surrounds us. The universe constantly and obediently answers to our conceptions; whether we travel fast or slow, the track is laid for us. Let us spend our lives conceiving then.[11]

In the earlier *Walden* passage, god and life are virtually competitors; the idea that life's purpose is to glorify god diminishes life. Here, life and god (and also truth, the sublime, and eternity) are nearly equated. We know Thoreau is speaking of immanent life because the passage begins with yet another critique of the pattern of transcendence. Counter to this pattern is the recognition that god in fact does not reside in a faraway time or place, and this recognition is not one of common sense but comes about through a practice, "the instilling and drenching of the reality that surrounds us"—consider this attention. Alongside it is the action of conceiving, that for which we are called to spend our lives. Since the universe answers to—that is, welcomes—our conceptions, we are to spend ourselves in the cultivating of conceptions (one might as well call this philosophy).[12] Attention brought about through the cultivation of concepts is precisely the philosophical and spiritual practice that Thoreau calls for. The philosophical quality of this activity is evident enough (after all, concepts are its medium), but its spiritual quality stems from the reality that emerges through attention. This reality (let us call it, once again, life) is divine, the source, or event, of value. And its existence is not argued for in the way other philosophers have argued (tried to prove) that the transcendent god exists. Life certainly exists, but saying so is meaningless without giving the attention that makes such existence matter. Then it makes sense to say (though it might sound strange) that immanent life exists with and through a practice that is both philosophical and spiritual.

It is worth emphasizing again that the spiritual practice of attending to immanent value does not amount to the selfish enjoyment of life as one finds it. Arguments of this kind are often heard: that without god, or some kind of transcendent principle, there is no cause for ethical action, nothing that stretches the self to concern beyond itself, nothing to stop humans from doing what they will; therefore, the path of righteousness calls for a return to religion in its conventional (tried-and-true) forms. Not only are such arguments made by conservative clerics, activists, and politicians; they are also increasingly made by academics and intellectuals who long for a version of transcendence that can stop the behemoth of capital. But god and monsters are not always at odds, as an observant reading of what Christians call the Old Testament attests.[13] In the current context, what this means is that, rather than being an ethical ground, transcendence is an ethical problem because it itself is the operation that allows humans to do what they will. The primary example used in this essay has been slavery: my contention that to look through another human as the means to the satisfaction of one's desires is the ultimate form of transcendence, and Thoreau's insistence (according to my reading) that a transcendent gaze prevents us from seeing the slavery in our midst.

Talk of slavery might seem antiquated, perhaps even trite or melodramatic. But Thoreau's insistence that an unacknowledged slavery is in our midst exceeds his own historical context. It speaks to us now, and I can hear it when I see the well-circulated photo of an Iraqi prisoner of war wearing a dog collar and leash that is held by a U.S. soldier. Such an image houses many stories. One of them is the story of how the United States and other world superpowers have for over a century used particular nations and peoples as mere resources for energy, as new markets for the maximizing of profits, and as proxies for war. Such transcendent polices have sown seeds of desperation so vigorous that human life itself has become a terrifying weapon, making monsters of us all.

To what are we now enslaved? What prevents us from giving attention to the unfurling of reality that goes on before us? By now a thoughtful reader might desire a directive, a call to specific actions that disrupt the fruitful marriage between fundamentalist religion and conservative, militaristic politics. Unfortunately (perhaps), I do not have one to offer. I believe, however, that when questions like those above are asked seriously and sincerely (not merely as part of a prescribed intellectual exercise), some kind of action is bound to follow. If the demand to know the ultimate effects of such action is released, if these effects are allowed to freely flow along an immanent plane rather than being projected through a transcendent one, then cynicism will have no place to grow. I consider this posture my philosophical faith.

Notes

1 Cf. Jacques Derrida, "Autoimmunity: Real and Symbolic Suicides," in *Philosophy in a Time of Terror*, ed. Giovanna Borradori (Chicago: University of Chicago Press, 2003), 85–91. Derrida observes that the immense repetition of the terms "September

11" or "9/11" serve the quasi-magical function of sheltering us from the trauma they are meant to signify.

2 Cf. Michelle Goldberg, *Kingdom Coming: The Rise of Christian Nationalism* (New York: Norton, 2006).

3 Cf. Gilles Deleuze, *Pure Immanence: Essays on a Life*, trans. Anne Boyman (New York: Zone Books, 2001), 26–27.

4 Such effect was not noticeable during Thoreau's own lifetime. His following consisted mostly of a small group of friends; his two published books were commercial failures; and he died young, at the age of 45. The lesson to take here is not the truism that the significance of a life becomes apparent only after death. Instead, it is that, when dealing in ideas, one can never know when and how they will take effect. This lack of certainty inhabits the edge between cynicism and hope.

5 Thoreau, "Slavery in Massachusetts," par. 1. Because of the many different published editions of Thoreau's writings, I will cite references by essay or chapter title and paragraph number. Cf. http://thoreau.eserver.org/slavery.html.

6 This is essentially the message of Thoreau's most famous political writing, "On Civil Disobedience," originally titled "Resistance to Civil Government." Cf. http://thoreau.eserver.org/civil.html.

7 Ibid., par. 43.

8 Ibid., par. 48.

9 In conversation, J. Daniel Brown gave me this thought.

10 "Where I Lived, and What I Lived For," par. 16; http://xroads.virginia.edu/~hyper/walden/walden.html.

11 Ibid., par. 21.

12 Cf. Gilles Deleuze and Felix Guattari's understanding of philosophy as the creation of concepts in their book *What Is Philosophy?* trans. Hugh Tomlinson and Graham Burchell (New York: Columbia University Press, 1994).

13 Cf. Timothy K. Beal, *Religion and Its Monsters* (New York: Routledge, 2002), esp. chaps. 2–6.

11

"An Army of One?"

Subject, Signifier, and the Symbolic

Melissa Conroy

You are not obliged to understand my writings. If you don't understand them, so much the better—that will give you the opportunity to explain them.

Seminar of Jacques Lacan 20.34

In the ongoing War on Terror, opponents to the agenda of the Bush administration have been labeled enemies, traitors, and even excrement.[1] Opponents to gay marriage claim that "gays are attacking marriage" and have "called war" on traditional marriage.[2] In another culture war, Rush Limbaugh has referred to abortion activists as "the original feminazis."[3] Throughout American culture are many examples of divisive rhetoric that uses binary opposition.

In this essay I will show how this rhetoric has power beyond its cultural context. Dualistic rhetoric speaks to the ingrained binaries that originally established our boundaries as human subjects. I examine how human subjects have the tendency to embody positive qualities in the Self while also projecting negative ones onto the Other (whether that Other is a Democrat, a gay rights activist, or an abortion rights activist). I will also look at how this tendency is apparent on the cultural scale where the "Self" (the United States) defines itself against the Other (who may be a rival country or, more currently, the terrorists).

Lacan: A Brief Sketch

Jacques Lacan (1901–81)[4] is considered the most important psychoanalytic theorist since Sigmund Freud. His theories have impacted such wide-ranging areas as literary theory, film theory, feminism, political theory, cultural studies, queer theory, gender studies, philosophy, and especially psychoanalytic theory and practice.

Lacan saw himself as a Freudian, and his lectures (recorded in a series called the "Seminars of Jacques Lacan") show a return to Freud's early writings, with an emphasis on the role of the unconscious. In analytical practice, Lacan showed a shift from focusing on the ego to examining the unconscious. Application of his work is often concerned with analyzing how the unconscious structures the subject and culture at large. Lacan was a radical psychoanalyst and theorist, as evidenced by his expulsion from psychoanalytic organizations for his unorthodox methods and his notoriously unsystematic lectures; terms he uses in his various seminars shift meaning over the years without warning, making a clear presentation of his ideas nearly impossible.

Here I do not intend to write a comprehensive survey of Lacan's system. Instead, my task is to show how some of the basic theories of Lacan can be used to examine the link between the subject and the religiopolitical realm. One of the great insights derived from Lacan's work is that he was able to make clear the connections between the subject (the human being as formulated by Lacan), the signifier (an individual word in a linguistic system), and the symbolic order (the realm of culture, language, and religion). I will show how the unconscious structures of the subject are linked to those of the larger cultural system. Lacan's work is indispensable for analyzing the subject's relationship to the political and religious realms because he "makes fully evident how the private, individual realm of subjectivity ultimately cannot be separated from the realm of public life."[5] I will explore some of Lacan's key ideas, such as the Mirror Stage, the Symbolic, and the quilting point, in order to provide theoretical tools for examining contemporary political and religious rhetoric, such as the commonplace idea of "Us versus Them," "Good versus Evil," or "USA versus the World."

The Subject in the Three Orders

My sketch of the Lacanian subject focuses on the experience of disharmony, fragmentation, and lack, and the consequent striving to attain a state of harmony, unity, and wholeness. Lacan's description of the subject is understood only by explaining the three orders of existence that Lacan posits. These three orders refer to different levels of existence that the subject operates in. The subject starts off as an unknowing and yet harmonious self that becomes alienated once it enters the other orders. Each order tries to reestablish the original harmony that was once (erroneously) felt.

The Real

In Lacan's depiction of the earliest experience of a child's life, he describes a world of oneness. The very young child does not have the ability to distinguish between itself and its environment. Freud described this state as an oceanic oneness, where the subject is intermingled with its world in a state of nondifferentiation. Lacan describes the subject as *l'hommelette* (the human omelet), whose sense of identity spreads out as far as it has experience. The child "does not differentiate between itself and the mother upon whose nature it relies, or the blanket whose warmth it enjoys."[6] This is the order of the Real, where the world is experienced without identity or difference. Eventually the child comes to realize that things in its environment are part of its own self. Once the child recognizes this, it comes to see itself as one element of its environment ("I am not the blanket/the mother/ the breast") and thus experiences itself as lacking. It senses itself as lacking because it holds the belief that it was once part of a greater whole. Thus the primordial experience of the child, the initial sense of unity, exists only in the misinformed mind of the child. It is this experience of wholeness that we constantly strive to return to, Lacan argues.

An example of this is found in Plato's *Symposium*, in a tale attributed to the ancient Greek Aristophanes. In this story of the origin of love, all creatures started off as "wholes": great blobs of humanoid creatures that had two heads, four arms, and four legs. Zeus cut these powerful beings in half; because of that, each human is now doomed to seek out its other half. This story nicely demonstrates Lacan's idea of the original sense of wholeness that we, in our now deficient state, think we can return to. Even now, in a world distant from the ancient Greeks, people refer to a spouse as one's "better half" and marriage as a union where "two become one." Even in the most intimate moments, you find Lacan's theory when one lover whispers to another, "You are everything to me." In popular culture we see this in countless romantic clichés, such as when Jerry

Macguire (Tom Cruise) tells Dorothy Boyd (Renée Zellweger), "You complete me."

The consequence of the Real, in terms of the signifier and the Symbolic, lies in the idea that in the Real, the subject has no way to distinguish itself from the Other. The order of the Real reveals the empty and arbitrary nature of signifiers. Words are simply labels used to distinguish one thing from another. This is evident in Lacan's account of the train station:

> A train arrives at a station. A little boy and a little girl, brother and sister, are seated across from each other in a compartment next to the outside window that provides a view of the station platform buildings going by, as the train comes to a stop.
>
> "Look," says the brother, "we're at Ladies!"
>
> "Imbecile!" replies his sister. "Don't you see we're at Gentlemen?"[7]

The example of the train station shows that the word one takes to identify oneself, whether one is a Lady or a Gentleman, is completely arbitrary and meaningless in and of itself. There is no intrinsic value to our bodies at the level of the Real. Lacanian analyst Juliet Flower MacCannell argues that Lacan's train station is not simply about the arbitrary nature of signifiers, but about the emptiness of the signifiers themselves. MacCannell suggests, "*Signifiers* carry the entire burden of gender identification—the sorting out of boys and girls: words, titles, clothes, accoutrements."[8] This example shows that sexuality, like other signifiers, exists only at the level of representation; there is nothing "under" the clothes that makes one a man or a woman. Signifiers, and chains of signifiers (such as those that go into producing genders such as masculinity and femininity), have no inherent meaning. The meanings of empty signifiers are only made clear once they are fully inscribed within the symbolic order.

The Imaginary

The Imaginary order refers not only to the realm of images, but also to something fictional or hallucinated. This is evident in the most famous visual metaphor of the imaginary order, the Mirror Stage. Lacan postulates that the moment a child recognizes its own image in the mirror is the crucial moment for ego formation. The child, at about six months or so, is an unwieldy creature, lacking motor coordination and a sense of self separate from the Other. The mirror image appears to the child to be complete and stable. This image becomes the child's *imago* of self, the child's ego ideal. The child, upon seeing its body reflected in a mirror, mistakes, and misrecognizes the mirror image for itself. It transfers the feelings of wholeness and completeness (experienced in the order of the Real) onto this stable body found in the mirror. It recaptures the sense of harmony, but the consequence is that the image is held as superior to its own body; its own material existence is doomed to fall short of this stable perfection. The child's happy recognition of itself in the mirror is always then a misrecognition; the child is alienated from its very self since its most ideal form is located *outside* of its own body. Leo Bersani and Ulysse Dutoit argue persuasively that the Mirror *Stage* is a misnomer because "we don't 'move beyond' the mirror stage; its self-misrecognition [is] the precondition of all object relations. Desire for the other depends on misrecognition of the self *in* the other."[9] This is important because it means that the Mirror Stage is repeated throughout one's life as subjects continually seek "ideal Others" to find themselves in. This is evident in the cultural myth of one's "true love" or of the ideal of finding a "soul mate." Not only in a subject's relation to other subjects, but also in the larger cultural order, the subject searches for an ideal Other, an image of harmony and wholeness to identify with.

Identification with the mirror image plays a primary role in understanding how Lacan conceives of the ego development of the self of the imaginary order. Even in the Mirror Stage, one sees that ego formation cannot be understood outside the organism's environment. Lacan writes, "The function of the Mirror Stage thus turns out, in my view, to be a particular case of the function of *imagos*, which is to establish a relationship between an organism and its reality."[10] The subject's idea of the self is formed through a negation of the outside world: things that are *not* me, establish me.

The Symbolic Order

The subject enters the third order, the symbolic order, because the imaginary order, with the subject as an alienated subject, does not create harmony for the subject. In Lacan's later phase (1950s onward) the role of the Symbolic, and the working of signifiers, came to replace his earlier emphasis on the Imaginary. The importance of the Symbolic is such that Lacan postulates that the subject is but an effect of the Symbolic, rather than an agent in it. Lacan explains the dynamics of the operation by which a subject appears as signifier: "The subject is born insofar as the signifier emerges in the field of the Other, but, by this very fact, this subject—which was previously nothing if not a subject coming into being—solidifies into a signifier."[11] In other words, it is in the realm of the Symbolic that the individual subject acquires a sense of a unique identity.

The symbolic order is particularly important because it is the realm of language. Recall the example of the train station. The interchangeable nature of "Ladies" and "Gentlemen" suggests that signifiers themselves are arbitrary. The combinations of letters that make up "Ladies" in English (or *femmes* in French or *señoras* in Spanish) are completely unconnected to the reality of the female sex (the thing signified). Yet signifiers do not appear so random. Because we are linguistically trained creatures, one already has the definite idea of what a "lady" or a "gentleman" connotes, and thus the association between the word and the object seems unquestionable. Why is this possible when signifiers are, in and of themselves, meaningless combinations of letters?

At this level, Lacan argues that a subject is quilted or knotted into a particular identity.[12] The *pointe de caption*, or quilting (anchoring) point, connects the signifier to the signified in the being's mind, quilting together this arbitrary reality. To be considered "normal," a person must be able to join together the right signifier and thing signified out of a range of possible meanings.[13] With the two properly joined, the individual's personal dilemma (for example, How do I, as a unique individual, answer the call of the Other?) is positioned in the whole of signification (How do I act as a "man"?).

In terms of the world of the Symbolic, the quilting point stitches together a signifier to a particular object or set of ideas. The quilting point "is the point with which all concrete analysis of discourse must operate. These signifiers fix the meaning of whole chains of signifiers."[14] An example of this would be how the signifier "communism" gives other signifiers, such as "democracy," "freedom," or "the state," specific cultural meanings.[15] In this case the quilting point, "communism," is a point that seems stable and ahistorical, and yet it only acquires its meaning at a specific time in history. Quilting points seem eternal and fixed (i.e., the idea of "America"), and yet when viewed historically, they change in relation to other quilting points. For example, the time of the Cold War and "communism" created a different idea of America than the current quilting point of "terrorism." Nonetheless the idea of America as a timeless entity, for example, as "the land of the free," seems to exist outside of the historical realities of the United States, whether these realities are threats to "freedom" such as communism and terrorism or the country's own past history of slavery and genocide.[16]

The Signifier and an Army of One

This stitching, however, is not always able to hold fast for the subject. Realizing that all that creates meaning are these multiple points of stitches, the individual must realize that all that makes oneself meaningful is this impersonal place the subject occupies in discourse. Lacan asks, "Where in the signifier is the person? How does a discourse hang together? Up to what point can a discourse that seems personal bear, on the level of the signifier alone, a sufficient number of traces of impersonalization for the subject not to recognize it as his own?"[17] This is the grammar of the Symbolic, where one participates in discourse, but the cost is becoming a mere interchangeable signifier.

Lacan supports his argument by the use of the linguistic concept of the floating signifier, the mechanism whereby the subject enters into language itself. Jacqueline Rose explains: "The 'I' with which we speak stands for our identity as subjects in language, but it is the least stable entity in language, since its meaning is purely a function of the moment of utterance. The 'I' can shift, and change places, because it only ever refers to whoever happens to be using it at the time."[18] Lacan's subject becomes a mere object in the signifying system because there is always a danger that speech will no longer be personal and that the subject itself will disappear: "The more functional language becomes, the less suited it is to speech, and when it becomes overly characteristic of me alone, it loses its function as language."[19] The subject's price for entry into language, and thus becoming a subject since subjects are formed through language, is becoming an object oneself: "I identify myself in language, but only by losing myself in it like an object."[20] For example, one must repeat the most intimate expressions, "I love you," over and over. The words exist everywhere so we must repeat them to try to make them our own: "The words we use are used by other people, on television, in books, in the media. The words do not belong to us."[21]

The quilting point is a way of explaining how the individual, through the ideology of the Symbolic, finds a way to think of oneself as having a unique place in the world. In his cryptic way, Lacan explains, "When the upholsterer's needle [the quilting point], which has entered at the moment of *God found faithful in all his threats*, reappears, it's all over; the chap says, *I'm going to join the faithful troops*."[22] The basis of the individual's ability to stitch oneself into the larger discourse is through the individual's fear of not having any identity. In other words, it is out of fear that the individual agrees to be part of the ideology.

We see this clearly on the Web site for the U.S. Army. The site uses an individual narrative, which emphasizes a sense of unique individuality. This instills the idea that the subject is not an interchangeable signifier. In the "Army of One" campaign, we encounter the most paradoxical rhetorical strategies, which try to reconcile the individual (and one's place as a replaceable signifier) with the larger order one is constructed in. For example, one of the values of the soldier is the idea of "Selfless Service": "Put the welfare of the Nation, the Army, and your subordinates before your own," while the site tells us that "the strength of the Army lies not only in numbers, but also in the individual Soldier." The site focuses on individual stories of actual soldiers, stressing the uniqueness of every soldier's path: "Tell us about your interests, and we'll show you the Army training that will help you find your strength." Individual stories of soldiers stress how they overcame personal adversity and fear to become what they are today: "I really didn't believe that I could pass the PT (Physical Training) test. I really didn't believe that I could shoot an M16. But once I got into it and believed in myself to do it, it happened."[23]

This stress on the unique individual is in direct opposition to the information provided about "Soldier Life" on the site. In addition to the required haircut, new recruits are made uniform in the rest of their appearance. They are told to bring "one pair of white, calf-length, athletic socks (no color bands, designs, or logos)," and if they wear glasses, to make sure it is not "faddish or stylish eyewear." Each "one" in the "Army of One" is, in some ways, completely interchangeable: "You'll take your place as a vital link in the chain, and become a Soldier, an Army of One." Each is a mere insignificant signifier, just in Lacan's schema, while seemingly individual and unique.

Transferring the Lack: Contemporary Religiopolitical Rhetoric

In this section, I will use Lacan's theories to understand how contemporary rhetoric addresses fundamental aspects of the subject. This rhetoric is so effective because it expresses deep-seated anxieties about the subject's fragmented subjectivity while also assuaging that uncertainty by producing a vision of the subject as whole. The rhetoric plays on our deepest fears about being human and frames those concerns in dualistic terms such as good and evil, civilized and uncivilized, life and death. The self embodies the positive qualities while the negative qualities are projected onto the Other.

The Signifier of Exclusion

One of the ways the binary logic of language and of the subject works is by dividing the subject from the Other. In Lacan's view, good and evil come from an initial experience of a sense of harmony and disharmony. The signifier of exclusion[24] creates a harmonious subject by espousing a narrative in which all evil (disharmony) belongs to the Other. The human condition is one that strives to idealize the ego in an effort to overcome its state of fragmentation. The vision of what is good, harmonious, and whole, that which it sees outside itself, is held on to as the true self, the original self, while the Other contains all the negative attributes of fragmentation and disharmony that threaten the subject's false sense of wholeness.

There are many cultural examples that show how the signifier of exclusion works. Consider the signifiers of man and woman. "Man" has traditionally been considered the complete human. This is evident in androcentric language, where the male is automatically assumed to be the subject. Man can be considered whole because his lack has been transferred onto the female. This is seen in various characterizations of woman as lacking in such things as reason, power, skills, intellect, ability, and/or emotional restraint. The idea of lack is so profound in the entity of woman that Lacan suggests that in the symbolic realm she can simply be defined as one lacking a penis.

Political analyst Yannis Stavrakakis gives several excellent examples of the way a signifier of exclusion makes possible a harmonious social order.[25] The self, in this case the United States, uses a signifier of exclusion to create a sense of wholeness or goodness. Ronald Reagan's description of the Soviet Union as an "evil empire" served to make the United States a "good" empire by transferring any "evil" to Russia. The USSR served as the opposite to the quilting point; it was a site of "pure negativity; what has to be negated and excluded in order for reality to signify its limits."[26] More recently, in his speech before the U.N. on September 18, 2007, George W. Bush referred to North Korea as a "brutal regime." More famous perhaps was Bush's reference to Iraq, Iran, and North Korea as "an axis of evil" in his State of the Union address on January 29, 2002. The vision of society as harmony, as an ideal Other, is dependent on the transfer of lack onto another. This can also be seen in the way "Nature" is presented as a thing of harmony, and yet things within Nature ("vermin," "weeds," "insects") are seen as a threat to Nature and must be eliminated because, paradoxically, they are perceived to threaten the "natural harmony" of nature. Yet, these "threats" are clearly part of nature and its balance.[27]

This impulse is clearly at work in contemporary political rhetoric in the aftermath of the Madrid bombings of 2004, such as President Bush's address of March 19, 2004: "There is no dividing line—there is a dividing line in our world, not between nations, and not between religions or cultures, but a dividing line separating two visions of justice and the value of life."[28] This statement paints an idealistic vision of America. It frames the fight against terror, the global fight between Good and Evil, in dualistic terms that serve to cover up the fragmented state of America and the world, and instill a vision of America as united, strong, and just. Bush has said, "There is no neutral ground—no neutral ground—in the fight between civilization and terror, because there is no neutral ground between good and evil, freedom and slavery, and life and death." This epic battle, so clearly delineated, stresses the absolute nature of the differences between the two forces. It serves to create a harmonious idea of "America" by excluding a scapegoat, whose form is any force thought to threaten the beatific ideal image of America, unto which force one can transfer any lack.

Although there are countless examples of this in the media,[29] I will confine my analysis to two examples that show how the idea of the nation is quilted in such a way that "the Nation" appears ahistorical and whole. The lack does not simply belong to the terrorists; also, in the age of political conservatism, any who question the quilting point, in its veracity or historicity find themselves aligned with the signifier of exclusion:

America is good, civilized, just, tolerant, and right; all words Bush used in his address to Congress on September 20. According to history, however, America is not so squeaky clean. History raises too many uncomfortable questions such as: What is terrorism, and have we in fact been terrorists? [It] means that anyone who raises such questions is "with the terrorists," and therefore is an uncivilized opponent of "progress and pluralism, tolerance and freedom."[30]

The late Susan Sontag related the reactions she received from a short article:

> I addressed the government and media rhetoric that quickly surrounded the event, deploring the self-congratulatory identification of the United States with "the world" and with "humanity" and with "civilization." I said: This is a political event, a response to the status of alliances contracted by the United States, not only a monstrous crime—which it certainly was. I suggested that not every negative adjective applied to the perpetrators of the attack. (Maybe "cowardly," I said, didn't apply.) . . . These rather banal observations won me responses that, in a lifetime of taking public positions, I've never experienced. They included death threats, calls for my being stripped of my citizenship and deported, indignation that I was not "censored."[31]

Just as the individual subject, for example, "man," transfers his lack onto "woman," so does the nation pass along its lack to its enemies. Just as in the imaginary order, where things that are *not* me, establish me, the nation forms itself by expelling what it does not perceive to be itself. Religious, and not just political, rhetoric is used (in the idea of good versus evil, for example) because the vision of the subject/nation is grounded in the order of the Real, where a primordial sense of harmony and unity (much like the garden of Eden) has been felt and lost. The subject or nation perceives that it can return to that original state of goodness, if the forces of evil do not win. Anything seen as threatening this return to wholeness is then not just an agent of fragmentation, but is, essentially, evil because it is seen as preventing the (false) state of unity in the self.

"Us versus Them" or "Consumers versus Terrorists"
In this section I look at one of Slavoj Žižek's arguments using Lacan's theories to deconstruct the popular dualisms that abound in today's world. In an article whose title recalls the blending of the subject and the Symbolic, "Enjoy Your Nation as Yourself!" Žižek writes:

This Nation-Thing is determined by a series of contradictory properties. It appears to us as "our Thing" (perhaps we could say *cosa nostra* [our thing]) as something accessible only to us, as something "they," the other, cannot grasp; nonetheless it is something constantly menaced by "them." It appears as what gives plenitude and vivacity to our life, and yet the only way we can determine it is by resorting to different versions of the same empty tautology. . . . The only consistent answer is [that] the Thing is present in that elusive entity called "our way of life."[32]

The signifier of exclusion, for Žižek, serves as a quilting point that unites several fears that the nation has at once and serves to unite "us" in "our way of life" from the Other. Žižek argues that the figure of the terrorist has been chosen as the current quilting point, unifying all the fears of fragmentation that America has. Earlier in this article, we have seen how people who oppose the idealistic image of "America" are construed as being aligned with anti-Americanism or terrorism. Žižek demonstrates how "terrorism" has now become the quilting point where all perceived threats converge: "Is not the figure of the terrorist Enemy also a condensation of two opposed figures, the reactionary 'fundamentalist' and the Leftist protester? . . . 'Terror' is thus gradually elevated into the hidden universal equivalent of all social evils."[33] The "war on drugs" in America, as Žižek points out, has also been subsumed into the War on Terror. The antidrug campaign of 2002 makes clear this equation: "'When you buy drugs, you provide money for the terrorists!'—'terror' is thus gradually elevated into the hidden universal equivalent of all social evils."[34]

Žižek's deconstruction of the "Us" versus "Them," or what is commonly called "the clash of civilizations," is useful for seeing how Lacan's theories can help us examine political rhetoric. Hence, Žižek argues that we fear the Other because he "wants to steal our enjoyment (by ruining our way of life)."[35] Simplistically, this enemy is felt as a threat to our "freedom" because of equating America with freedom. The actual reality of the American way of life is much more complicated. Progressive Muslim Farid Esack details the larger context of the terrorist attacks of 9/11 that disappeared from the discourse: "It sadly appeared as if issues of globalization, the rise of the new empire and corporate power, the unbridled exploitation of the earth's limited resources, global warming, consumerism and its twin sister poverty, as well as HIV/AIDS, belonged to another planet. Flushed away were all memories of the cooperative relationship between the Taliban and the U.S. administration and oil industry nexus."[36] The idea of the American "way of life" is so deeply quilted to such signifiers as democracy and freedom that the American "way of life" does not signify the actual realities of living an American life.

Instead of dealing with the realities, the self or nation perceives a threat from the outside force in a superficial way: the self or nation thinks that the enemy cannot grasp "our" ways. This gap between "Us" and "Them" is evident in Žižek's analysis of the "surprise of the average American," who asks, "How is it possible that these people display and practice such a disregard for their own lives?" Žižek counters this logic by asking, "Is not the obverse of this surprise the rather sad fact that we, in First World countries, find it more and more difficult even to imagine a public or universal Cause for which we would be ready to sacrifice our lives?"[37]

Žižek questions the very divide that separates "Us" versus "Them." Is it really a fight between the uncomplicated dualisms of good and evil, civilized and uncivilized? He argues that the split between first and third worlds "runs more and more along the lines of the opposition between leading a long and satisfying life full of material and cultural wealth, and dedicating one's life to some transcendent Cause."[38] Instead of looking at the easy divisions of "Us" versus "Them," Žižek suggests that the forces of global capitalism, economics, and geopolitics are factors in what has simply been reduced to a "clash of civilizations." By analyzing the practices and history of the United States,[39] as well as the motivation and nature of terrorism, Žižek questions the simple divide where the self is good and the signifier of exclusion is pure evil.

Conclusion

Lacan's work is highly useful for understanding the facile dichotomies that surround much of the religiopolitical debates of our times. His theories demonstrate not just why we construct an ideal Other and a signifier of exclusion; they also show why we cling to these dualistic models of harmony and disharmony. The quilting point helps us examine why certain words are invested with particular meanings, and because we can see that those stitches can be loosened and indeed broken, we can also step back and examine how one is quilted into a particular ideology. All signifiers, whether it is "America" or "terrorist," are culturally and historically bound and thus ultimately mutable.

Notes

1 See Kevin Baker, "Stabbed in the Back: The Past and Future of a Right-Wing Myth," *Harper's Magazine*, June 2006, 31–42.

2 Dana Milbank, "For the Foes of Same-Sex Marriage, It's the Thought That Counts," *Washington Post*, June 7, 2006, A02.

3 See http://mediamatters.org/items/200508100005 (accessed November 24, 2007).

4 The reader may consult Darian Leader and Judy Groves, *Introducing Lacan* (Cambridge, UK: Icon Books, 1995), for a brief introduction to the life and work of Lacan. For a more detailed, historical sketch of Lacan's life, see Elisabeth Roudinesco and Jeffrey Mehlman's *Lacan and Co.: A History of Psychoanalysis in France, 1925–1985* (Chicago: University of Chicago Press, 1990), as well as Roudinesco's biography on Lacan simply titled *Jacques Lacan* (New York: Columbia University Press, 1997).

5 Tim Dean, *Beyond Sexuality* (Chicago: University of Chicago Press, 2000), 1.

6 Kaja Silverman, *The Subject of Semiotics* (New York: Oxford University Press, 1983), 155.

7 Jacques Lacan, *Écrits: A Selection*, trans. Bruce Fink (New York: W. W. Norton, 2004), 143.

8 Juliet Flower MacCannell, *Figuring Lacan: Criticism and the Cultural Unconscious* (Lincoln: University of Nebraska Press, 1986), 51 (italics in original).

9 Leo Bersani and Ulysse Dutoit, *The Arts of Impoverishment* (Boston: Harvard University Press, 1993), 156.

10 Lacan, *Écrits: A Selection*, 6.

11 Jacques Lacan, *The Four Fundamental Concepts*, trans. Alan Sheridan (New York: W. W. Norton, 1998), 199.

12 Slavoj Žižek explains how the quilting point is what ties the subject into a particular relation to ideology. See *The Sublime Object of Ideology* (New York: Verso, 1989). Žižek argues that identity is sustained by the quilting point, which stabilizes the signifier and signified, thus fixing their meaning (87).

13 The psychotic individual is unable to create meaning between a given signifier and what is being signified; for the psychotic person, the two "present themselves in a completely divided form" (Jacques Lacan, *The Psychoses*, trans. Russell Grigg [New York: W. W. Norton, 1997], 268).

14 Yannis Stavrakakis, *Lacan and the Political* (New York: Routledge, 1999), 60.

15 See ibid., 78.

16 These quilting points are so powerful that they make it quite impossible to think outside of them. As Žižek writes, "We lack the very language to articulate our 'unfreedom.' . . . 'War on terrorism,' 'democracy and freedom,' 'human rights,' and so on—are false terms, mystifying our perception of the situation instead of allowing us to think it" (*Welcome to the Desert of the Real: Five Essays on September 11 and Related Dates* [New York: Verso, 2002], 2).

17 Lacan, *The Psychoses*, 269.

18 Rose, "Introduction—II," in *Feminine Sexuality: Jacques Lacan and the école freudienne*, ed. Juliet Mitchell and Jacqueline Rose (New York: W. W. Norton, 1982), 31.

19 Lacan, *Écrits: A Selection*, 84.

20 Ibid.

21 Leader and Groves, *Introducing Lacan*, 127.

22 Lacan, *The Psychoses*, 268.

23 SSG Lee Priest at http://www.goarmy.com/paths/508_path_1.jsp (accessed November 24, 2007).

24 The term "signifier of exclusion" is from Stavrakakis, *Lacan and the Political*, 33.

25 See ibid., 65–80.

26 Ibid., 81.

27 Stavrakakis relates how in 1907 alone the Roosevelt administration destroyed 1,700 wolves and 23,000 coyotes in an attempt to make "Nature" balanced and harmonious (ibid., 63–64).

28 George W. Bush, March 19, 2004, in the East Room of the White House.

29 This "Either you are with us or you are against us" attitude was also apparent in an editorial by Lance Morrow in *Time* magazine. Morrow presented a dichotomy of world systems, where the enemy, not surprisingly, was presented as an insect needing extermination: "Anyone who does not loathe the people who did these things, and the people who cheer them on, is too philosophical for decent company. . . . [We need to] exterminate men like Osama bin Laden. . . . The worst times, as we see, separate the civilized . . . from the uncivilized. . . . Let the civilized toughen up, and let the uncivilized take their chances in the game they started." See April Eisman's "The Media of Manipulation: Patriotism and Propaganda—Mainstream News in the United States in the Weeks Following September 11," *Critical Quarterly* 45, nos. 1–2 (2003): 55–72, quote on 60.

30 Ibid., 64. Cf. http://ics.leeds.ac.uk/papers/pmt/exhibits/1760/Eisman2.pdf.

31 See http://www.soros.org/resources/articles_publications/publications/osn _aftertheattacks_20020101/aftertheattacks.pdf.

32 Žižek, "Enjoy Your Nation as Yourself!" in *Theories of Race and Racism: A Reader*, eds. Les Back and John Solomos (New York: Routledge, 2000), 594–606, quote on 595.

33 Žižek, *Desert of the Real*, 111.

34 Ibid.

35 "Enjoy Your Nation as Yourself!" 596.

36 Farid Esack, "In Search of Progressive Islam Beyond 9/11," in *Progressive Muslims: On Justice, Gender and Pluralism*, ed. Omid Safi (Oxford: Oneworld, 2003), 78–97, quote on 83–84.

37 Žižek, *Desert of the Real*, 40.

38 Ibid.

39 Not only does Žižek bring up the well-known connections between the United States and Osama bin Laden, but he also questions U.S. policy when he notes that the lip service paid to ideals such as "democracy" and "freedom" are questionable when one sees the support the U.S. gives to conservative Arab regimes such as Saudi Arabia: "They stand for the point at which the U.S.A. is forced explicitly to acknowledge the primacy of economy over democracy" (*Desert of the Real*, 42–43).

12

Let Freedom Free
Politics and Religion at the Heart of a Muddled Concept

Mary-Jane Rubenstein

Freedom under Fire

Of the varied political slogans one sees on T-shirts, billboards, and bumper stickers these days, of the sundry platitudes crooned over the country music airwaves, perhaps none is more puzzling than "Freedom isn't free."[1] This strange, self-sabotaging declaration has rather hazy origins, but it dates back at least to the United States' entrance into the Second World War, when the government asked civilians to support the effort through the "personal sacrifice" of buying war bonds.[2] At this particular historical juncture, however, it is not entirely clear what the locution means. Six-plus years into the long War on Terror(ism), the American public spends its money more or less the way it did seven years ago, having been entreated, infamously, to have faith in the economy and go shopping in response to September 11. President Bush even assured ordinary Americans that they would not have to make any monetary sacrifices "whatsoever," and one month after the attacks, he proved it by granting a sizeable tax cut to the wealthiest segment of the population.[3]

To be sure, President Bush makes regular reference to the personal sacrifices that military families and personnel have made and continue to make "for liberty."[4] These, however, are sacrifices from which the general population has been carefully shielded: Americans are neither advised to reduce their level of material comfort to provide adequate protection for soldiers, nor are they permitted to see the flag-draped coffins flown home in the middle of the night. Nor has there been a surge of enrollment in the military or the Red Cross; to the contrary, as one soldier has recently said of his fellow Americans, "We're nowhere near to sharing the sacrifice. . . . And it's only in that sharing that our society will truly care about what's going on over there."[5] On the surface, then, the civilians of the United States are being led to believe that, for civilians at least, freedom *is*, in the crudest sense of the word, "free"; that all we need to do to support the war effort is to go about our usual consumerist business. After all, the Global War on Terrorism is being waged in the uncontestable name of "freedom." Surely there could be no better aid to the cause of freedom than to exercise it. And so buying a flat-screen television amounts to making a sacrifice for the freedom America is defending.

What, however, does freedom *mean*? This question was taken up in force by seventeenth- and eighteenth-century European philosophers from all persuasions (Hobbes, Locke, Rousseau, Kant, Hegel, Schelling, Tocqueville),[6] who did not exactly come to a consensus on the matter. In fact, as Isaiah Berlin has famously demonstrated, the height of freedom in the eyes of some often coincides with the height of unfreedom in the eyes of others; for example, John Stewart Mill and Benjamin Constant railed against the purported freedom of Rousseau's "general will," arguing that "the sovereignty of the people could easily destroy that of individuals."[7] More recently, cognitive scientist George Lakoff has argued that there are two fundamentally incompatible notions of freedom competing for control of the contemporary American political landscape: a "progressive" model based on interdependence, and an emerging "conservative" model based on independence.[8] So the meaning of freedom as invoked in any given song, slogan, or speech is far from self-evident, and yet this does not often prompt President Bush, for one, to define his terms. Indeed, one gets the faint impression that freedom's conceptual murkiness is part of the reason he tends to invoke it so readily and so tirelessly.[9]

From the first sentence of his evening address on September 11, and with very little explanation, President Bush described the events of that morning as an assault on freedom: "Good evening. Today, our fellow citizens, our way of life, our very freedom came under attack in a series of deliberate and deadly terrorist attacks."[10] Now clearly, our fellow citizens had come under attack. But the leap from "our fellow citizens," through the indeterminate middle ground of "our way of life," to "our very freedom" goes unexplained in this speech. How exactly is it that "freedom came under attack" when planes flew into the World Trade Center and the Pentagon? The only clarification offered in this particular address is that "America was targeted for attack because we're the brightest beacon for freedom and opportunity in the world."[11] What one is left to deduce is that freedom here stands metonymically for the nation itself: America was attacked, and America *is* freedom, so freedom is under attack. One can assume from this point on that, insofar as "America" and "freedom" have been established from the outset as functionally coextensive, any response to the events of September 11 on the part of the United States will be phrased as an expression of freedom itself.

This explains how, with very little clarification, the President has been able to refer to the invasions of Afghanistan and Iraq as efforts both to defend and to spread liberty.[12] Granted, the American military is waging this war, but only as an instrument of freedom itself. Conversely, the true adversary is not the leaders, armies, or citizens of any particular nation, but the terror that instrumentalizes them. "Freedom and fear are at war," Bush told the nation in the same speech that accused the terrorists of "hating freedom."[13] Consolidating the opposition between freedom and terror, Bush has assured the public that "this will not be an age of terror; this will be an age of liberty." "The terrorists will not stop the march of freedom." "Hope and liberty" are "the great alternatives to terror."[14] By means of a few rhetorical sleights of hand, then, a terrorist attack on New York and Washington comes to launch and justify a cosmic battle between the forces of freedom and the forces of terror, with the former providing a convenient cover for any action on the part of the United States military.

So, is President Bush's idea of freedom merely an empty signifier? This is certainly a tempting conclusion: the President's constant conflation and unclarified repetition of the words "freedom" and "liberty" could well lead one to believe they are nothing more than conceptual Trojan horses, ready to be filled with all manner of ideological foot soldiers. In this essay, however, I hope to demonstrate that "freedom" not only has a specific meaning for Bush; it has *two* meanings. Piecing together the scattered characteristics of "freedom" in Bush's public addresses, one witnesses the emergence of two incompatible meanings, intertwined with one another.[15] On the one hand, the President's notion of "freedom" is fully reducible to particular political criteria. On the other hand, however, this freedom exceeds all criteria, to such an extent that it is lifted out of the category of the political entirely, and into the category of the religious. There is, in other words, a contradiction within Bush's understanding of freedom, which performs a simultaneous assertion and effacement of the political. Although this slipperiness has been deployed to justify recent American foreign policy—whitewashing political and economic aims in "religion," "faith," or "the design of nature"—I maintain that if Bush's own double logic is fully fleshed out, it gives way, surprisingly, to a notion of freedom that fundamentally undermines the self-assertion of the American Empire.

Conditioning Freedom

As unevenly sketched throughout George Bush's public speeches, freedom on one hand is measured by certain conditions. These include "the rule of law, limits on the power of the state, respect for women, private property, equal justice, religious tolerance,"[16] access to global markets,[17] freedom of speech, political pluralism, labor unions, independent media, privatized economies, and above all, popular sovereignty ensured by a representative government.[18] Presumably, American citizens of even the most diverse political persuasions would count most of these as instances of freedom. What signals Bush's own political bent, however, is that for Bush each of these criteria relies upon the singular integrity of the autonomous individual. This is evident above all in the tautological linchpin of Bush's second inaugural address: "Self-government relies, in the end, on the government of the self."[19]

By hinging freedom on the individual and one's unimpeded pursuits, Bush is able to set forth the "ownership society" as the model of fully realized liberty. Under this system, all social ills from poverty to shift-lessness will be solved by each person's active participation in the market. Once everybody has a mortgage and everybody is an entrepreneur, each citizen will achieve "economic independence," and the rest will take care of itself.[20] Once in a rare while, Bush gives a nod to interpersonal relationships, saying for example that "our nation relies on men and women who look after a neighbor and surround the lost with love."[21] But looking after *a* neighbor hardly addresses the systematic economic injustices of the "ownership society," and loving the lost cannot stand in for the social services that have been cut for the sake of tax breaks and low interest rates (not to mention the War on Terror).[22] Understood in this manner, freedom places upon individual subjects the sole responsibility for hauling themselves into the "free-market society," while eroding the infrastructural supports upon which they might rely in order to get there. One begins to wonder just how free freedom is.

This concern becomes intensified by the realization that each of Bush's criteria of freedom—from women's rights to the right of dissent to the rule of law—corresponds to a specific civil liberty or democratic process that the past five years have seen severely eroded. As George Lakoff asks,

> How . . . can Bush mean anything at all by "freedom" when he imprisons hundreds of people in Guantánamo indefinitely with no due process in the name of freedom; when he sanctions torture in the name of freedom; when he starts a preemptive war on false premises and retroactively claims it is being waged in the name of freedom; when he causes the deaths of tens of thousands of innocent Iraqi civilians in the name of freedom; when he supports oppressive regimes in Saudi Arabia, Egypt, and Pakistan, while claiming to promote freedom in the Islamic world; when he sanctions the disenfranchisement of African-American voters in Florida and Ohio in the name of freedom; when he orders spying on American citizens in America without a warrant in the name of freedom; when, in the name of freedom, he seeks to prevent women from making their own medical decisions, to stop loving couples who want to marry, to stop families from being able to remove life supports when their loved ones are all but technically dead?[23]

If one adds to this list the suspension of habeas corpus for terror suspects, the widespread intimidation of members of the press, and the threats leveled against scholars and teachers who criticize American foreign policy,[24] it becomes a challenge even to separate the terms of the battle between freedom and fear. Viewed from this angle, Bush's conditional construal of freedom again undermines itself, this time with the cause of freedom becoming indistinguishable from the "tactics of terror" so carefully opposed to freedom.

But there is a third way that freedom collapses when understood as a set of enforceable standards: freedom's simple reduction to a set of enforceable standards. As Bush made clear in his second inaugural address, if a nation's economy, government, and culture behave in a particular set of ways, then America stamps it "free"; if not, then the nation remains "enslaved," "oppressed," "tyrannized." What's more, there are rewards and punishments that attend the fulfillment or neglect of freedom's criteria: "When you stand for liberty," Bush told the "unfree" world in early 2005, "we will stand with you. . . . Start the journey of progress and justice, and America will walk at your side."[25] The reward for meeting the conditions of freedom is America's friendship,[26] but this comes with a further set of conditions: "Iraq will be a free nation, and a strong ally in the war on terror."[27] If a nation chooses not to meet America's conditions, then it will quite literally be "forced to be free."[28] Freedom, in other words, is the punishment for its own refusal. Whether chosen or imposed, however, Bush insists that freedom will prevail: "As the twentieth century ended, there were around 120 democracies around the world—and I can assure you, more are on the way."[29]

As we have seen, conditional freedom inscribes individuality while effacing the very "freedoms" upon which "individuals" rely. More fundamentally, however, one might want to ask: If freedom can be reduced to any conditions, any political laundry list at all—if it can be rewarded, punished, and inflicted by military force—can it be said to be freedom? It could be argued that the notion of an imposable freedom not only can but *did* perform an auto-deconstruction the moment "Operation Iraqi Freedom" was launched by means of "shock and awe," a tactic meant to terrify the enemy into early submission.[30] Long after the abject failure of this maneuver, the sentiment behind shock and awe still found its way into a speech commemorating the fifth anniversary of September 11. "One of the strongest weapons in our arsenal is the power of freedom," the President told the nation. "The terrorists *fear* freedom as much as they do our firepower. They are thrown into *panic* at the sight of an old man pulling the election lever, girls enrolling in schools, or families worshiping God in their own tradition."[31] Overlooking for a moment the ridiculous imagery of these scenarios, the point is clear: far from being "at war" with fear, freedom operates *by means of fear*; far from providing an "alternative to terror," freedom instills "panic" among its enemies.[32] *Fear* is at war with fear in the Middle East. So much for the conceptual integrity of conditional freedom.

Unconditioning Freedom

There is, however, another understanding of freedom that can be distilled from Bush's public addresses, one that purports to exceed not only the political expectations of a given nation, but also nationhood and even the political itself. This is the "freedom" Bush usually invokes in the *second* half of his speeches on the matter, when he refers to the inexorable "direction of history," the "permanent hope of humanity,"[33] the order of nature, and/or the design of a benevolent God.[34] According to this line of thinking, freedom cannot be measured against any particular instance of freedom because, as universal, it can take an infinite number of forms: "Representative governments in the Middle East will reflect their own cultures," Bush told the National Endowment for Democracy (NED) in 2003. "They will not, and should not, look like us."[35] In this address, Bush explicitly unbinds freedom from the specifications to which he had tied it moments earlier (women's rights, political pluralism, capitalist participation), chastising those who might measure and reward a nation's freedom "as if freedom were a prize you win for meeting our own Western standards of progress."[36]

Perhaps in an attempt to seem cosmopolitan, Bush has even gone so far as to *dissociate* "freedom" from "America," proclaiming in May of 2004 to the United States Army War College, "I sent American troops to Iraq to make its people free, not to make them American."[37] Likewise, Bush said in Brussels that "this strategy is not American strategy, or European strategy, or Western strategy. Spreading liberty for the sake of peace is the cause of all mankind."[38] And just in case "mankind" isn't sufficiently transcendent, there is always one more rung up the ontological ladder: two weeks before declaring war on Iraq, Bush told the Associated Press (AP), "Liberty is not America's gift to the world; it is *God's* gift to each and every person."[39]

Once freedom is thus established as unconditional, universal, unlimited, and irresistible, the work of "spreading liberty" can be announced not as a political agenda, but rather as a service to humanity, inscribed within the very order of nature and history. Furthermore, in Bush's worldview, this service is underwritten by a divine command, or a *call*: "The advance of freedom is the *calling* of our time; it is the *calling* of our country," he proclaims, a call whose proper response is nothing less than a creed: "*We believe* that liberty is the design of nature; *we believe* that liberty is the direction of history. *We believe* that human fulfillment and excellence come in the responsible exercise of liberty. And *we believe* that freedom—the freedom we prize—is not for us alone; it is the right and the capacity of all mankind."[40] At this point, freedom is not a matter of economic policies or civil rights; it is a matter of *belief.* And so the logic of unconditional freedom soars above the boundaries of nations and politics, through the category of the universal, and into the realm of . . . Protestantism.

The President would surely make the ecumenical gesture of extending freedom's realm to "religion" itself, at least the kind of religion that can be safely identified as *faith* in *one* God. And as it turns out, the category of the religious undergoes careful purification during the course of these addresses, as if in preparation for its eventual reception of the concept of freedom. Ever since his address to the nation on September 20, 2001, Bush has tried to dissociate the "religion" of Islam from "Islamic extremism," a purportedly *political* program that "perverts the peaceful teachings of Islam." To Muslims in that September speech, the President said, "We respect your faith. It's practiced freely by many millions of Americans, and by millions more in countries that America counts as friends. Its teachings are good and peaceful, and those who commit evil in the name of Allah blaspheme the name of Allah. [Applause.] The terrorists are traitors to their own faith, trying, in effect, to hijack Islam itself. The enemy of America is not our many Muslim friends; it is not our many Arab friends. Our enemy is a radical network of terrorists, and every government that supports them. [Applause.]"[41] The enemy thus is terror; the enemy is politics; the enemy is *not* religion.

Bush told the NED in 2003, "Islam—the *faith* of one-fifth of humanity—is consistent with democratic rule." Explaining this compatibility, Bush went on to make Islam look like a hypothetical page out of Martin Luther's biography, sitting on Max Weber's desk: "[Muslims] succeed in democratic societies, not in spite of their faith, but because of it. A religion that demands individual moral accountability, and encourages the encounter of the individual with God, is fully compatible with the rights and responsibilities of self-government."[42] "Religion," in other words, is never to blame, insofar as it consolidates the autonomous subject that performs with and for the market.

By holding up independence and individualism as the marks of genuine "faith," Bush is able, first of all, to hide economic motivations behind a religious veil. One might cite here Bush's subtle announcement to the NED that "successful societies guarantee religious liberty—the rights to serve and honor God without fear of persecution. Successful societies privatize their economies and secure the rights of property"[43]—as if one followed necessarily from the other. Second, by attributing all the fruits of *freedom*— from peace to privatization—to religion, Bush is able to load all the mechanisms of *terror* onto politics. Thus, in elucidating the designs of the architects of "theocratic terror," Bush explains, "Behind their language of religion is the ambition for absolute political power." Again, religion is blameless, as it is among all nations that remain unfree: "These are not the failures of a culture or a religion. These are the failures of political and economic doctrines."[44] During the course of a typical speech, then, Bush—or his writer—gradually moves freedom from the conditional to the unconditional, while simultaneously clearing "religion" as a signifier. By the end of the address, freedom leaps into the purified category of the religious, at which point freedom is asserted as the incontrovertible will of everybody's God: "The author of freedom," Bush concludes, "is not indifferent to the fate of freedom."[45]

The upshot of this transformation is that the initial adversarial couple, freedom/liberty/democracy versus terror/oppression/fear, now also maps on to the distinction between ethereal, incorruptible religion on one hand, and base, dirty politics on the other. They have politics; we transcend politics. They hijack religion; we are religion. This is the framework that supports the distinction Bush makes in his second Inaugural Address between "oppression, which is *always* wrong" and "freedom, which is *eternally* right."[46] It's a long way from always to eternity, and once eternity is on our side, God cannot be far behind: "Freedom and fear, justice and cruelty, have always been at war, and we know that God is not neutral between them."[47]

Freeing Freedom

On the one hand, then, Bush's understanding of freedom is exchangeable with a set of political, economic, and cultural expectations that can ostensibly be imposed upon nations that do not meet them. On the other hand, Bush insists that freedom exceeds all concrete political, economic, and cultural factors, so that neither America nor the West has any particular claim to it. Freedom is actually in *such* excess of these determinations that its proper domain is that of "faith," "religion," and the "Author of Liberty."[48] As we have seen, freedom conditionally understood collapses in one manner or another into the "fear" to which it is ostensibly opposed.

Conversely, freedom understood unconditionally, even transcendently, exceeds all efforts to circumscribe it either politically or conceptually. Bush surely wants to hold both of these configurations together at once. He wants freedom to be particular and universal—imposable and transcendent—at the same time. This is evident in a 2002 address to the ROTC, in which the President enumerated specific attributes of freedom, from the rule of law to private property, and then said, "No nation owns these principles. No nation is exempt from them."[49] In other words, freedom can be articulated as a specific set of political expectations that nevertheless applies to everyone, at all times and in all places. This is the reason Bush can send the ROTC to join the violent scene in Afghanistan with a charge to "advance the cause of freedom around the world."[50]

At this point, one might be tempted to say that Bush cannot have it both ways. It cannot be the case that freedom transcends the limits of America, the West, politics, and economics, *and* that the American government can determine and impose freedom. Either freedom exceeds the control of human institutions or it does not. Either freedom is, at the end of the day, merely a political projection, subject to threats and conditions and enforced by smart bombs and Humvees; or freedom genuinely transcends the whole politico-econo-military complex of nationhood—in which case freedom would necessarily slip through the fingers of any given nation, coalition, or president, and ultimately throw into question *any* supposed instances of freedom. It is a stark option: Either there is nothing we can truly know about freedom, or freedom is just politics in a fancy dinner jacket.

Or perhaps there is a third possibility. Perhaps Mr. Bush's contradictory inscription of the term "freedom" actually reflects a tension inherent in freedom itself. Arguably, a truly free freedom would indeed transcend all interests and boundaries of nation, personality, or culture. And doubtless, there are certain conditions under which the emergence of this excess is either helped or hindered—conditions more or less favorable to the freeing of freedom. These might well include freedom of speech, free exercise, civil rights for women and minorities, and any number of other familiar "freedoms." Yet freedom also exceeds these particular instances and conditions. Recognizing this excess would mean constantly expanding and reimagining the context, number, and extent of the conditional freedoms that fall short of the very freedom they instantiate. There are always more freedoms to extend; more people to be counted as fully human; more communities to be respected rather than being demonized.

But expanding freedom's scope in this manner is never an innocent endeavor, precisely because "freedom-itself" cannot appear independently of conditional, highly imperfect freedoms. On one hand, then, particular freedoms must undergo constant revision in conversation with unconditional freedom. And on the other hand, "the cause of freedom" as articulated by any particular text, nation, or charismatic figure is never pure, never disinterested; and perhaps most important, never a direct expression of some unmediated divine will.

Surprisingly, then, we can distill from George Bush's recent political speeches two strands of "freedom" that are, as Derrida would say, not reducible to one another, yet cannot be dissociated from one another. Neither wins out over the other, and neither can exist without the other. The concept is, in other words, *inherently* ambivalent. Such ambivalence makes of "freedom" a ceaselessly autocritical dynamic: it only *is* itself insofar as it evaluates and revises itself. Taken seriously, then, freedom could only unsettle the international agenda Bush calls upon it to support. To admit that freedom exceeds the contours any nation assigns to it means admitting that no nation can have sufficient mastery over it to impose it upon others; as we have seen, this effort has actually resulted in collapsing "freedom" into the "terror" to which it has been rhetorically and militarily opposed. At the same time, freedom's reliance upon particular political conditions of freedom undermines all pretense to divine sanction for one nation's military initiatives, however lofty its stated aims.

Even more fundamentally, freedom understood as a constant conversation between the conditional and the unconditional would shatter the confines of the autonomous subject that conditional freedoms purport to secure: the autonomous individual who pursues one's own economic interests and occasionally "looks out for a neighbor." If freedom *truly* belongs to no one, takes an infinite number of forms, and is constantly reshaped by the conditions it in turn reshapes, then freedom cannot support the consolidation of any simple "self-governing self" or, for that matter, any other-governing nation. Rather, a truly free freedom would surprise and reform the very conditions under which it emerges, unsettling all pretensions to autonomy while freeing unforeseen possibilities of intercultural and interpersonal alliance. Or, taking a realistic view, it is always possible that "freedom" just marks a set of political and economic expectations, policed by the nation with the biggest arsenal and purchased at the expense of civil liberties, the social support structure,

and countless military and civilian lives. But then we might as well admit
what should be self-evident: if freedom is not free, it is not freedom.

Notes

1 For their comments on earlier drafts of this chapter, I thank my colleagues in the
Religious Studies Working Group at Wesleyan University (2006–7), especially
Karen Anderson, Jacob Dorman, Jodi Eichler-Levine, Elizabeth McAlister, and Sara
Ritchey. All remaining shortcomings are products of my own myopia—or
stubbornness.

2 See, for example, "Display Ad 29: 'If You Can't Fight on One, Invest in One! Buy
War Bonds," *New York Times*, April 15, 1943. The text of the advertisement begins,
"Freedom isn't free. We must fight for it," and ends, "Compared with the contri-
bution made by the armed forces, sacrifices on the Home Front are of little moment.
If a sacrifice is necessary, the government asks that you make it. Buy War Bonds
now!"

3 See Frank Rich, "Whatever Happened to the America of 9/12?" *New York Times*,
September 10, 2006, http://www.cslproductions.com/scrapbook/NYTimes-
Frank_Rich-whatever-happened-to-9-12/; George W. Bush, "Statement by the
President in His Address to the Nation," September 11, 2001, http://www.
whitehouse.gov/news/releases/2001/09/print/20010911-16.html; and idem, "Address to a Joint Session of Congress and the American People," September 20, 2001,
http://www.whitehouse.gov/news/releases/2001/09/print/20010920-9.html. Later
references to this and other public addresses will include the title of the address and
the date of delivery rather than the date of publication; e.g. Bush, "Address to the
Nation," September 11, 2001.

4 See George W. Bush, "Advancing the Cause of Freedom: Progress Is Measured Day
by Day," address to the George C. Marshall ROTC Award Seminar, Virginia Military Institute, Lexington, Virginia, April 17, 2002, *Vital Speeches of the Day* 67, no.
14 (May 1, 2002): 419; and idem, "Freedom in Iraq and Middle East: Some History
of Democracy," address to the Twentieth Anniversary of the National Endowment
of Democracy, Washington, DC, November 6, 2003, *Vital Speeches of the Day* 70,
no. 4 (December 1, 2003): 99.

5 Sgt. Mike Krause, quoted in Bob Herbert, "Sacrifice of the Few," *New York Times*,
October 12, 2006.

6 See Thomas Hobbes, *Leviathan*, ed. J. C. A. Gaskin (Oxford: Oxford University
Press, 1998), esp. 86–95; John Locke, *Second Treatise of Government*, ed. C. B.
Macpherson (Indianapolis: Hackett, 1980); Jean-Jacques Rousseau, *On the Social
Contract*, in *The Basic Political Writings*, trans. Donald A. Cress (Indianapolis:
Hackett, 1987), 141–227; Immanuel Kant, *Critique of Practical Reason*, trans.
Werner S. Pluhar (Indianapolis: Hackett, 2002), esp. 77–87; F. W. J. Schelling,
Philosophical Inquiries into the Nature of Human Freedom, trans. James Guttmann
(La Salle, IL: Open Court, 1989); G. W. F. Hegel, *Introduction to the Philosophy of
History*, trans. Leo Rauch (Indianapolis: Hackett, 1988), 19–56. Alexis de Toc-

queville, *Democracy in America*, trans. Gerald E. Bevan (New York: Penguin, 2003), esp. 290–305, 593–595.

7   Isaiah Berlin, "Two Concepts of Liberty," in *Liberty: Incorporating "Four Essays on Liberty,"* ed. Henry Hardy (Oxford: Oxford University Press, 2002), 208. See Rousseau, *Social Contract*, 148–50.

8   Lakoff, who argues that the "progressive" understanding of freedom is the "traditional" one, opens his book by suggesting that "freedom defines what America is— and it is now up for grabs." George Lakoff, *Whose Freedom? The Battle over America's Most Important Idea* (New York: Farrar, Straus & Giroux, 2006), 5. Cf. Eric Foner's similar schematic in *The Story of American Freedom* (New York: W. W. Norton, 1999).

9   As Lakoff (*Whose Freedom?* 9) points out, Bush used the words "freedom" and "liberty"—which are interchangeable for him, as for many political theorists—a total of *forty-nine times* in his twenty-minute inaugural address in 2005. See Bush, "Second Inaugural Address," January 20, 2005, http://www.whitehouse.gov/news/releases/2005/01/print/20050120-1.html.

10 Bush, "Address to the Nation," September 11, 2001.

11 Ibid.

12 In his declaration of war against Iraq, President Bush declared, "We will defend our freedom. We will bring freedom to others. And we will prevail"; Associated Press, "Bush Declares War," CNN, March 19, 2003, http://www.cnn.com/2003/US/03/19/sprj.irq.int.bush.transcript.

13 Bush, "Address to a Joint Session," September 20, 2001.

14 Ibid.; Bush, "Working Together: Every Person Has the Right and Capacity to Live in Freedom," address delivered at Concert Noble, Brussels, Belgium, February 21, 2005; in *Vital Speeches of the Day* 71, no. 10 (March 1, 2005): 293.

15 In thematizing this sort of ambivalence, I am entirely indebted to Jacques Derrida, whose "conceptual genealogies" locate an irreducible tension between conditional and unconditional valences of terms that often go uninterrogated in contemporary parlance, such as "gift," "forgiveness," "friendship," "hospitality." For a brief introduction to this phase of Derrida's work, see Simon Critchley and Richard Kearney et al., "Preface," in Jacques Derrida, *On Cosmopolitanism and Forgiveness* (New York: Routledge, 2001), vii–xii.

16 Bush, "Advancing the Cause of Freedom," April 17, 2002, 420.

17 Bush, "The Right to Live in Freedom: Working Together," address to the Leon H. Sullivan Summit, Abuja, Nigeria, July 21, 2003, *Vital Speeches of the Day* 69, no. 20 (August 1, 2003): 611.

18 Bush, "Freedom in Iraq and Middle East," November 6, 2003, 100–101.

19 Bush, "Second Inaugural Address," January 20, 2005.

20 Ibid. See also Lakoff, *Whose Freedom?* 154.

21 Bush, "Second Inaugural Address," January 20, 2005.

22 See Jason Furman, "Treasury Dynamic Scoring Analysis Refutes Claims by Supporters of the Tax Cuts," Center on Budget and Policy Priorities, July 27, 2006 (revised August 43, 2006), http://www.cbpp.org/7-27-06tax.htm. The Treasury study to which this report refers is titled "A Dynamic Analysis of Permanent

Extension of the President's Tax Relief," Office of Tax Analysis, United States Department of the Treasury, July 25, 2006, http://www.treasury.gov/press/releases/reports/treasurydynamicanalysisreporjjuly252006.pdf. See also "Tax Cuts: Myths and Realities," Center on Budget and Policy Priorities, September 27, 2006, http://www.cbpp.org/9-27-06tax.htm#m2.

23 Lakoff, *Whose Freedom?* 6–7.

24 On the issue of the administration's manipulation of the press and seizure of suspected terrorists among them, see David Barstow and Robin Stein, "The Message Machine: How the Government Makes News; Under Bush, A New Age of Prepackaged News," *New York Times*, March 13, 2005, http://query.nytimes.com/gst/fullpage.html?res=9A03E5DD153CF930A25750C0A9639C8B63; and Tom Curley, letter to the editor, *New York Times*, September 20, 2006, http://www.nytimes.com/2006/09/22/opinion/l22ap.html. For an introduction to the accusations launched against college and university professors by the American Council of Trustees and Alumni (chaired by Lynne Cheney) and their associates, see Jerry L. Martin and Anne D. Neil, "Defending Civilization: How Our Universities Are Failing America and What Can Be Done about It," American Council of Trustees and Alumni, February 2002, http://www.goacta.org/publications/Reports/defciv.pdf. For differing views on this controversy, see David Horowitz, *The Professors: The 101 Most Dangerous Academics in America* (Washington, DC: Regnery Publishing, 2006); and Michael Bérubé, *What's Liberal about the Liberal Arts? Classroom Politics and "Bias" in Higher Education* (New York: W. W. Norton, 2006).

25 Bush, "Second Inaugural Address," January 20, 2005.

26 On the paradox of conditional friendship, see Jacques Derrida, *The Politics of Friendship* (New York: Verso, 2006).

27 Bush, "President's Address to the Nation," September 11, 2006 [fifth anniversary of 9/11], http://www.whitehouse.gov/news/releases/2006/09/print/20060911-3.html.

28 This infamous phrase is Rousseau's. Once each member of a community is bound under the social contract, "whoever refuses to obey the general will will be forced to do so by the entire body. This means merely that he will be forced to be free" (Rousseau, *Social Contract*, 150). While this utterance has been roundly criticized on its own terms, it seems even more dangerous to hold people or nations to a "contract" to which they have not agreed in the first place.

29 Bush, "Freedom in Iraq and Middle East," November 6, 2003.

30 See Harlan K. Ullman and James P. Wade Jr., *Shock and Awe: Achieving Rapid Dominance* (Washington, DC: Center for Advanced Concepts and Technology, 1996), http://purl.access.gpo.gov/GPO/LPS29021; Associated Press, "Iraq Faces Massive U.S. Missile Barrage," *CBS News*, January 24, 2003, http://www.cbsnews.com/stories/2003/01/24/eveningnews/main537928.shtml; and Not in Our Name Project, *The "Shock and Awe" Experiment: Compilation, Analysis, and Discussion of Available Information on the Pentagon's "Shock and Awe" Plan for Iraq*, http://www.notinourname.net/war/shock_awe.html. For criticism of the plan's failure (or nonimplementation), see Eric Schmitt, "Top General Concedes Air Attacks Did Not Deliver Knockout Blow," *New York Times*, March 26, 2003,

http://query.nytimes.com/gst/fullpage.html?res=9C0CE2DB1030F935A15750C0-A9659C8B63 and Paul Sperry, "No Shock, No Awe, It Never Happened," *World Net Daily*, April 3, 2003, http://www.wnd.com/news/article.asp?ARTICLE_ID=31858.

31 Bush, "President's Address to the Nation," September 11, 2006, with emphasis added.

32 Bush, "Working Together," February 21, 2005, 294.

33 Ibid.

34 Bush, "Second Inaugural Address," January 20, 2005.

35 Bush, "Freedom in Iraq and Middle East," November 6, 2003, 101.

36 Ibid., 100.

37 Bush, "We Will Not Fail: President Outlines Steps to Help Iraq Achieve Democracy and Freedom," address to the United States Army War College, Carlisle, PA, May 24, 2004, *Vital Speeches of the Day* 70, no. 16 (June 1, 2004): 485.

38 Bush, "Working Together," February 21, 2005, 294.

39 "President George Bush Discusses Iraq in National Press Conference," March 6, 2003, http://www.whitehouse.gov/news/releases/2003/03/print/20030306-8.html, emphasis added.

40 Bush, "Freedom in Iraq and Middle East," November 6, 2003, 102, emphasis added.

41 Bush, "Address to a Joint Session," September 20, 2001.

42 Bush, "Freedom in Iraq and Middle East," November 6, 2003, 100, emphasis added.

43 Ibid., 101.

44 Ibid., 100.

45 Ibid., 102.

46 Bush, "Second Inaugural Address," January 20, 2005, emphasis added.

47 Bush, "Address to a Joint Session," September 20, 2001.

48 Bush, "Second Inaugural Address," January 20, 2005.

49 Bush, "Advancing the Cause of Freedom," April 17, 2002, 420.

50 Ibid., 421.

13

Incongruent Beliefs and the Vitality of Fantasy

The New Politics of Religion

Neal E. Magee

When I say that I "believe" something, what exactly is going on? I can believe in God, I can believe in justice, and I can tell my son that I believe in him before he steps up to the plate. What then is the stuff of our various beliefs? How do I justify them? Certainly my beliefs relate to what I know, my sense of what is right or important, and how I see the world. At the same time, I can believe in aliens, in demon possession; I can believe that the Illuminati control global financial markets, or that the spirit of a deceased relative is watching over me. "Belief" is therefore quite a flexible category, with at least one important feature: though my beliefs can intimately inform my life and experience of this world, they do not necessarily trade in the currencies of truth or fact. We might say that someone's beliefs are really "out there," but we lack any precise way to measure if they have gone too far.

This book is in part an attempt to analyze how certain beliefs have borne themselves out in recent American political and religious history, a time when conservative politicians and evangelical Christians have come together with unforeseen (but perhaps imaginable) effectiveness. Much can be said about the ways this was a long-term project slowly coming to fruition, how this alliance might not remain in both parties' best interests, and the ways these partners have forever changed each other.[1] Perhaps most striking culturally and historically is the political invigoration of a large bloc of the population that previously felt disenfranchised. Beyond this history, however, I am even more interested in what constitutes belief itself. A nagging fear in the back of my mind is that readers of this book may dissociate themselves, focusing only on those two groups "out there"—Republicans and evangelicals—and so miss the opportunity to see this as an opportunity to better understand themselves and their society.

It is, I admit, quite American to make everything about ourselves, and while I do not mean to detract from the fine essays above that focus our gaze outward and help unravel the dynamics of the past several years, I want to draw out a new lesson about the ways we ourselves are caught up in this dynamic. That lesson is this: this latest politicoreligious alliance should be understood as only one example of the nature of belief at the beginning of the twenty-first century. What can we learn about our world by understanding the nexus of religious and political? And in what ways do they help us in "worlding our world"? What does this alliance teach us about how we ourselves understand and relate to politics? To religion? Or most important, how does this mobilization of "belief" already explain some of the ways that we ourselves believe?

To answer these questions, we should recognize two dynamics common to contemporary American Christianity and politics. The first is the way in which belief and the things we believe are no longer easily understood as singular, indivisible, or monolithic. Instead, it seems to me that belief is at best a "bundle" or collection of various threads: religion, politics, ideology, class, morality, and so on. Beliefs are not simply described in statements on "What I believe," just as most Christians today would not think that a historical creed or confession of the church can fully encapsulate what they believe. Our beliefs are not singular or monolithic; we should recognize them as multiple, polyvalent, sometimes tangential, and sometimes conflicting. Ultimately, the things we believe are not always congruent. (This is G. E. Moore's famous paradox—when I assert something like "It is raining, but I don't believe it"—a phenomenon that he thought was not easily explained.) Even choosing to believe that our beliefs are congruent cannot make up for the fact that their inner tensions, various allegiances, and hidden desires pull them naturally in several directions at the same time. This is not a new feature of belief, not a sudden arrival to the plane of our convictions: it has always been present, even if effectively masked over by comprehensive or overarching names.

This leads to the second dynamic of belief today: given this incongruity, we continue to create those singular names, paradigms, and systems, to gather them together. The anxiety created by the contradictions, gaps, or incongruities in what we believe is eased by fashioning what theorist Slavoj Žižek calls a "fantasy," which emphasizes coherence and harmony and helps give structure to how we perceive our world.[2] Both political parties (under rubrics like platforms) and Christian thinkers (under names like systematic theology) have worked hard at delineating core values, unifying themes, and recruiting logical support to shore up what they stand for. In this way party members or the faithful "knew what they believed" and were quite ready to argue how it all fit together. Indeed, was not much of the modern era concerned with selling the idea that our ideas and beliefs *must* fit into such unified systems? Through such litmus tests, a person could tell where one stood in relation to church or party and then either reform one's beliefs or transfer allegiances elsewhere. So much energy was devoted to creating unifying frameworks and examinations of how well each part fit in with the big picture. How we narrate our beliefs to ourselves is in part an effort to cover over the incongruity and lend some stability or purity to what seems at best a disarray of convictions.

Before elaborating on these two dynamics, I do recognize that belief is a strange, complex, yet utterly important endeavor. In arguing that belief is often incongruent, my point is that belief does not naturally emerge as the result of analytical reflection. I do not adopt a system of ideas first, which then filters, sorts, keeps, and discards my beliefs accordingly. Belief is not the same thing as reason, though they are obviously related, nor is it the same thing as knowledge, though they are related as well. But belief does not stop there: do we not also understand it as fundamentally related to desire? As informed by the largest and smallest ways we see and experience the world and other humans? As related to our deepest motivations and impulses? There is also a danger in placing "belief" in the same sentence as "fantasy." Ludwig Feuerbach (1804–72), the nineteenth-century German thinker, argued for just such a construction, seeing religion as simply an illusion or construct, a purely anthropomorphic projection: the object of belief is never really real. Unlike Feuerbach, I have no desire to reduce faith to a mere illusion or to do away with the things in which we believe. My concern is the nature of belief itself. Though belief does not consist solely of fantasy, it would be equally mistaken to think that it plays no part at all. Although fantasy does not dominate the field of belief, it is always present.

The upshot or critical gift of understanding belief in this way, as (1) fundamentally multiple and incongruous and (2) drawn together under grand names, is that it helps us recognize and remember that the field of belief is in continuous relationship with other parts of the social sphere, and that these relationships are much more complicated than direct reflection allows. If we want to explain *what we believe* as well as *how we come to believe it*, then we must put some effort into exposing everything at play in the process; yet such an effort may indeed never truly find completion. In what follows I want to explore these dynamics further, drawing mainly from political examples to illuminate religious belief, hopefully drawing out a larger and more general sense of "belief" itself.

The Incongruity of Our Beliefs

During the U.S. presidential campaign of 2004, the Republican National Committee (RNC) was experimenting with a new tool for connecting with voters. Dubbed "microtargeting," this tool relies on the collection of data, assembling them into highly sophisticated databases, correlating various data points, and then producing lists of various smaller subgroups that might be open to particular political messaging and action. The essence of microtargeting is identifying potential voters and determining what messages might best garner their votes. And so the RNC began focusing on voters much the same way that Visa or Land's End targets potential customers. To begin, one simply needs to purchase volumes of personal consumer data, essentially the shopping histories of individuals, the "residue" left behind after every transaction. Next, that consumer data must be related to any known political data, such as campaign contributions, party affiliation or activism, or frequency of voting. Then, the tantalizing and difficult process of finding connections between bits of data begins. For example, Republicans tend to drink Coors beer; they are the majority of viewers of the Golf Channel; and if you read *Field and Stream*, you are much more likely to vote Republican. These small discoveries help campaign strategists divide the electorate into increasingly small "slices," cut along economic, racial, religious, cultural, and ideological lines. Finally, once these slices are identified, campaigns try to "speak" to each one with a *precise* message tailored to their tastes and anticipated political interests.

The results of microtargeting are surprisingly effective. Because of this new tactic, campaigns no longer blanket the airwaves with singular, monolithic messages ("Vote for Smith for President") or uniform campaign literature. Instead, they produce a variety of specific messages

("Join other Cleveland Latinos and vote for Smith because of his stance on Cuba," or "Like you, Smith wants to maintain a vibrant arts community in the city and opposes drastic NEA cuts"). The specificity of this sort of approach transforms what were previously broad, generic campaigns into those tied to issues that particular communities care about. An early success story in microtargeting was Karl Rove's 2002 mobilization of usually unenthusiastic rural white male voters in Georgia, fueled by their strong opposition to changing the Georgia state flag.[3] In the world of microtargeting, however, "communities" are no longer necessarily geographic. As RNC Chair Ken Mehlman explains, "We used to target them based on their geography. We now target them based on what they do and how they live."[4] The art of political campaigning now relies not on singular, monolithic "broadcast" messages but on manifold and varied messages targeted to these many subgroups.

There is also a powerful fringe benefit to this process. Not only are political messages custom-fit to anticipated voters, but the process of data collection and correlation also produces lists of doors to knock on, people to persuade, e-mail addresses and cell-phone numbers to send text messages to. This is the much-vaunted "get out the vote" ground effort deployed by the RNC during the last seventy-two hours of a campaign. The end effects of microtargeting and the ground effort are statistically clear: though in the 2000 election the Bush campaign was able to reach approximately half of eventual Bush voters in Iowa and Florida, in 2004 it reached 92 percent in Iowa and 84 percent in Florida.[5]

Microtargeting illuminates for us something beyond the RNC, presidential campaigns, and even the political realm itself: organizations and individuals themselves keep in balance a variety of values and beliefs that do not necessarily agree. This is evident in an example from Karl Rove, President Bush's chief political strategist, who used microtargeting to try to gain every possible advantage in the general election of 2004 against Democrat John Kerry:

When the [Republican] campaign learned that the sitcom *Will & Grace* was wildly popular with younger Republican and swing voters, especially young women, it larded the series with its commercials—473 of them in all. It was a neat trick: the Bush campaign managed to ratchet up turnout among one core group of voters by touting the president's proposal for a constitutional amendment banning gay marriage, and at the same time to attract another

group of voters by running commercials on a television comedy
that sympathetically portrayed urban gay life.[6]

Here we find the perfect case of what anyone would normally consider
to be a contradiction: On the one hand, the RNC appealed to social progressives (*Will & Grace* fans), leaving out talk of antigay legislation and
making specific appeals to this younger, more-tolerant audience. On the
other hand, the campaign simultaneously rallied social conservatives by
championing a constitutional amendment declaring marriage to be solely
"between a man and a woman." The conflict here is on at least two levels:
First, the campaign sought to garner support from a population that
probably would not agree with President Bush on gay rights, but might
support him nevertheless on what they consider to be more pressing issues. But the second, greater conflict is that here the party favoring states'
rights proposed a sweeping constitutional amendment that would deny
states the very right to decide this issue for themselves.

Political doublespeak is, of course, not new: saying two different things
to two different groups of voters is part of the electoral process. Com-
promise is equally vital to the art of politics. How we read the doublespeak, however, is what interests me. In many cases, avowing two
different causes is likely an effort to please or appease, or it may signify a
politician simply hedging his bets. These cases are probably best understood as being disingenuous, as a bit of a lie, even if not so intended. But
the example of *Will & Grace* evidences something different: it exposes
that the beliefs of both social organizations (like religious groups and
political parties) and individuals themselves are inherently full of contradictions and conflicts. Our social institutions and groups thus operate,
as individuals do, in the full awareness that not everything "lines up." Our
ideas about economics might not exactly go hand in hand with our
thoughts on the size of government, social issues, the military, or the poor.
Likewise, our religious sensibilities might not appear in lockstep: our
sense of "ultimate concern," to borrow a term from Paul Tillich, might
not match so well with how we understand worship, piety, or sacred texts.
There once was a day when such misalignments could cost one dearly or
expose one as insincere, but today they actually help to describe how
we believe.

What does microtargeting teach us about belief? It is evidence of the
ways belief emerges as multiple, for both groups and individuals. Or put
another way, no single thread of logic can ever account for or call forth

what groups of people or individuals believe. With microtargeting, congruity of belief no longer matters. Such targeting seeks to exploit this fact and capitalize on communicating directly to increasingly specific convictions. But as both parties by now have surely realized, the drilling down to smaller slices and correlating more data points must, at some point, stop. Karl Rove and others are well aware that though such deep digging will teach one more and more about the electorate, effective campaigning has only to discern the *key* points to push and explore, enough to get you elected. Similarly, political platforms never fully enshroud a particular party's membership: many or most will disagree with a plank or two, if not more, but go along for the sake of party success. Even the affirmation of these planks, these various political convictions, stands apart from another set of beliefs about *how best* to enact and embody them in law and practice.

In their book *Politicians Don't Pander* (2000), Lawrence Jacobs and Robert Shapiro address a pair of contradictory political beliefs that Americans hold. The first is that public-opinion polls have grown in influence and have led to politicians "abdicating true leadership in favor of slavishly following polls." The second is that the steady influx of partisan money into the political sphere leads elected officials to ignore the wishes of the public. After carefully examining the facts, Jacobs and Shapiro, two prominent political scientists, argue that this contradiction in beliefs cannot be sustained; they support the second belief as the only factual choice. While troubled by the fact that politicians are only listening to the moneyed interests, I am more interested, for its theoretical significance, in how they explore with amazement the intense conviction with which Americans hold these two beliefs.[7]

The fragmentation of so-called postmodernity has spilled over into our own political and religious beliefs. We do not, in general, formulate beliefs based solely upon their accord with all of our other beliefs, but upon how appealing or convincing they are to each of us. And those beliefs do not always go all the way down. Our religious and political attachments are often quite ambivalent, and in some cases *undecidable*. Here I am reminded of what John Caputo wrote at the start of this volume: that the "event" stirring within the political and the religious, which goes by the name of "the impossible," surprises us and shatters our horizon of expectation. Likewise, theological conviction that claims knowledge of God can never end or be complete, but continue ad infinitum. As a result, we make ample room for exceptions, and some of the beliefs or values we hold dear do not completely jibe with other parts of ourselves. Perhaps in certain moments our beliefs do not feel contradictory, or perhaps we hold on to some beliefs a bit more firmly than other "half beliefs." But when we step back, it seems to me that we hold amalgamations or collections of political and religious beliefs that seem plainly in conflict with one another. These gaps and inconsistencies are disturbing. Rather than a linear, building effort—as in the hard sciences, where knowledge builds progressively—political and religious belief can meander and perambulate, form cul-de-sacs or take detours. (For example, the neoconservatives of today began mostly as liberal democrats with socialist leanings, then came to conservatism as outsiders.[8])

Perhaps for some of us, this is not a great problem. Perhaps those individuals in some way need and even thrive upon the lack of full integration between all the parts of their thinking. Maybe the cognitive dissonance and tension between their most extreme edges are somehow productive. For the rest of us, however, this does not sit so well. Those of us who are students of philosophy and theology in particular know well the great traditions of the past: how one piece of a theory informs the next piece; how well they fit together is important; how these traditions rely upon the metaphor of building—with foundational beliefs and those that sit on top. To ease the anxiety of not quite having all our ducks in a row, we tell others and ourselves a certain story about how they all fit together. We narrate our beliefs as somehow whole, integrated, and harmonious. Because of this, we spin a fantasy, one that helps us both deny the contradictions within ourselves and form some clear sense of identity. This fantasy is useful in the realms of politics and religion not only because the things and ways that we believe are not easily boiled down or made clear, but because such fantasy actually enables belief to deepen and unfold into action.

Fantasies of Clarity and Conviction

As Jacobs and Shapiro point out, President Bill Clinton was infatuated with polling data. He well knew the political importance of how one appears, and early on he mastered the art of offering up the right image as a leader, at the right place, and at the right time. As a result, he polled on every major and minor decision: for how Americans felt about certain domestic or foreign policy issues; for their attitudes toward their leaders; for the right language to package a new proposal or speech. He even polled for the appropriate place for the first family to vacation. This had two opposing effects: if you know what people want, and then you give it to them, that tends to produce favorable results and attitudes. But at the same time, when you ask people what looks best all the time, you tend to look as though you lack convictions of your own as a leader.

So when then-Governor George W. Bush began to organize his campaign for President in the late 1990s, his political team looked for ways to offer Bush as different from Clinton on every level, since Bush also knew the importance of image and presentation. They realized that since Clinton spoke with precise verbosity and flourish, Bush should capitalize on being as plainspoken and humble. Clinton's foreign policy was multilateral and often tediously complicated, so Bush's should be unilateral and clearly defined. Clinton could appreciate and speak to the many sides and ambivalences of a problem, so Bush would excel as a decisive, no-nonsense MBA ready to cut through the red tape and make government work "as an outsider." Therefore, it was not surprising when Bush told reporters early on that he "doesn't govern by polls," or when, amid his second term, he declared himself "the decider." Without ever referencing Clinton, Bush could telegraph himself as a clear voice, who leads by principle, who sticks by his decisions, and who does not bend to popular opinion—all of which, in moderation, are generally ideal qualities in a leader. The irony is that Bush discovered the brilliance of this position primarily through polls and focus groups as well, and he in fact *does*, despite repeated assertions that he does not, have regular polling done on a range of issues large and small.[9] This is because the stakes are too high not to know how certain actions, legislation, meetings, speeches, or even phrases will play out with the public. Each election cycle, Bush is actually quite a student of polling numbers, frequently bouncing statistics for particular congressional districts off his aides for their assessment.[10]

Here is a wonderful case of covering over the anxiety of belief with fantasy. The two beliefs held by Bush's camp are that (1) we must present ourselves as principled and not prey to public opinion, and (2) we must poll to be certain that we are on the right track. Rather than expose these two beliefs, however, the second is masked over through the fantasy that he "does not govern by polling," that he thus is "the decider." Without this fantasy, the contradiction would be rather distasteful and only make it harder to project the image of Bush as a strong leader. Beyond appearances, there is a more-pressing reason for Bush to assert that he "does not govern by polls" and that he is "the decider": *they are fantasies or self-deceptions that a President must tell himself in order to govern.* My point is not really that the President is a liar, though these two lies are important for him to keep up. Rather, Bush is the real audience of these two declarations, since he is the one who must hear them most clearly. This is not simply in order to comfort Bush amid his anxieties, but to enable him to "go ahead and act that way."[11]

In the realm of conservative Christianity, the same phenomenon appears. In many evangelical and fundamentalist circles, there is an attitude about the work of interpreting Scripture that claims: "The Bible says what it means and means what it says."[12] In a way, this is a version of "literalism" (claiming that the Bible is to be read literally, and that it does not incorporate myth or metaphor) and perhaps also a version of "infallibility" (that the Bible is a perfect and unfailing guide for life and faith). Yet conservative Christians primarily argue that the Bible is clear, straightforward, and unambiguous. This view also claims that the work of interpretation is, in essence, no work at all: the Bible interprets itself. In this position, an interesting split occurs: on one level, Scripture is entirely plain, simple, accessible, and graspable. On another level it operates as a fantastic abstraction or code for the reader, a universal key to transcendental knowledge, which circumvents all things human. In either case it quite easily becomes idealized, becoming reified to access things divine, serving as a moral yardstick, and is taken to be filled with "signs" for "those with eyes" to see. Here, like the tensions masked by Bush's facade as a "strong leader," are many contradictions and questions as well: if the Bible says what it means, how do I know when I "have" it or not? Does the text provide its own litmus test for this? What then is my role as reader? Is it fair then to ask questions of the text? If it reads itself literally, does this happen for all translations of the Bible? (or only for the Greek and Hebrew? or only for the King James Version?) Most important, what am I to do when I read a part that does not seem to make sense; does it still have "meaning" then? What am I to do when my friend or spouse or minister seem to read it differently?

The real fantasy in such a reading strategy is less about the actual words on the page and more about the strategy itself: *If only everyone would read this like we do, . . . then everything would be all right.* Such a strategy essentially consolidates interpretation by trying to forbid and cut off difference. Though these biblical readers are often understood (or present themselves) as returning to a more "natural" or historically accurate attitude toward the text ("This is how it *used* to be read, so let's reclaim it"), they are actually like everyone else: readers reliant upon complex networks of abstraction and meaning. These networks have been mounting for many centuries and culminate in the way we moderns cherish textuality itself.[13] To claim that it "says what it means and means what it says" is actually a marvelous and elaborate theoretical fantasy, saying attests more about a *desire* for textual certitude than about the ease with which Semitic and Greek narratives of the Old and New Testaments can be interpreted well or accurately. Moreover, the claim that such a reading strategy is a *return* would require us to know just how people used to read it thus, which in turn requires still more layers of explanation and justification.

So once again, who is the real audience of the fantastic statement? The readers themselves making this affirmation are the audience: they seek not to convince others how to read or to find the beginning of an interpretive strategy, but to assure themselves that this text—or really this *collection of texts*, since the Bible's literary unity is itself a fantasy—can be read and easily understood. This fantasy in effect lets them let themselves off the hook, saves them from having to open up the interpretive can of worms within this sacred (or any) text. Most of all: this belief allows them to *go ahead and read.*

The Real Audience of Our Fantasy

Marx's famous quote about ideology is that "they do not know what they are doing, but still they are doing it." This is not the result of bad choices or coercion, but of what Marx called "misrecognition." Through a person's interactions with various products in one's world, the subject misrecognizes those products as the primary social relation—a relation between things—rather than one's relations with other people. To understand this, however, we are not limited only to Marx's discussion of "commodities" or products. Feudal society gives us another case, which has its own misrecognitions, as Žižek points out:

> "Being-a-king" is an effect of the network of social relations between a "king" and his "subjects"; but—and here is the fetishistic misrecognition—to the participants of this social bond, the relationship appears necessarily in an inverse form: they think that they are subjects giving the king royal treatment because the king is already in himself, outside the relationship to his subjects, a king;

as if the determination of "being-a-king" were a "natural" property of the person of a king.[14]

Here Žižek's argument is that a certain forgetfulness or denial allows the subject to *misrecognize* itself. The king's subjects misrecognize him *as a king* rather than recognizing that he is a king because they treat him as such. Likewise, the king comes to see himself as a king not because the subjects treat him that way, but because *he is a king*. However, we cannot simply shake this process of misrecognition. We could unmask it, but we would still be forced to acknowledge that it is "unavoidable—that is, we must accept a certain delusion as a condition of our historical activity, of assuming a role as agent of the historical process."[15] Misrecognition, the product of fantasy, is woven into belief and even thought itself, not just as a persistent stain, but also as a necessary part of their work.

Marx recognized the societal shift away from "relations between people" and toward "relations between things," which we can now also see as a mysterious process of *substitution*. Žižek asks, "How is it . . . possible that the innermost 'relations between people' can be displaced onto (or substituted by) 'relations between things'?"[16] The effect of such a substitution is found not in what people *think* they are doing, but in what they actually *do*. The substitution of fantasy works just like the symbol: as a stand-in for something else, and like the political and religious fantasies above, the power of symbolic identification is that "it is by definition a misidentification."[17] To explain this better, Žižek offers a personal example:

> As a father, I know I am an unprincipled weakling; but, at the same time, I do not want to disappoint my son, who sees in me who I am not: a person of dignity and strong principles, ready to take risks for a just cause—so I identify with this *misperception* of me, and truly "become myself" when I, in effect, start to act according to this misperception (ashamed to appear to my son as I really am, I actually accomplish heroic acts).[18]

Here is an excellent example of the misidentifying effects of fantasy, and how it begins to structure how one perceives the reality of the situation. At some point the father takes on the misperception to the point that he essentially *forgets* his former self-perception.

Unlike a simple mask, however, this misperception is not just made up of the "false" (external) and "genuine" (internal) self: "It occurs when the way I appear to others becomes more important to me than the psychological reality 'beneath my social mask,' forcing me to do things I would never be able to accomplish 'from within myself.'"[19] So for Žižek, it is no longer a *wish* that I would act a particular way. I *go ahead and act that way*, stepping into the shoes of the misperception and forgetting the ways this was made up in the first place. To what extent, then, might the sense of divine expectation—of pleasing God, of not wanting to disappoint—raise up individuals to do things (believing, praying, serving) they would never be able to accomplish from within themselves? Or, if I were an elected official, might this enable me to lead with conviction and a purity of principle? Political strategists work hard during campaigns for their candidate to "look presidential": one must be centered, unflappable, and convey a certain gravitas while always appearing natural. In short, the candidate, before ever being elected (or losing in the end), must *go ahead and act like a President* in order to become one.

Symbolic identification, working in this way as a misidentification, seems important in the monotheistic faiths: trying to see oneself as God might and acting accordingly. Are not the airwaves, books, and sanctuaries of so many Christian churches ringing with the challenge to deliberately misrecognize ourselves by trying to gain a God's-eye point of view? To truly understand and love yourself, the message goes, you must know and love as only God can; we must love ourselves and each other as God would love us. This provocative idea clearly holds power over a certain theological imagination, even though individuals are usually captivated by the "appearance" of the misrecognition (where I affirm myself as a child of God) more than the "genuine" reality beneath it (I am a desperate individual who is trying to imagine what God must think of me, which is something I can never really know). Mark 12:31 provides just such a construction, "Love your neighbor as yourself," which then raises the question *How do I come to know what the Other/other thinks?* This is no simple interpretive leap, and considerable obstacles remain in accessing such knowledge. Perhaps for the moment it is enough to say that fantasy and misrecognition are always already at work in the field of belief.

Does fantasy simply authorize any behavior? It does not. Returning again to Žižek, we can look to his example of anti-Semitism, since racist scapegoating always comprises just such a fantasy: "*If only we could rid ourselves of them, then everything would be all right.*" Foisting all social problems onto "the Jews" serves to ameliorate the fractured social field and ensure a smooth and comforting edifice. The core of this equation (If only X, then Y) that is always left out is that, in this example, the Jews are never blocking society from "achieving its full identity; . . . it is prevented by [society's] own antagonistic nature, by its own immanent blockage, and it 'projects' this internal negativity into the figure of the 'Jew.'"[20] When antagonism cannot be reconciled through a more positive fantasy, it often emerges in other more destructive ways. Scapegoating places blame on an individual or group while at the same time affirming the fundamental social hostility by scapegoating in the first place.

When fantasy is so deeply involved, where and how does its critique begin? How can I be critical of someone else's fantasies or of my own? In the world of events, fantasy does not often prevail. As defense analyst Anthony Cordesman puts it, "When it comes to a contest between ideology and reality, reality always wins."[21] But in the realms of belief and meaning, which admittedly play a part in how we perceive reality, fantasy is not so easily undone. I am reminded of present-day politicians who stay "on message," drawing from talking points dictated to them by staffers and strategists. Talking points also are simply thumbnail versions of fantasy, since the audience and the speaker know quite well that such fantasies never tell the full story. Although we might try to interrupt fantasy with questions or examples from reality, trying to shake it loose and expose the ways it fails to account for what is going on, seasoned speakers who are fast with their tongues can always "stay on message." That is, they can always uphold the fantasy. The more productive approach might be to *enter the fantasy itself*, in the hopes of exposing its truest desires, recognizing that the fantasy structuring belief never had much to do with truth or fact. When Bush declares that he is "the decider," it is not a point for debate, but a reminder to himself that his job centers on making executive decisions on the grandest of scales, and that he fervently wishes those decisions to be principled and well reasoned, since that must be how Presidents make decisions. Entering the fantasy does not mean trying to prove it wrong; instead, it is an effort to decode at least part of the belief it helps to sustain.

Conclusion

We thus might say that the twin poles of this book, politics and religion, have been "born again." For the *new religion of politics*, faith has entered the scene, and one must now profess some sort of belief to be elected. Moreover, we can see a new influx of belief beyond the religious—belief in country, in epic struggles, in freedom—even if the rhetoric surrounding these beliefs often rings hollow (for example President Bush's dictum that freedom is "on the march"). Political belief of this invigorated form has played a part in exceptional demonstrations of sympathy and unity (for example September 11, 2001, which ushered in a short period where globalism was a good thing for everyone) as well as substantial, albeit disorganized, dissent (taking the form of new political action committees [PACs], or the liberal intolerance of religious intolerance). Likewise, a *new politics of religion* has emerged, wherein we are reminded once again of the innately political nature of religious belief. Whether that politics should or can be contained or redirected is a matter to be taken up elsewhere; yet recent history has shown that belief of this variety can manifest itself in real, this-world politics. This terrain of belief also makes use of fantasy: it must do so, in the sense that only fantasy allows for and justifies envisioning the impossible or unimaginable, which is the very stuff of theistic faith. The struggle for the new politics of religion, no matter who is elected to office in 2008 and beyond, will be the struggle to interpret and justify both belief and fantasy, now folded over and multiplied into one another. Here the fantasy contained within belief is not going to go away or even diminish, but will increasingly dominate the scene. Thus the emerging point of contention—in both churches and houses of state—will center not on the question *Do you believe?* but rather on asking, *How do you come to believe it?*

Notes

1 For an excellent historical retelling of evangelicals' political travails before 2000, see Melani McAlister's *Epic Encounters: Culture, Media, and U.S. Interests in the Middle East, 1945–2000* (Berkeley: University of California Press, 2001), esp. chap. 4, "The Good Fight: Israel after Vietnam, 1972–1980," 155–97. I also point to E. J. Dionne, Jean B. Elshtain, and Kayla M. Drogosz, *One Electorate under God: A Dialogue on Religion and American Politics* (Washington, DC: Brookings Institution Press, 2004).

2 Slavoj Žižek, *The Sublime Object of Ideology* (London: Verso, 1989), 33.

3 Jeffrey Gettleman, "The 2002 Elections: Georgia: An Old Battle Flag Helps Bring Down a Governor," *New York Times*, November 7, 2002, B2, http://topics.nytimes.com/top/reference/timestopics/people/g/jeffrey_gettleman/index.html?offset=20&s=oldest.

4 Todd S. Purdum, "Karl Rove's Split Personality," *Vanity Fair*, December 2006, 202–19, http://www.vanityfair.com/politics/features/2006/12/rove200612.

5 Yochi J. Dreazen, "Democrats, Playing Catch-Up, Tap Database to Woo Potential Voters," *Wall Street Journal*, October 31, 2006, A1, http://online.wsj.com/article/SB116226051099508453.html.

6 Purdum, "Karl Rove's Split Personality," 202–19.

7 See Lawrence R. Jacobs and Robert Y. Shapiro, *Politicians Don't Pander: Political Manipulation and the Loss of Democratic Responsiveness* (Chicago: University of Chicago Press, 2000).

8 See Michael Lind, "A Tragedy of Errors," review of *An End to Evil: How to Win the War on Terror*, in *The Nation* (February 23, 2004). In this review, Lind, who no longer considers himself a neoconservative, traces the left-liberal origins of that movement to anti-Soviet liberals and social democrats usually called "paleoliberals."

9 Bush's White House has been a regular client of Matthew Dowd, who is a principal with ViaNovo, an "international communications and brand-positioning firm": http://www.vianovo.com/.

10 Purdum, "Karl Rove's Split Personality," 202–19.

11 Žižek, *The Fragile Absolute* (London: Verso, 2000), 49–50.

12 For an example of this position, see *60 Minutes*, CBS News, "Faith, Hope, and Politics: The Beliefs and Political Power of Evangelical Christians," February 8, 2004.

13 Certain nations, particularly the United States, have a deep affinity for texts and how we read or change them. Take, for example, the elaborate steps necessary to amend the United States Constitution or Bill of Rights, but also the multitiered judicial system, which takes on the difficult task of "interpreting" these texts and their meaning for our present society. Even in this microcosm there are fundamentalists, usually called "constructionists" or "originalists," and their liberal counterparts, so-called "activist" judges. The former, like Christian fundamentalists, claim to read "naturally," or as these texts "used to be read" or were intended, before being diluted when readers of another stripe entered the scene.

14 Žižek, *Sublime Object*, 25.

15 Ibid., 2.

16 Žižek, *The Plague of Fantasies* (London: Verso, 1997), 105.

17 Žižek, *Fragile Absolute*, 49.

18 Ibid.

19 Ibid., 49–50.

20 Žižek, *Sublime Object*, 127.

21 Michael Kirk and Jim Gilmore, "The Lost Year in Iraq," *Frontline* series, WGBH Boston: Frontline, originally aired October 17, 2006, http://www.pbs.org/wgbh/pages/frontline/yeariniraq/etc/credits.html.

Postface

Better Dead Than Red—Again!

Slavoj Žižek

The blood-dimmed tide is loosed, and everywhere
the ceremony of innocence is drowned;
the best lack all conviction, while the worst
are full of passionate intensity.

William Butler Yeats, "The Second Coming" (1920)

Recall the diagnosis of the twentieth century proposed long ago by William Butler Yeats, the archconservative, given in the epigraph above. The key to this diagnosis is contained in the phrase "ceremony of innocence," which is to be taken in the precise sense of Edith Wharton's *Age of Innocence* (1920): Newland Archer's wife, the "innocent" the title refers to, was not a naive believer in her husband's fidelity. She well knew of his passionate love for Countess Ellen Olenska; she just politely ignored it and staged the belief in his fidelity.

In one of the Marx brothers' films, Groucho Marx, when caught in a lie, answers angrily: "Whom do you believe, your eyes or my words?" This apparently absurd logic renders perfectly the functioning of the symbolic order, in which the symbolic mask-mandate matters more than the direct reality of the individual who wears this mask and/or assumes this mandate. This functioning involves the structure of fetishist disavowal: "I know very well that things are the way I see them, that this person is a corrupt weakling, but I nonetheless treat him respectfully, since he wears the insignia of a judge, so that when he speaks, it is the Law itself which speaks through him." So in a way, I effectively believe his words, not my eyes: I believe in Another Space (the domain of pure symbolic authority) which matters more than the reality of its spokesmen. The cynical reduction to reality thus falls short: when a judge speaks, there is in a way more truth in his words (the words of the institution of law) than in the direct reality of the person of judge. If one limits oneself to what one sees, one simply misses the point.

This paradox is what Lacan aims at with his "*les non-dupes errent*": Those who do not let themselves be caught in the symbolic deception/ fiction and continue to believe their eyes are the ones who err most. What a cynic who "believes only his eyes" misses is the efficiency of the symbolic fiction, the way this fiction structures our experience of reality. The same gap is at work in our most intimate relationship to our neighbors: we behave *as if* we do not know that they also smell badly, secrete excrement, and so forth; thus a minimum of idealization, of fetishizing disavowal, is the basis of our coexistence.

Does not the same disavowal account for the sublime beauty of the idealizing gesture discernible from Anne Frank to American communists who believed in the Soviet Union? Although we know that Stalinist communism was appalling, we nonetheless admire the victims of the McCarthy witch hunt, who heroically persisted in their belief in communism and support for the Soviet Union. The logic is here the same as that of Anne Frank, who in her diaries expresses belief in the ultimate goodness of man in spite of the horrors accomplished by men against Jews in World War II. What renders such an assertion of belief (in the essential goodness of humanity; in the truly human character of the Soviet regime) sublime is the very gap between it and the overwhelming factual evidence against it: the active will to disavow the actual state of things. Perhaps therein resides the most elementary metaphysical gesture: in this refusal to accept the real in its idiocy, to disavow it and to search for Another World behind it. The big Other is thus the order of lie, of lying sincerely. And it is in this sense that "the best lack all conviction, while the worst are full of passionate intensity": even the best are no longer able to sustain their symbolic innocence, their full engagement in the symbolic ritual, while "the worst," the mob, engage in (racist, religious, sexist . . .) fanaticism. Is this opposition not a good description of today's split between tolerant but anemic liberals, and the fundamentalists full of "passionate intensity"?

"Fundamentalism" concerns neither belief as such nor its content; what distinguishes a "fundamentalist" is the way he relates to his beliefs; its most elementary definition should focus on the *formal status of belief.* In "Faith and Knowledge," Derrida deploys the inherent link between these two terms: knowledge always relies on a preceding elementary act of faith (into the symbolic order, into the basic rationality of the universe), while religion itself more and more relies on the scientific knowledge, although it disavows this reliance (the use of modern media for the propagation of religions, religious exploitation of the newest scientific advances, and so forth). Perhaps this link reaches is apogee in the New Age cyber-gnosticism, the spirituality grounded in the digitalization and virtualization of our life-world. What if we add another twist to this link? What if the neoobscurantist faith in all its versions, from conspiracy theories to irrational mysticism, emerges when faith itself, the basic reliance on the big Other, the symbolic order, fails? Is this not the case today? This brings us to the formula of fundamentalism: *What is foreclosed from the symbolic* (belief), *returns in the real* (of a direct knowledge). A fundamentalist does not believe; a fundamentalist *knows*: the proper tension and anxiety of an authentic belief are lost there.

As to the direct ideological content of the fundamentalist struggle, it is more than obvious that they are fighting a war that simply *cannot be won.* If Republicans were effective in totally banning abortion, prohibiting the teaching of evolution, imposing federal regulation on Hollywood and mass culture—this would mean not only their immediate ideological defeat, but also a large-scale economic depression in the United States. The outcome is thus a debilitating symbiosis: although the "ruling class" disagrees with the populist moral agenda, it tolerates their "moral war" as a means to keep the lower classes in check. The ruling class enables them to articulate their fury without disturbing their economic interests. What this means is that *culture war is class war* in a displaced mode. So much for those who claim that we leave in a postclass society.

This, however, makes the enigma only more impenetrable: how is this displacement *possible*? "Stupidity" and "ideological manipulation" are not an answer. It is clearly not enough to say that the "primitive" lower classes are brainwashed by the ideological apparatuses so that they are not able to identify their true interests. If nothing else, one should recall how, decades ago, the same Kansas which is today the focus of fundamentalist populism was the hotbed of *progressive* populism in the United States. People certainly did not get more stupid in the last decades.

And neither would do a direct "psychoanalytic" explanation in the old Wilhelm Reich style (people's libidinal investments compel them to act against their rational interests): it confronts too directly libidinal economy and economy proper, failing to grasp their mediation.

The first thing to recognize here is that it takes two to fight a culture war: culture is also the dominant ideological topic of the "enlightened" liberals, whose politics focus on the fight against sexism, racism, and fundamentalism, and for multicultural tolerance. The key question thus is, Why is "culture" emerging as our central life-world category? With regard to religion, we no longer "really believe," we just follow (some of the) religious rituals and mores as part of the respect for the lifestyle of the community to which we belong (nonbelieving Jews obeying kosher rules out of respect for tradition, and so forth). "I do not really believe in it; it is just part of my culture" effectively seems to be the predominant mode of the disavowed/displaced belief characteristic of our times. What is a cultural lifestyle, if not the fact that, although we do not believe in Santa Claus, there is a Christmas tree in every house and even in public places every December? Perhaps, then, the nonfundamentalist notion of "culture" as distinguished from "real" religion, art, and so forth *is* in its very core the name for the field of disowned/impersonal beliefs. "Culture" is the name for all those things we practice without really believing in them, without taking them seriously.

The second thing to recognize is how, while professing their solidarity with the poor, liberals encode culture war with an opposed-class message. More often than not, their fight for multicultural tolerance and women's rights marks the counterposition to the alleged intolerance, fundamentalism, and patriarchal sexism of the "lower classes." The way to unravel this confusion is to focus on the mediating terms, whose function is to obfuscate the true lines of division. The way the term "modernization" is used in the recent ideological offensive is exemplary here: first, an abstract opposition is constructed between "modernizers" (those who endorse global capitalism in all its aspects, from economic to cultural) and "traditionalists" (those who resist globalization). Into this category of those who resist are then thrown all, from the traditional conservatives and populist Right to the "old Left" (those who continue to advocate welfare state, trade unions, and so forth). This categorization obviously does comprise an aspect of social reality; recall the coalition of church and trade unions that, in Germany in early 2003, prevented the legalization of stores being open also on Sunday. However, it is not enough to say that this "cultural difference" traverses the entire social field, cutting across different strata and classes. It is not enough to say that this opposition can be combined in different ways with other oppositions (so that we can have conservative "traditional values" resistance to global capitalist "modernization," or moral conservatives who fully endorse capitalist globalization). In short, it is not enough to say that this "cultural difference" is one in the series of antagonisms that are operative in today's social processes.

The failure of this opposition to function as the key to social totality does not only mean that it should be articulated with other differences. It means that it is abstract, and the wager of Marxism is that there is one antagonism (class struggle) that overdetermines all others and thus is the concrete universal of the entire field. The term "overdetermination" is here used in its precise Althusserian sense: it does not mean that class struggle is the ultimate referent and horizon of meaning for all other struggles; it means that class struggle is the structuring principle that allows us to account for the very "inconsistent" plurality of ways in which other antagonisms can be articulated into "chains of equivalences." For example, feminist struggle can be articulated into a chain with progressive struggle for emancipation, or it can (and it certainly does) function as an ideological tool of the upper-middle classes to assert their superiority over the "patriarchal and intolerant" lower classes. And the point here is not only that the feminist struggle can be articulated in different ways with the class antagonism, but that class antagonism is doubly inscribed here. It is the specific constellation of the class struggle itself that explains why the feminist struggle was appropriated by upper classes. (The same goes for racism: it is the dynamics of class struggle itself that explains why direct racism is strong among the lowest white workers.) Class struggle is here the "concrete universality" in the strict Hegelian sense: in relating to its otherness (other antagonisms), it relates to itself: it (over)determines the way it relates to other struggles.

The third thing to recognize is the fundamental difference between feminist, antiracist, antisexist, or other struggle and class struggle. In the first case (struggle over specific issues), the goal is to translate antagonism into mere difference (peaceful coexistence of sexes, religions, ethnic groups). The goal of the class struggle is precisely the opposite: to aggravate class difference into class antagonism. The point of subtraction is to reduce the overall complex structure to its antagonistic minimal difference. So what the series race-gender-class obfuscates is the different logic of the political space in the case of class: while the antiracist and antisexist struggles are guided by the striving for the full recognition of the other, the class struggle aims at overcoming, subduing, even annihilating the other. Even if not a direct physical annihilation, class struggle aims at the annihilation of the other's sociopolitical role and function. In other words, it is logical to say that antiracism wants all races to be allowed to freely assert and deploy their cultural, political, and economic strivings. Yet it is obviously meaningless to say that the aim of the proletarian class struggle is to allow the bourgeoisie to fully assert its identity and strivings. In one case, we have a horizontal logic of the recognition of different identities; in the other case, we have the logic of the struggle with an antagonist.

The paradox here is that the populist fundamentalism retains this logic of antagonism, while the liberal Left follows the logic of recognition of differences, of defusing antagonisms into coexisting differences. In their very form, the conservative-populist grassroots campaigns took over the old Leftist-radical stance of the popular mobilization and struggle against upper-class exploitation. Insofar as, in the present U.S. two-party system, red designates Republicans and blue Democrats, and insofar as populist fundamentalists vote Republican, the old anticommunist slogan "Better dead than red!" now acquires a new ironic meaning. The irony resides in the unexpected continuity of the red attitude from the old Leftist grassroots mobilization to the new Christian fundamentalist grassroots mobilization.

This unexpected reversal is just one in a long series. In today's United States, the traditional roles of Democrats and Republicans are almost inverted: Republicans spend government money, thus generating record budget deficits, de facto build a strong federal state, and pursue a politics of global interventionism. Meanwhile Democrats pursue a tough fiscal politics that, under Clinton, abolished budget deficit. Even in the touchy sphere of socioeconomic politics, Democrats (the same as with Blair in the United Kingdom) as a rule accomplish the neoliberal agenda of abolishing the welfare state, lowering taxes, privatizing, and so forth. Meanwhile Bush proposed a radical measure of legalizing the status of the millions of illegal Mexican workers and made health care much more accessible to the retired. The extreme case here is that of the survivalist groups in the West of the United States. Although the survivalists' ideological message is that of religious racism, their entire mode of organization (small illegal groups fighting the FBI and other federal agencies) makes them an uncanny double of the Black Panthers from the 1960s. According to an old Marxist insight, every rise of fascism is a sign of a failed revolution. No wonder, then, that Kansas is also the state of John Brown, the *key* political figure in the history of United States, the fervently Christian radical abolitionist who came closest to introducing the radical emancipatory-egalitarian logic into the U.S. political landscape:

> John Brown considered himself a complete egalitarian. And it was very important for him to practice egalitarianism on every level.... African Americans were caricatures of people, they were characterized as buffoons and minstrels, they were the butt-end of jokes in American society. And even the abolitionists, as antislavery as they were, the majority of them did not see African Americans as equals. The majority of them, and this was something that African Americans complained about all the time, were willing to work for the end of slavery in the South but they were not willing to work to end discrimination in the North.... John Brown wasn't like that. For him, practicing egalitarianism was a first step toward ending slavery. And African Americans who came in contact with him knew this immediately. He made it very clear that he saw no difference, and he didn't make this clear by saying it, he made it clear by what he did.[1]

His consequential egalitarianism led him to get engaged in the armed struggle against slavery: in 1859, Brown and twenty-one other men seized the federal armory at Harper's Ferry, hoping to arm slaves and thus create a violent rebellion against the South. However, after thirty-six hours the revolt was suppressed and Brown was taken to jail by a federal force led by none other than Robert E. Lee. After being found guilty of murder, treason, and inciting a slave insurrection, Brown was hanged on December 2, 1859. And, today even, long after slavery was abolished, Brown is the dividing figure in American collective memory. This point was made most succinctly by Russell Banks, whose magnificent novel *Cloud-splitter* retells Brown's story:

> The reason white people think he was mad is because he was a white man and he was willing to sacrifice his life in order to liberate Black Americans.... Black people don't think he's crazy, generally—very few African Americans regard Brown as insane. If you go out onto the street today, whether you are speaking to a school kid or an

elderly woman or a college professor, if it's an African American person you're talking to about John Brown, they are going start right out with the assumption that he was a hero because he was willing to sacrifice his life—a white man—in order to liberate Black Americans. If you speak to a white American, probably the same proportion of them will say he was a madman. And it's for the same reason, because he was a white man who was willing to sacrifice his life to liberate Black Americans. The very thing that makes him seem mad to white Americans is what makes him seem heroic to Black Americans.[2]

For this reason, those whites who support Brown are all the more precious. Among them, surprisingly, is Henry David Thoreau, the great opponent of violence. Against the standard dismissal of Brown as bloodthirsty, foolish, and insane, Thoreau[3] painted a portrait of a peerless man whose embracement of a cause was unparalleled; he even goes as far as to liken Brown's execution (he states that he regards Brown as dead before his actual death) to Christ. Thoreau vents at the scores of those who have voiced their displeasure and scorn for John Brown. The same people cannot relate to Brown because of their concrete stances and "dead" existences; they are truly not living; only a handful of men have lived.

When talking about the Kansas populists, one should bear in mind that they also celebrate John Brown as their saint.[4] We should thus not only refuse the easy liberal contempt for the populist fundamentalists (or even worse, the patronizing regret of how "manipulated" they are). We should reject the very terms of the culture war. As to the positive content of most of the debated issues, a radical Leftist should support the liberal stance (for abortion, against racism and homophobia, and so forth). Yet one should never forget that it is the populist fundamentalist, not the liberal, who in the long term is the true ally of the Left. In all their anger, they are not radical enough to perceive the link between capitalism and the moral decay they deplore. Recall how Robert Bork's infamous lament about our "slouching towards Gomorrah" ends up in a deadlock typical of ideology: "The entertainment industry is not forcing depravity on an unwilling American public. The demand for decadence is there. That fact does not excuse those who sell such degraded material any more than the demand for crack excuses the crack dealer. But we must be reminded that the fault is in ourselves, in human nature not constrained by external forces."[5]

In what, exactly, is this demand then grounded? Here Bork performs his ideological short circuit. Instead of pointing toward the inherent logic of capitalism itself—which to sustain its expanding reproduction has to create new and more demands—and thus admitting that, in fighting consumerist decadence, he is fighting a tendency entwined in the very core of capitalism, he directly refers to "human nature." Left to itself, human nature ends up wanting depravity and thus needs constant control and censorship: "The idea that men are naturally rational, moral creatures without the need for strong external restraints has been exploded by experience. There is an eager and growing market for depravity, and profitable industries [are] devoted to supplying it."[6]

What moral conservatives fail to perceive is thus how, to put it in Hegelese, in fighting the dissolute liberal permissive culture, they are fighting the necessary ideological consequence of the unbridled capitalist economy that they themselves fully and passionately support. Their struggle against the external enemy is the struggle against the obverse of their own position. (Long ago, intelligent liberals like Daniel Bell formulated this paradox under the title of the "cultural contradictions of capitalism.") This throws an unexpected light onto the Cold Warriors' moral crusade against communist regimes. The embarrassing fact is that the Eastern European Communist regimes were overthrown by forces that "represented the three great antagonists of conservatism: the youth culture, the intellectuals of the '60s generation, and the laboring classes that still favored Solidarity over individualism."[7] This feature returns to haunt Bork: at a conference, he "referred, not approvingly, to Michael Jackson's crotch-clutching performance at the Super Bowl. Another panelist tartly informed me that it was precisely the desire to enjoy such manifestations of American culture that had brought down the Berlin wall. That seems as good an argument as any for putting the wall back up again."[8] Although Bork is aware of the irony of the situation, he obviously misses its deeper aspect.

Recall Jacques Lacan's definition of successful communication: in it, I get back from the Other my own message in its inverted—that is, true—form. Is this not what is happening to today's liberals? Are they not getting back from the conservative populists their own message in its inverted/true form? In other words, are conservative populists not the symptom of tolerant enlightened liberals? This is why the present volume is so important. It breaks the vicious cycle mutual implicating "the best who lack all conviction" and "the worst who are full of passionate intensity." It returns the passion to the best.

Notes

1 Margaret Washington, http://www.pbs.org/wgbh/amex/brown/filmmore/reference/interview/washington05.html.
2 Russell Banks, http://www.pbs.org/wgbh/amex/brown/filmmore/reference/interview/banks01.html.
3 See Henry David Thoreau, *Civil Disobedience and Other Essays* (New York: Dover Publications, 1993).
4 Some antiabortionists draw parallels between Brown's fight and their own. Brown acknowledged blacks as fully human though the majority counted them as less than human and thus denied them basic human rights. Similarly, antiabortionists claim, they acknowledge the unborn child as fully human.
5 Robert H. Bork, *Slouching towards Gomorrah: Modern Liberalism and American Decline* (New York: Regan Books, 1997), 132.
6 Ibid., 139.
7 Quoted from *The American Prospect*, www.prospect.org.
8 Bork, *Slouching toward Gomorrah*, 134.

Notes on Contributors

J. Heath Atchley teaches in the Department of Religion at Mount Holyoke College. He is author of the forthcoming *Encountering the Secular: Philosophical Endeavors in Religion and Culture.*

John D. Caputo is Thomas J. Watson Professor of Religion and Humanities and Professor of Philosophy at Syracuse University and the David R. Cook Professor Emeritus of Philosophy at Villanova University. His most recent books are *The Weakness of God: A Theology of the Event, Philosophy and Theology, After the Death of God* (coauthored with Gianni Vattimo), and *What Would Jesus Deconstruct?*

Melissa Conroy is an Assistant Professor at Muskingum College in New Concord, Ohio. She focuses on issues involving the intersection of gender, film theory, and religion. She has had articles published in the international journal *Revista Literalis* and the *Journal of Religion and Film.* Currently she is working on a book on religious visuality in contemporary cinema.

Clayton Crockett is Assistant Professor in the Department of Philosophy and Religion at the University of Central Arkansas. He is the author of *Interstices of the Sublime* (Fordham University Press, 2007) and *A Theology of the Sublime* (Routledge, 2001) and the editor of *Religion and Violence in a Secular World* (University of Virginia Press, 2006), as well as a coeditor of the book series Insurrections: Critical Studies in Religion, Politics, and Culture for Columbia University Press.

Creston Davis is Assistant Professor in the Department of Philosophy and Religion at Rollins College. He is the coeditor (with Clayton Crockett and Slavoj Žižek) of the forthcoming *Religion, Politics, and the Dialectic: Hegel and the Opening of the Infinite* (with John Milbank and Slavoj Žižek) and of *Theology and the Political: The New Debate*. He is the guest editor (with Clayton Crockett) of "The Political and the Infinite: Theology and Radical Politics" in *Angelaki: The Journal for the Theoretical Humanities* (12, no. 1). He is also the coeditor of two book series: Insurrections: Critical Studies in Religion, Politics, and Culture with Columbia University Press and New Slant with Duke University Press.

Rocco Gangle is Assistant Professor of Philosophy at Endicott College. He received his PhD from the University of Virginia in 2007 and has taught philosophy, modern religious thought, and interdisciplinary studies at Oberlin College and the University of California, Merced. His publications include work on phenomenology, semiotics, political theology, and the philosophy of science, and he is cofounder of the philosophical organization Synousia.

Peter Goodwin Heltzel is Assistant Professor of Theology at New York Theological Seminary. He is the editor of *Theology in Global Context: Essays in Honor of Robert C. Neville* (T&T Clark, 2004).

Chrisopher Haley is an independent researcher. His interests include international development, neoliberalism, and interstate conflict. He is currently researching the politics of terrorism in relation to U.S. foreign policy. Chris lives in Austin, Texas.

Neal E. Magee received his doctorate from Syracuse University and studies the intersections of religion, philosophy, culture, and politics. His writings particularly explore the traces of theology in Western culture and history. He has taught religion at Syracuse University and philosophy at Le Moyne College. He also serves as the technical editor for the online *Journal for Cultural and Religious Theory* (www.jcrt.org). He currently works in Washington, DC, and lives in Charlottesville, VA, with his wife Diana and their two children.

Anna Mercedes is Instructor of Theology and Gender at the College of Saint Benedict / Saint John's University in central Minnesota, and a doctoral candidate in theological and religious studies at Drew University in Madison, New Jersey. She specializes in feminist theology.

Adam S. Miller is a Professor of Philosophy at Collin College in McKinney, Texas. He is the author of *Badiou, Marion, and St Paul: Immanent Grace* and has published a number of articles addressing the intersection of religion, ethics, and politics. He is also the founder of *The Journal of Philosophy and Scripture.*

Jeffrey W. Robbins is Assistant Professor of Religion and American Studies at Lebanon Valley College, where he also directs the college colloquium series. He is the author of *Between Faith and Thought* and *In Search of a Non-Dogmatic Theology*, and editor of *After the Death of God*. He is the associate editor of the *Journal for Cultural and Religious Theory* and a regular contributor on religion, politics, and culture to the Huffington Post.

Mary-Jane Rubenstein is Assistant Professor of Religion at Wesleyan University, where she teaches primarily in the areas of philosophy of religion and modern Christian thought. Her work on Kierkegaard, Heidegger, Derrida, poststructuralist retrievals of apophaticism, and sex and gender in the Anglican Communion can be found in *Modern Theology, Telos, The Journal of the American Academy of Religion*, the *Journal for Cultural and Religious Theory*, and a number of edited volumes. She is the author of the forthcoming book with Columbia University Press, *Wondrous Strange: The Closure of Metaphysics and the Opening of Awe.*

Andrew Saldino is Assistant Professor of Philosophy at Lees-McRae College in beautiful Banner Elk, North Carolina. His dissertation is titled "Just Speech: The Grammar of an Ethics beyond Essence," and that work plus other recent writings are available online at http://www.lmc.edu/faculty/saldinoa/.

Ben Stahlberg is a lecturer at Colgate University, specializing in Modern Western Religious Thought.

Slavoj Žižek is a professor at the Institute for Sociology, Ljubljana, Slovenia, and at the European Graduate School EGS in Switzerland. He has published widely in philosophy, critical theory, psychoanalysis, politics, and religion. His most recent books include *Universal Exception* and *Interrogating the Real*, both with Continuum.

Index